Anonymous

Manual Of Police Regulations

For The Guidance Of The Constabulary Of Queensland

Anonymous

Manual Of Police Regulations
For The Guidance Of The Constabulary Of Queensland

ISBN/EAN: 9783744650526

Printed in Europe, USA, Canada, Australia, Japan

Cover: Foto ©Lupo / pixelio.de

More available books at **www.hansebooks.com**

MANUAL

OF

POLICE REGULATIONS

FOR THE GUIDANCE OF THE

CONSTABULARY OF QUEENSLAND.

Brisbane:
JAMES C. BEAL, GOVERNMENT PRINTER, WILLIAM STREET.

1876.

MANUAL

OF

POLICE INSTRUCTIONS AND DUTIES.

The following Instructions for the guidance of the Members of the Police Force, in the performance of their duty, are published by the Commissioner of Police.

ACCIDENTS.

1. In all cases of accidents or illness in the streets, the Police are to render all assistance in their power, and if necessary, remove the sufferer to the hospital.

2. The number of a sergeant or a constable who witnesses an accident is to be given to the person injured or aggrieved.

3. The full particulars are to be reported by the police concerned in each case, with statement whether witnessed by police, but if only known to them by the accounts of others, the names and addresses of informants are to be stated; all such particulars shall be entered in the Occurrence Book.

APPOINTMENTS OF POLICE.

1. Each member of the Force will be furnished at the expense of the Government with the arms, ammunition, and appointments named in one of the following lists, according as he may be attached to the mounted or foot police, and which will be marked with a number and the letter of the District.

2. The mounted police appointments consist of:—
   Saddle
   Saddle cloth
   Crupper
   Stirrup leathers
   Stirrup irons
   Carbine bucket and straps
   Surcingle
   Three cloak straps
   Three valise straps
   One carbine stay strap
   Valise
   Valise pad
   Breast plate
   Girth
   Bridle
   Bridoon
   Bit
   Curb
   Regulation head collar
   Halter
   Japanned iron manger log and chain
   Carbine, rifled
   Sword
   Sword belt and slings
   Pouch belt
   Revolver
   Baton
   Hand-cuffs
   Number and letter

3. The foot police appointments are:—
   Rifle
   Sword bayonet and sheath
   Pouch belt
   Waist belt and frog
   Number and letter
   Manual of Police Regulations
   Extracts from Acts of Parliament
   Baton
   Hand-cuffs
   Duty badge

4. Numbers and letters will only be supplied to members of the Force below the rank of Sub-Inspector.

5. On being supplied with these or such other articles as it may be deemed advisable to supply him with, each constable will be required to sign a certificate containing a list of them, the date of issue, statement of condition when issued, together with any other remarks it may be necessary to insert, which certificates will be countersigned by the officer issuing the articles, and must be retained by the party supplied, and be produced prior to receiving his monthly pay, and the officer by whom the pay is issued, after examining the articles, will enter in the Station Occurrence Book, certificates to the following effect:—

> I certify that on paying the men of this station I carefully examined all the articles mentioned in their certificates, and found they were all in good serviceable order.

6. In the event of any member of the Force, on leaving the service, taking with him any of the articles mentioned in the certificates he will be liable to be prosecuted.

7. Any constable losing or defacing the certificate will be charged two shillings and sixpence for a new one, and it will be presumed that he has been provided with every article mentioned in it.

8. In case any of the articles be lost or damaged, the amount of the cost of the article lost, or the damage, will be charged to him.

9. When any sergeant or constable receives his discharge, or is dismissed from the Force, the officer in charge of the station must see that his arms, accoutrements, or any other Government property in his possession are returned to the store in a clean and proper state, and not used until his successor is appointed; and must state on the back of the certificate in what condition the arms and other things were returned, and must forward the certificate to the Commissioner's office.

10. Each man will be instructed by the sergeant, or other officer under whose immediate charge he is placed, in the proper manner of cleaning and keeping his arms and accoutrements in good order.

11. He will be supplied with twenty rounds of ammunition, and in the event of the quantity being unaccounted for at any time, the amount of threepence for every missing cartridge will be deducted from his pay. When applying for more, he will state in writing how and when that previously issued had been expended.

12. The sword and carbine should not be used on ordinary police duty. The baton, with the addition of a revolver, when it is probable fire-arms will be required, will generally be sufficient, except on gold escort.

13. A certain number of handcuffs will be supplied to each watchhouse-keeper, for which he will be responsible. Twelve pairs will be supplied to the office of each officer in charge of a District, for which the clerk will be responsible.

14. No constable is to load or discharge his fire arms, unless ordered to do so by his superior officer, or in case of emergency.

15. Every mounted constable will be held strictly responsible for the state of the saddlery in his charge, and any breakages or damage done to any articles, unless satisfactorily accounted for as having occurred in the execution of his duty, and not through any carelessness, will be repaired at his expense.

ARMLETS.

1. Constables are to wear their armlets on all occasions when on duty, also at theatres, and all places of public amusement, and whether their services are paid for by private individuals or otherwise.

2. The armlets are to be worn on the left arm, about three inches above the lower end of the sleeve of the jumper.

ARMS, USE OF, BY POLICE.

1. The police are armed to enable them successfully to overcome opposition to lawful arrests, and to protect themselves against armed interference in the execution of their duty. It is therefore of great importance that they

should clearly understand under what circumstances they are justified in resorting to the use of the weapons with which they are entrusted.

2. It is only in the apprehension or detention of felons that a constable is justified in proceeding to extremities, that is, when the constable is armed with a warrant for a felony, or when a felony is committed in his own view, or when he is in immediate or fresh pursuit of a person known to have committed a felony. Being satisfied on this point, the resort to firearms must be owing to some unavoidable necessity to which he is reduced in the execution of his duty.

3. If a person having actually committed a felony will not suffer himself to be arrested, but stand on his own defence, or fly so that he cannot possibly be apprehended alive by those who pursue him, with or without a warrant from the magistrate, the constable in pursuit is justified in using his weapon to secure him. The necessity (viz., that he cannot otherwise be taken) must be clearly apparent.

4. A police constable on duty at a gaol, or any other place in which prisoners are confined is only justified in firing on a prisoner attempting to escape, who assaults or resists the person endeavoring to retake or secure him, or on a prisoner committed for or convicted of felony, who persists in flying from the gaol or other place of confinement, after reasonable efforts have been unsuccessfully made to capture him.

5. The above remarks do not apply to cases of riot, &c., in which the police are called upon by the magistracy to act as an armed body, as on these occasions they will obey the orders of the magistrates, with whom the responsibility will rest.

See "Appointments," "Baton."

ARRESTS.

1. It is necessary that the police should inform themselves in what cases they ought to arrest, and what legal powers they possess to effect the object in case they meet with resistance. To assist the police constables in the

discharge of their duties, the following observations are prepared for their attention, perusal, and study.

2. It will be first shown for what offences of more ordinary occurrence a party may be arrested and detained in custody. With this object, offences may be divided into "felonies" and "misdemeanors."

3. Murder, rape, housebreaking, robbery, picking pockets, receiving stolen goods knowing them to have been stolen, assaulting any one with intent to rob, wounding, with intent to do murder or some grievous bodily harm, setting fire to any church, house, or other building, are some of the principal felonies, besides a great many more, too numerous to be inserted here.

4. Persons guilty of any of these offences are called felons.

5. Slighter offences, such as common assaults, affrays and riots, and various kinds of fraud, with numerous other offences, are called misdemeanors.

6. The first duty of a constable is to *prevent* the commission of crime.

7. A constable, by his appointment as such, has power to arrest without warrant from a Magistrate, any person who is found in the commission of, or charged with, or suspected of certain offences.

8. A constable may arrest any one whom he has just cause to suspect to be about to commit a felony; thus when a drunken person or a man in a violent passion threatens the life of another, the constable should interfere and arrest.

9. He should arrest any person having in his possession any picklock, key, crow, jack, bit, or other implement, with intent feloniously to break into any dwelling house, warehouse, coach house, stable, or out building; or any person armed with any gun, pistol, hanger, cutlass, bludgeon, or offensive weapon, or having upon him any instrument with intent to commit any felonious act, or any person found in or upon any dwelling house, warehouse, coach house, out house, or stable, or in any enclosed yard, garden, or area, or found in and on board any vessel when lying in any place within this

colony for any unlawful purpose, or any suspected person or reputed thief, frequenting any river, canal, or navigable stream, dock or basin, or any quay, wharf, or warehouse, near or adjoining thereto, or any street, highway, or place adjacent, with intent to commit felony.

10. If any party draw a weapon upon another, attempting to strike, the constable should take him into custody; if persons are merely quarrelling or insulting each other, the constable has in general no right to take them into custody, but should be ready to prevent a breach of the peace.

11. In cases where an offence has not been actually committed, a constable must judge from the situation and behaviour of the party what his intention is; in some cases no doubt can exist, as when the party is a notorious thief, or acting with those who are thieves or when the party is seen to try persons' pockets in a crowd, or to attempt to break into a house, or to endeavour to take any property secretly from another; the constable must not act hastily in case the intention is not clear, but content himself with watching closely the suspected party, that he may discover his design.

12. A constable should arrest any person whom he sees in the act of committing a felony, or any one whom another positively charges with having committed a felony, or whom another suspects of having committed a felony, if the suspicion appear to the constable to be well founded, and provided the person so suspecting go with the constable.

13. Though no charge be made, yet if a constable suspect a person to have committed a felony, he should arrest him, and if he have reasonable grounds for his suspicion he will be justified, even though it should afterwards appear that no felony was in fact committed; but the constable must be very cautious in thus acting upon his own suspicions.

14. Generally, if the arrest was made discreetly and fairly in pursuit of an offender, and not from any private motive or ill-will, a constable need not doubt that the law will protect him.

15. On the apprehension of any person for felony, if there is any reason to believe that any property connected with the felony will be found in the house or place in which the prisoner last resided, the arresting constable should, in the presence of the person so arrested, search the premises the prisoner has been occupying, and open any boxes, cases, or other receptacle of property belonging to the prisoner.

16. If after sunset and before sunrise a constable should see any one carrying a bundle of goods which he suspects to have been stolen, he should stop and examine the person, and may detain him; but here also he should judge from circumstances, such as the appearance and manner of the party, his account of himself, and the like, whether he really has stolen goods in his possession, before he takes him into custody.

17. He may also arrest any person whom he may find between sunset and sunrise lying or loitering in any highway, yard, or other place, and not giving a satisfactory account of himself.

18. A constable, when justified in making an arrest, must use every exertion to effect it. If the felon, or party accused of felony, fly, he may be immediately followed wherever he goes; and if he takes refuge in a house, the constable may break open the doors, if necessary, to get in, first stating who he is, and his business; but the breaking open outer doors is so dangerous a proceeding, that the constable should never resort to it except in extreme cases, and when an immediate arrest is necessary.

19. If a constable finds his exertions insufficient to effect the arrest, he ought to require all persons present to assist him, and they are bound to do so, on his stating that he is a constable, and has lawful authority for what he is doing.

20. If a prisoner, on whatever charge lawfully taken, should escape, he may be retaken, and in immediate pursuit the constable may follow him into any place or any house; and if the escaped prisoner take refuge in a

house, the doors may be broken open after demand of admission, and after notification by the constable of his office and object in coming.

21. In cases of misdemeanor the powers of the constable are not so extensive; he cannot generally arrest without a warrant unless for offences committed within his own view, and when the arrest is specially authorised by law; and in executing the warrant and pursuing the offender, he must be specially careful to act with the greatest forbearance.

22. A constable may take into custody without warrant all loose, idle, and disorderly persons whom he shall find disturbing the public peace, or whom he shall have good cause to suspect of having committed, or being about to commit any felony, misdemeanor, or breach of the peace.

23. A constable has power to apprehend and carry immediately, or as soon as possible, before a justice of the peace any person whom he may find wilfully damaging any public building, parapet, wall, sluice, bridge, road, street, sewer, watercourse, or other public property; also any person who in his view commits any malicious injury to private property, and he should take charge of any person given into his custody who may have been arrested by the owner of the property damaged, or by his servant, or any person authorised by him.

24. In the following cases, also, constables are empowered to arrest without warrant, but they are to be specially careful not to do so upon light grounds:—

(1.) Any person found in the streets and public places in a state of intoxication, or behaving in a riotous and indecent manner, or incapable of taking care of himself.

(2.) Every common prostitute wandering in any street or public highway, or being in any place of public resort, who shall behave in a riotous or indecent manner.

(3.) Every person wandering abroad, or placing himself or herself in any public place to beg or gather alms, or causing or procuring or encouraging any child or children to do so, or endeavoring by the exposure of wounds or deformities to obtain alms, or endeavoring to procure charitable contributions under any false or fraudulent pretence.

(4.) Every person wilfully exposing to view in any public place, or who shall expose or cause to be exposed to public view in the window or other parts of any shop or other building situate in any public place any obscene book, picture, or other indecent exhibition or representation.

(5.) Every person wilfully or obscenely exposing his or her person in any street or road, or in the view thereof, or in any place of public resort.

(6.) Every person playing or betting at any unlawful game.

(7.) Every person playing or betting in any street, road, highway, or other open and public place, at or with any table or instrument of gaming at any game or pretended game of chance.

(8.) Any person who shall sing any obscene song or ballad, or write or draw any indecent or obscene word, figure, or representation, or use any obscene language in any public place, or within the view or hearing of any person passing therein.

(9.) Any person who shall use any threatening, abusive, or insulting words or behaviour in any public place with intent to provoke a breach of the peace, or whereby a breach of the peace may be occasioned.

(10.) Or any person who shall cruelly beat, illtreat, over-drive, abuse, or torture, or cause or procure to be cruelly beaten, illtreated, over-driven, abused, or tortured, any animal.

25. In all these cases constables are not only empowered to arrest without a magistrate's warrant, but on fair and sufficient grounds it is their duty to do so, and they are also bound to receive into their custody any person found committing any of these offences, who, having been apprehended by another, is delivered to them; and any refusal or wilful neglect to take such offender into their custody

or to take or convey him or her before some justice of the peace will be a neglect of duty, and will render them liable to the penalty attached to such neglect.

26. In cases where any soldier or member of any other public service shall appear intoxicated, it is advisable that the constable should communicate on the subject, through his superior officer, with the officer under whose command such person is, and to refrain, except in cases of strong necessity, from taking him into custody.

27. The police are not to arrest or unnecessarily interfere with any person unless some specific act has been committed by which the law has been broken.

28. To deprive a person of liberty is a very serious matter, and great discretion is necessary in trifling cases where one person charges another with having committed an offence.

29. After the arrest the constable is in all cases to treat a prisoner properly, and impose only such restraint upon him as may be absolutely necessary for his safe custody.

ASSAULTS.

1. In cases of affrays in the streets, assaults upon the police, attempts to rescue, or obstruction to the police in the performance of their duty, it is most desirable that persons should not be taken into custody at the time, *if they are known to the police*, and can be apprehended afterwards, on warrant, obtained from a magistrate.

2. When the residence of persons is known, it can rarely be a proper step for the police to take them into custody during the excitement of an affray or disturbance, and when resistance by others, as well as by the persons themselves, may be caused by the attempt to take into custody. This does not apply to those cases in which it is necessary to take persons into custody in order to put an end to a disturbance or prevent acts of violence being committed.

3. When a person escapes into his own residence or lodging, or any place where he may be found or traced, forcible entrance to apprehend him on a charge of assault,

disturbance, or the like, is strictly forbidden. A warrant is to be applied for as soon as possible.

4. The police are not to interfere unnecessarily between a man and his wife who are quarrelling, unless it is absolutely necessary to prevent serious violence to either party or public disturbance.

5. Charges preferred by constables of assaults on themselves are to be strictly investigated by the officer on duty or lockup-keeper, and discouraged as much as possible, especially when the assaults are trifling and the accused are known, so that a warrant may be afterwards obtained.

6. The police are not authorised to arrest, or assist in arresting, or take into custody, a person charged by another with assault, when the assault was not committed in the presence or within view of the police. The person complaining is to be referred to a magistrate to obtain a summons.

7. If there is corroborative evidence of wounds or injury, by which the police may have good reason to believe that a serious or aggravated assault has been committed, although not within their view, they are then to take into custody a person charged by any other person with having committed such offence.

8. When any special case of assault on the police occurs, the circumstances should be reported to the Commissioner.

9. The police are to take into custody any person charged by another with having committed an indecent assault, unnatural crime, or rape, although the offences were not committed in their presence; such prisoners are to be confined in separate cells.

10. In cases of actual breaches of the peace, as riots, affrays, assaults, and the like, committed within view of the police, they should immediately interfere (first giving public notice of their office if they be not already known), separate the combatants, and prevent others from joining in the affray. If the riot, &c., be of a serious nature, or if the offenders do not immediately desist, they should take them into custody, and do everything in their power to restore quiet.

11. A justice of the peace may by word of mouth command any constable or any other person to arrest another who should be guilty of an actual breach of the peace in his presence, and such command is a good warrant without writing, and must be obeyed accordingly.

12. The police may arrest anyone assaulting or opposing them in the execution of their duty, or anyone aiding or assisting any person so to assault or resist them.

13. When an offence has not yet been committed, but a breach of the peace is likely to take place (as when persons are openly preparing to fight), the police should desire them to desist, and if they do not do so should take them into custody. If they fly into a house and are making preparations to fight within, the police should enter to prevent them, and take the parties into custody; and should the doors be closed they may break them open, if admission is refused, after giving notice of their office and their object in entering.

14. But in all such cases, if the parties are known, and no very violent breach of the peace has been committed, it is more advisable that they should be summoned before a magistrate.

ATTENTION.

1. When the Commissioner, Inspector, or Sub-Inspector enters any room at a Police Station, the police in the room are to stand to attention.

2. The first man who perceives the officer's approach is to give notice to the others by calling "Attention!"

BAIL.

1. The officer in charge of a Police Station may admit to bail, persons charged with any petty misdemeanor, or any offence for which they are liable to be summarily convicted by a Magistrate, or with having carelessly done any hurt, or damage; who, without the warrant of a Magistrate are in custody when the Police Court is closed.

2. Persons charged with drunkenness only, may be admitted to bail as in any other case, though still apparently drunk, if the sureties, on bailing such person, undertake to have him or her sent home or properly taken care of until sober.

3. If prisoners in custody for a bailable offence, wish to send for bail, and are willing to pay a messenger, the officer in charge of the Station will, so far as possible, comply with their request.

4. No bail is to be sent for, except with the sanction of the officer in charge of the Station.

5. If application is made for bail, and not complied with, the cause and other particulars of bail being refused, are to be entered in the Occurrence Book.

6. In every instance where the police grant bail, the usual recognizance must be made out and signed by the principal, and where there are sureties, the bail bond is to be signed by them also.

7. When the amount of the bail is deposited, *i.e.*, after the necessary recognizance has been entered into, and signed by the principal, it must be in cash, and as a rule, never less than the maximum fine that might be inflicted in the case.

8. Persons apprehended on warrants can only be admitted to bail with the sanction of a Magistrate.

9. In all cases where the Magistrates wish it, the police are to make the necessary inquiries, as to persons offering to become bail.

10. A surety who has reason to fear that his principal is about to abscond, is justified in causing him to be re-arrested, in order that he may surrender him at the Court at which the bail was taken. To enable him to do so, he is entitled to claim the assistance of the police, and that assistance may be given without a warrant from a Magistrate; but if it should be found necessary to *break open doors* in order to make the arrest, the police are not to resort to that force without having previously obtained a warrant from a Magistrate. If necessary, observation may, in the mean time, be kept on the house in which the principal is supposed to be.

BAILIFF.

(See "Distraint of Goods," and "Sheriff.")

BARRACKS.

1. The officer in charge of a station will be held strictly responsible for the state of the quarters, which must always be orderly, cleanly, and fit for inspection; the arms, accoutrements, clothing, and barrack furniture, being regularly arranged, and kept in good and serviceable repair and order.

2. All damages must be promptly reported to the officer in charge of the district; and when occurring through carelessness or negligence, the officer in charge at the time will be responsible for the cost of the repairs being defrayed by the person through whom the damage has occurred, and in the event of his failing to discover the offender, he will be liable to defray it himself.

3. A board, with a list of all articles the property of the Government, will be hung up in each room, and the officer, sergeant, or constable in charge of the station, will be held responsible for the articles mentioned therein; and in the event of such officer, sergeant, or constable being removed, the officer relieving him will take care that the articles correspond with the list, and are in serviceable condition; if not, a report must be forwarded to the Inspector of the District.

4. The officer in charge is to make an immediate report of any man who absents himself (unless illness be the cause of such absence), from quarters at night, whether in barracks or not.

5. No constable shall leave his barracks without acquainting the sergeant or constable in charge where he is to be found, nor go from his station any greater distance than a quarter of a mile, without permission from the officer in charge; constables living out of barracks must not be absent from their quarters after ten p.m. without permission.

6. Except when on duty, no greater number than one-half the Force at a station shall leave their quarters, or their immediate vicinity.

B

7. The constables are to keep every part of the barracks, approaches, passages, and yards, clean and in good order, and are to study to maintain neatness and regularity in everything connected with their post.

8. The windows must be kept clean, and should be opened when the weather will admit of it, and must be repaired when they require it.

9. As regards hours, the following should, where practicable, be observed at all police stations in the colony:—All constables, with the exception of those who have been employed on night duty, should rise in the morning not later than six, they should be dressed and their bedding neatly folded during the next half-hour, and the rooms should be swept and set in order immediately afterwards.

The hour for breakfast should be eight a.m.; for dinner, one p.m.; and for tea or supper, six p.m. At half-past nine such men as have not leave, or are not on duty should go to bed, and all lights and fires, except such as are authorised to be kept up during the night, should be extinguished by ten o'clock.

From the great variety in the different police duties, it cannot be expected, nor is it intended that these hours should be adhered to in all cases and at all times, but only when regularity of hours does not interfere with the performance of police duties.

10. During the summer months no fire will be allowed in any of the apartments except the cook-house or kitchen.

11. The officer in charge will be held strictly responsible for seeing that the relatives of policemen, or other persons not connected with the establishment, be not allowed to sleep in the barracks; and that no person, except on business relating to the public service, be allowed to frequent police premises.

12. A man who has been dismissed from the Force must never be allowed to enter police quarters, on any excuse whatsoever; nor is any member of the Force to associate with such person, if the offence for which he was dismissed was of such a nature as to attach disgrace to the Force.

13. Every article in a barrack-room is to have its appointed place, and when not in use is not to be out of that place. Provisions are not to be exposed to view, nor are mess utensils to be left unarranged or uncleansed.

14. The officer in charge of a station is to take into his possession the private effects of any policeman who dies at such station; and he is to make a careful inventory of such effects in the presence of a subscribing witness, and to give a true copy of such inventory to the Inspector of his district, who is to transmit the same, with all necessary information on the subject, to the Commissioner, with a view to the proper disposal of such private effects.

15. All sergeants and constables living in barracks, unless suffering from sickness, or absent on duty, or leave, must attend roll call every night at 9.30 p.m.

16. Smoking is strictly prohibited in barracks, as are also card-playing and every other species of gambling.

17. Officers in charge will be held strictly responsible for the enforcement of the foregoing regulations respecting barracks, and for the immediate report of any infraction of them.

BATHING.

1. The police are authorised, under the 21st section of the Act 2 Vic., No. 2, to apprehend without warrant, any person found bathing near or within view of, any public wharf, quay, bridge, street, road, or other public place within the limits of any of the towns proclaimed in accordance with the provisions of the 1st section of the aforesaid Act, between the hours of 6 o'clock in the morning and 8 o'clock in the evening.

2. It is not lawful for the police to arrest persons bathing outside the boundary of a proclaimed town. Bathers, however, who indecently resort to public places, seldom fail to bring themselves within the law; as, whatever outrages public decency, and is injurious to public morals, is indictable as a misdemeanor. Hence, stripping oneself naked, and bathing near a highway, or place of public resort, or near inhabited houses, so that the persons doi so can be distinctly seen from there, is a misdemeanor

3. Printed notices cautioning persons against bathing, can be obtained on application to the Commissioner's office, and they are to be posted at public places frequented by bathers.

4. A police constable should caution any person who may be about to bathe within that part of any river reserved to the public use for the supply of water, and report any person who shall so bathe, or who shall throw into the water, any offal, carrion, or other offensive thing, or obstruct any watercourse, or public sewer, either by casting any filth or rubbish into the same, or in any other manner.

BATON.

1. In all ordinary cases of police duty the baton is the weapon to which the constable should have recourse, and the use of this should be avoided as much as possible.

2. If a constable is likely to be overpowered he may draw his baton and use it, *taking care to avoid striking anyone on the head.* The arms and legs should be aimed at to disable a prisoner as parts of the frame least likely to suffer serious injury.

BEATS.

1. In Brisbane, and in other towns where a certain system of police duty is followed, a beat is committed to the care of a constable, who will be informed by his sergeant of the names of the streets and roads forming his beat.

2. He is responsible for the security of life and property, and for the preservation of the peace, and general good order within his beat during the time he is on duty.

3. As a general rule, constables performing street duty will work their beats so as to have their right hand next the houses.

4. Sergeants and senior constables in charge of sections, when visiting the men, will work the beats in the opposite direction, so as to have their left hands next the houses.

5. Constables on night-duty beats are to walk on the inside of the footway near to the houses, and are not to make unnecessary noise or disturbance to cause annoyance to the inhabitants.

6. Constables are to walk their beats at a uniform rate of about two-and-a-half miles per hour; they are not to loiter or gossip, but be active and attentive to their duties.

7. Constables may leave their beats to act in cases of fire, or accidents, or other emergencies, but they are to return to them as soon as possible.

8. Constables should see every part of their beats in the time allotted; and this they will be expected to do regularly, so that any person requiring assistance, by remaining in the same spot for that length of time, may meet a constable.

9. The police on duty are strictly forbidden to idle or gossip with each other, or with any persons, especially female servants, at houses on their beats.

10. This regularity of moving through their beats shall not, however, prevent their remaining at any particular place, if their presence there be necessary for the due performance of their duty, to observe the conduct of any suspected person, or for any other good reason; but they will be required to satisfy the sergeant or superior officer that there was sufficient cause for such apparent irregularity.

11. It is indispensably necessary that the constables should make themselves perfectly acquainted with all the parts of their beats or sections, with the streets, thoroughfares, courts, and houses.

12. They will be expected to possess such a knowledge of the inhabitants of each house as to enable them to recognise their persons; and thus prevent mistakes, and be enabled to render assistance, when called upon, to the inhabitants.

13. When a constable takes anyone into custody during the night, he should, if possible, before he leaves his beat, give notice to another constable who can supply his place

while he is taking the party to the watch-house; and he will return again as soon as possible to his beat.

14. If at any time a constable requires immediate assistance, and cannot in any other way obtain it, he must blow his whistle; but this is to be done as seldom as possible, for, though he be provided with one, and may sometimes find it necessary to use it, such alarms frequently create the inconvenience they are intended to avert—viz., the assembling of a crowd. He will be required to report to his sergeant any occasion of using his whistle.

15. A constable is not to leave his beat during his tour of duty, unless under the circumstances already mentioned or others which make it necessary. He shall not enter any house except in the execution of his duty.

16. He will pay particular attention to all public-houses within his beat, reporting the hour at which each is closed, and also whether they appear to be kept in good order.

17. On no pretence shall he enter any public-house except in the immediate execution of his duty. Such a breach of positive order will not be excused; the publican himself is subject to a severe fine for allowing him to remain in his house.

18. If he observes anything in the street likely to produce danger or public inconvenience, or anything which seems to him irregular and offensive, he must report it to the sergeant. (See "Constable," "Reliefs," &c.)

19. The Sub-Inspector or sergeant in charge of each division should, both by day and by night, visit all parts of his division, and see that the sergeants and constables are alert and understand their duties properly; he is also responsible that the men in reserve both by day and by night are prepared to turn out at a moment's notice.

20. Each officer in charge of a division is expected occasionally to visit all parts thereof at uncertain hours during the day and night, and, when on duty, to attend the court and visit the watch houses at least once during the day and once after midnight.

21. Each officer in charge of a division will be held responsible for that division, and will also take the imme-

diate charge of the lock-up situated in it; he must also consider it his duty to make himself acquainted with all the inhabitants resident in his division, to whatever class they may belong, and with all the lanes and alleys in such division : he should pay particular attention to the manner in which his sergeants and constables perform their duty, and by examination and enquiry, find out whether each constable is acquainted with the purpose for which he is placed on beat, and whether he exerts himself to the utmost of his ability to discover all that is going on within its limits, and whether he also makes himself acquainted with the inhabitants.

22. Should any suspicious characters, either arrive at, or leave any parts of the town within a constable's beat, it is his duty to report it to his sergeant, who will report the same to the Sub-Inspector, with a view to its being brought to the notice of the Inspector.

23. As the detection of offences depends very much on the support and assistance which the Detectives receive from the constables on duty, every endeavor must be made by the constables to assist the Detectives, by promptly affording them all the information in their power respecting offences committed within the limits of their beats. In all cases of offences of a serious nature, the constable within whose beat the offence was committed, should immediately report the matter to the sergeant of his section, who will at once proceed to the station of his division, and fill up the proper forms with full particulars of the case, description of parties to be apprehended, and so forth, and forward one copy to the Detective Police Office, and one to each of the other divisions. The constable, on being relieved, should go to the Officer in charge of Detectives, and explain to him personally what has taken place. (See " Detectives.")

BEDDING.

1. Where bedding is supplied to police by the Government, each article will be branded with the letters Q.G. and the broad arrow.

2. To each man living in barracks will be supplied one tick, one rug, two pillow cases, two blankets, and two sheets.

3. Blankets are to be washed in the month of January each year, bed ticks at least twice a-year, sheets and pillow-cases at least once a month, at the cost of the men using them.

4. The price of any article not accounted for or rendered useless, except by fair wear or tear, will be deducted from the pay of the sergeant or constable using it.

5. When any man is transferred to another District, or discharged from the Force, he must return his bedding into store; the sheets, ticks, and pillow-cases being properly cleansed, or leave with the sergeant in charge a sum of money to pay for their being so cleansed.

BEGGARS.

1. Beggars in the streets are to be apprehended and charged with the offence under "*The Vagrant Act.*"

2. Persons in the streets who under various pretences seek to obtain alms, although they do not actually beg or ask charity, seem to come within the second clause, 15 Victoria, No. 4, which enacts "That every person wandering abroad or placing himself or herself in any public place street highway court or passage to beg or gather alms or causing or procuring or encouraging any child or children so to do shall be deemed an idle and disorderly person within the true intent and meaning of the Act." The gathering of alms, therefore, without begging constitutes an offence

3. Beggars—deformed, blind, or suffering from offensive or contagious diseases—are to be especially noticed and charged with the offence.

BELL-PULLS AND BRASS PLATES.

1. The police are to prevent persons attempting to steal bell-pulls, knockers, door plates, or such things, and endeavour to detect the thieves, if the offence has been committed.

2. Where brass plates are insecurely fastened, the police are to caution the proprietors to take the necessary steps to secure them effectually.

BOOKS.

1. The officers in charge of districts are to send in requisitions on the thirty-first day of March and the thirtieth of September in each year for the number of each description of book which will be required during the ensuing half-year, and if approved they will be delivered at the head-quarters of each district with the supply of forms and stationery.

2. The Inspectors, when visiting or inspecting stations, will examine the various books, to ascertain if they are properly and neatly kept; and any carelessness, errors, or omissions are to be reported.

3. The following is a list of the books approved to be used, and none others are to be introduced unless with the special sanction of the Commissioner :—

No.	Name.	Where kept.
1	Alphabetical and Numerical	Inspector's Office
2	Bail Book	Every Watchhouse
3	Charge Book	Ditto
4	Contingent Account Book ...	Inspector's Office
5	Criminal Offence Book ...	Every Police Station
6	District Order Book, to contain copies of all other orders	Inspector's Office
7	Diary and Occurrence Book	Every Police Station
8	Forage Store Account Book	Every Station where Government horses are stabled
9	Forage Reference Book ...	Inspector's Office, to contain balance of forage in hand at each Station as given in the returns forwarded periodically to the Commissioner's Office

No.	Name.	Where kept.
10	General Order Book	Inspector's Office, to contain copies of all General Orders that may, from time to time, be received from the Commissioner's Office
11	Letters and Minute Book	Every Station
12	Miscellaneous Property Book	Inspector's Office
13	Occurrence Book	Ditto
14	Police Pay Book	Ditto
15	Postage Stamp Account Book	Every Station
16	Property Inventory	Inspector's Office
17	Property Unclaimed Book	Ditto
18	Refused Charge Book	Every Watchhouse
19	Register of all Police in the Districe	Inspector's Office
20	Register of Conduct	Ditto
21	Register of Convicts	Detective Office
22	Register of Crime, C	Ditto
23	Register of Crime, I	Ditto
24	Register of Horses and Cattle Stolen	Ditto
25	Register of Stolen Watches	Ditto
26	Register of Horses	Inspector's Office
27	Register of Thieves and Suspects	Ditto
28	Register of Warrants	Every Station
29	Requisition Books	Every Station and Watchhouse
30	Store Account Book	Inspector's Office
31	Stud Book	Ditto
32	Summons Book	Inspector's Office, and every Station at which there is a Court of Petty Sessions
33	Telegraph Message Book	Every Station where there is a Telegraph Office
34	Warrant Book	Every Station.

4. A book will be kept at each out-station, in which General Orders will be copied on one side and District Orders on the other.

BOX.

1. Every unmarried constable, if so directed, shall, on entering the Force, furnish himself with a box (of the pattern approved by the Commissioner of Police) of the following dimensions, viz. :—Exterior measurement. length, 30 inches; breadth, 18 inches; depth, $14\frac{1}{2}$ inches; flat top.

2. This box is the only baggage which will be conveyed for sergeants and constables from one station to another at Government expense.

BRANDS ACT.

1. It is the duty of any constable, when necessary to inspect any travelling stock, and compare the brands thereof with the brands set forth in the way-bill or delivery note of the drover.

2. The constable inspecting such stock, and being satisfied with the correctness of the way-bill or delivery note thereof, shall endorse such way-bill or delivery note with his name, designation, address, and date.

3. As the signature of an endorsee is apt to prevent further challenge, the police are to refuse to endorse any way-bill unless the owner of stock or person in charge gives every facility for having the stock properly inspected in a stock-yard.

4. If any travelling stock are not fully and accurately described in the way-bill, the constable may impound the same in the nearest pound to the place where the inspection was made.

5. The proprietor of stock not fully and accurately described may be arrested *on warrant*.

6. Should the way-bill or delivery note be accidentally lost or destroyed, it is imperative upon the drover of such travelling stock to apply in writing to the nearest inspector of brands, or officer in charge of the nearest police station, for an *interim* way-bill.

7. On satisfactory proof of such loss, the officer in charge of the police station shall grant an *interim* way-bill to the person so applying, on the payment of one pound.

8. Under "*The Brands Act*," no constable, unless he be in charge of a station, can grant an *interim* way-bill.

9. The money received by officers in charge of police stations for *interim* way-bills should be forwarded through the proper channel to the Commissioner's office.

10. All police acting as inspectors of slaughter-houses shall furnish the Inspector of Brands for the district in which such slaughter-houses may be situate, with a weekly list of the brands of the stock about to be slaughtered or which may have been slaughtered.

11. A book will be kept by the member of the Force in charge of each police station, in which the brands and description of all stock inspected by the police shall be entered. It shall contain the following headings :—date, name of owner of stock, name of drover, place from whence stock came, number, sex, color, brands, and other description of stock, and remarks.

12. The constable making the inspection shall sign the book when these particulars are entered therein. (See "*Brands Act of* 1872," 35 Vic., No. 4.)

BREAKING OPEN WINDOWS OR DOORS.

1. In every case, whether civil or criminal, in which doors may be broken open in order to effect an arrest, there must be a previous notification by the constable of his business, a demand by him to enter, and a refusal, before the constable can proceed to that extremity.

2. Doors may be forced in the following cases :—
    (1.) Where one known to have committed a treason or felony or to have given a dangerous wound, is pursued, and takes refuge in a house.
    (2.) Where a minister of justice is armed with process founded on a breach of the peace.
    (3.) Where an officer is charged with the execution of a process of contempt committed in the shape of an insult to any Court of Justice.

(4.) Where an officer is executing a warrant to take forcible possession.
(5.) Where the proceeding is on a warrant of a Justice for levying a penalty on a conviction grounded on a statute which gives the whole or any part of the penalty to the Queen.
(6.) When an officer *is armed with a warrant grounded on a suspicion* that the party is guilty of felony.
(7.) Where there is an affray in a house (the doors being closed) whereby manslaughter or bloodshed is likely to ensue.
(8.) Where there is disorderly drinking or noise at an unseasonable time of night, in hotels or public houses especially, and in cases elsewhere noticed.

3. If an officer find the outward door open he may break any inner door to execute his process.

BRISBANE.

1. The city of Brisbane police consists of several Divisions, with a Sub-inspector or a sergeant in charge of each, and to each Division is entrusted a certain portion of the city and suburbs.

2. Each Division is sub-divided into two sections, each of which is under the immediate charge of a sergeant or a senior constable, and the sections are divided into beats, for the safety of which the constables on duty are held responsible.

BUILDINGS, ERECTION AND REPAIR OF.

1. In every case where a member of the Force recommends a police building, paddock fence, &c., &c., to be erected or repaired, a detailed estimate of the proposed expenditure must accompany the application, otherwise the communication will not be noticed.

2. This rule will apply to every case where expenditure is recommended that has no connection with the supplying of articles, &c., from the Colonial Store.

BURGLARIES.

1. The breaking into or breaking out of occupied premises between the hours of 9 p.m. and 6 a.m. constitutes the offence of burglary, and where any violence is used to persons, the offence is to be described as "burglary with violence."

2. In investigating cases of burglary, the police should ascertain the following particulars:—

> 1st. Who was last up in the house, and whether the doors and windows were all shut before retiring to rest.
> 2nd. How and by what means the entrance to the house was effected.
> 3rd. A careful search should be made for the instrument by the aid of which the breaking in or out was accomplished.
> 4th. The ground outside the house should be particularly examined for foot or other marks which might give a clue to the offenders. (See "Foot-marks.")
> 5th. Any article, however small, left behind by offenders should be carefully preserved by police, as it may lead to their identification.

3. When a burglary has been committed, a superior officer is to proceed at once to the premises and obtain all the particulars as to the entry, description, and value of the property stolen, and also of any suspicious characters seen loitering near. Full particulars are to be circulated to out-stations, and, if necessary, telegraphed to Commissioner's Office.

4. Immediate inquiries are also to be made in the neighborhood, and any clue which may be obtained is to be followed up, where practicable, by the Detectives, with a view to discover the thieves and recover the property.

5. A rough sketch of the situation of the premises will sometimes be found useful in following up an inquiry, and when necessary, it is to be made by Police.

6. In cities and towns, the full particulars are to be entered on the morning report, and the officers in charge

of districts or stations are to be careful not to state the crime of a lower degree than the circumstances warrant.

7. Officers in charge of stations are to call attention to watchmakers' and jewellers' shops, and take any special measures practicable to prevent, as far as possible, burglaries being committed at them, and to warn the owners of all such shops to use every precaution they can adopt, and point out any mode of access by thieves which may be guarded against, also to remind the whole of the Police, before being sent on duty, to pay special attention to places where valuable property is deposited, and to watch suspicious persons in the immediate neighborhood.

CANDIDATES.

1. The condition under which candidates are admitted into the Police Force are stated here, that no complaint may be made hereafter, upon their being enforced; but the Commissioner has the power, subject to the approval of His Excellency the Governor in Council, to alter or annul any of these conditions, and also to make such new Rules as may be found expedient.

2. Candidates for the Force must be under the age of thirty years, unless they have previously been engaged in Police duty, in which case they may be admitted up to the age of thirty-five years. They must stand clear five feet eight inches without their boots.

3. They must be of strong constitution, and free from any bodily complaint.

4. They must be able to read and write well.

5. They must produce satisfactory testimonials of character, either from those under whom they have served at home, or from persons of respectability in the colony.

6. If the constable has been in any Public Service, he must produce a certificate of good conduct in that service.

7. Candidates are to understand that in engaging for service in the Police Force, they are engaged not only for Police duties, but for fatigue, or any other work they may be ordered to perform by their superior officers.

8. They will be taken on for General Police Service, and those who are best adapted will be selected for mounted duty, but are liable at any time, on its being considered advisable, to be dismounted.

9. They will be taken on, in the first instance, for not less than three days on trial, without pay; but before enrolment they must be certified to, by the medical officer appointed for the purpose, as being physically fit for the service.

10. During the period of probation, which is always passed at the depôt, they can leave at any time, by giving notice to the officer in charge.

11. After the period of probation, they are, if considered suitable, required to fill up, in their own handwriting, answers to the following queries, attaching their signature thereto, and to take and subscribe, in the presence of a Magistrate, the following oath, as required by the Act 27 Victoria, No. 11:—

QUESTIONS.

Have you been in any Police or Public Service; if so, in each case, state what and where?
For what time?
When discharged, and why?
By whom last employed, and where?
By whom recommended?
Married or single?
Do you belong to any secret society?
Signature:

OATH.

I, , do swear that I will well and truly serve Our Sovereign Lady the Queen in the office of constable, without favor or affection, malice or ill-will, for the period of one year from this date, and until I am legally discharged; that I will see and cause Her Majesty's peace to be kept and preserved, and that I will prevent, to the best of my power, all offences against the same; and that while I shall continue to hold the said office I will, to the best of my skill and knowledge, discharge all the duties thereof faithfully, according to law—So help me God.

12. In order that all newly-appointed constables may have an opportunity of acquiring a knowledge of drill, and the more simple duties of the Service, a certain number of supernumeraries will always be maintained at the Depôt, for the purpose of supplying such vacancies as may occur in the various Districts.

13. Constables are to serve and reside wherever they may be ordered, and must be ready, at all times, to move in any direction that may be found necessary.

14. They are to appear in the police dress, at all times, unless leave be given to the contrary.

15. They are to promptly obey all lawful orders, which they may receive from the persons placed in authority over them.

16. They are to conform themselves to all the Regulations which may be made, from time to time, for the good of the Service.

17. They are not, upon any occasion, or under any pretence whatever, to take money or any gratuity from any person, without the express permission of the Commissioner.

18. Persons appointed to the Force will be sworn in for one year, in the first instance, during which period they cannot voluntarily leave the Force; but when they have served a year, they may leave, upon giving three months' notice.

19. Constables who have served in the Police, and voluntarily resigned, will not be re-admitted, except under very special and exceptional circumstances.

20. No married man will be accepted as a candidate, unless he has previously served in a Military or Police Force.

21. No man in the Police Force shall marry without permission from the Commissioner.

22. Any constable who questions or disobeys the orders he may receive from a superior officer, will be severely punished; every officer or sergeant in charge is held

c

strictly responsible that he immediately reports any subordinate who refuses to obey him in any matter of duty. At the same time, the men are informed (although obedience is their first and most especial duty), that they have a right respectfully to complain of any officer from whom they may receive any improper orders.

23. Police constables in uniform, whether on duty or not, are prohibited from smoking in the streets or public places.

24. No candidate who belongs to any secret order or society, excepting the order of Freemasons, will be admitted into the Police Force.

CAPES.

1. No cape is to be worn at any time over the police uniform, except the approved glazed cape.
2. Capes, when folded, are to be worn on the left side of the waistbelt.
3. During wet or changeable weather, the sergeants and constables are to take their capes with them going on duty.

CARD PLAYING.

1. The police are forbidden to play at any game of cards in a Police Station, or Watchhouse, or to meet anywhere for the purpose of playing cards.
2. The officers, sergeants, and senior constables at each station are responsible that this order is obeyed, and are to report any violation of it. (See "Card-playing" at Public-houses.)

CARTS AND WAGGONS.

(*See* 19 *Victoria*, *No.* 24, *Section* 21.)

1. In places in which the Towns Police Acts have been proclaimed to be in force, the police are to notice any carts or waggons used in any public street or road without having the name and place of abode of the owner duly painted thereon, and* are to obtain the name and address of every person driving any cart, waggon, or carriage whatsoever who shall not keep the left or near side of

the road, or street, except when passing another vehicle, or who shall wilfully prevent any person from passing him, or interrupt the free passage of any carriage or person, or who shall drive any wain, waggon, cart, dray, or van out of a walking pace.

2. The practice of persons riding on the shafts of vehicles without having and holding the reins, is to be prevented, and drivers are to be summoned for the offence. If the drivers have reins they are to be cautioned as to the danger.

CATTLE.

1. It is contrary to the Act 16 Vic., No. 23, sec. 1, for any person to drive or cause to be driven, any cattle intended for sale, slaughter, or shipment, into or through any part of any town or place to which the Act applies, at any hour except between 6 p.m. and 8 a.m.

The provisions of the Act are to be strictly enforced by the police.

2. It is the duty of the police to impound any horse, cow, sheep, goat, or swine, found straying in the streets within the boundaries of any proclaimed town or municipality.

3. Under the provisions of 17 Vic., No. 3, sec. 6, it is illegal for any person to take, use, or in any manner work any cattle the property of any other person, without consent of the owner or other person in lawful possession thereof.

4. Every effort is to be used by the police to enforce the provisions of this section of the Act.

5. If the evidence disclose a question of disputed property, or if it appear that the accused took the animal under the *bonâ fide* belief that it was his own property, the Act does not apply.

CELLS.

1. The cells are to be kept very clean and ventilated as much as possible. The carbolic acid supplied for disinfecting purposes, is to be freely used.

2. The wicket in cell doors is to be closed and carefully bolted after each visit, when prisoners are confined,

who have been charged with any offence greater than that of being drunk and disorderly.

3. The door of every cell is always to be carefully locked when prisoners of any description are confined.

4. The keys of the cells are to be hung up in the lock-up keeper's room, when not required for locking or unlocking the doors.

5. No person is to be allowed to visit the cells from curiosity, except with the sanction, and authority of an officer, above the rank of sergeant.

6. One cell at each station will be fitted with a raised boarded floor, higher at one end than the other, in which drunken persons are to be confined.

CERTIFICATES OF CONDUCT.

1. Police who have served more than twelve months are granted certificates on resignation, in accordance with their conduct, during their period of service.

2. The certificates of conduct are of five classes, viz.:—
    I. Very good.
    II. Good.
    III. Generally good.
    IV. Gives the date of joining and resignation without alluding to his conduct.
    V. Gives dates, and states "he was required to resign."

3. A certificate of good conduct in the Police Service, is not granted by the Commissioner:—
    I. If the constable is dismissed the service.
    II. If the constable has been frequently guilty of misconduct, although of a light nature.
    III. If the constable has been guilty of *any* misconduct of a serious nature.
    IV. If the constable has quitted the service without giving due notice of his intention to do so.
    V. If the constable has served less than twelve months.

4. If a certificate is lost, or mislaid, no duplicate of it can be obtained, unless on explanation approved by Commissioner, and in each of such cases payment of two shillings will be required.

CHARGES.

1. When prisoners are brought to Police Stations, and charged with any offence, the statements of persons charging, of witnesses, and of Police, are to be made to the watchhouse-keeper on duty, in the presence and hearing of the prisoners.

2. Good order is to be strictly preserved whilst the witnesses are giving evidence, and their statements, and any made by the persons charged, are to be patiently and attentively heard.

3. If there be more than one Police witness in a case, each constable is to make his statement out of the hearing of the other when it is so desired by the person charged, and if there be any material discrepancy in the evidence, the charge is to be refused, or a note made of such discrepancy, if not sufficient to make it proper to refuse the charge, and a verbal report made to the Police Magistrate, and a written one to the Inspector in charge of the District.

4. The watchhouse-keepers on duty at a Station, are, before receiving a charge, to ascertain that there is a reasonable ground for preferring the complaint against the accused; and unless the circumstances be such as entitle the accuser to be believed, a charge is not to be taken.

5. Charges by constables of assaults on themselves, or of obstruction in the prosecution of their duty, are to be strictly investigated at the Station, and discouraged, especially when persons are known, so that a summons or warrant may be afterwards obtained.

6. When a person is brought to the Station, accused of having committed a felony or misdemeanor, the watchhouse-keeper on duty to whom the complaint is made, is only to ascertain from the person preferring it, that the act charged constitutes a felony or misdemeanor as the case may be, and that there is reasonable ground for pre-

ferring the complaint against the accused. Such enquiry is only to be made of the person who prefers the complaint, who does so on his own responsibility, and is not to be made of any other persons, although they may be cognizant of the facts, and may be heard as witnesses in a subsequent stage of the proceedings before the Magistrates; for this purpose their names and addresses, if they are in attendance at the Station, are to be entered on the Charge Sheet.

7. If a complainant after having given a person into custody on a criminal charge, should refuse to sign the Charge Sheet, supposing the charge to have been made in the first instance, to any constable, the constable, if he saw the offence committed, is to sign the charge himself, and the prisoner is to be detained; and the complainant may be summoned before the Magistrate to substantiate the charge. The watchhouse-keeper is for this purpose always to ascertain the name and address of the complainant, previously to his making any enquiry of him; if the constable is himself unable to establish the charge, and the complainant refuses to support it and sign the Charge Sheet, the accused is not to be detained.

8. If the charge or complaint in the first instance, whether made by a third person, or by a constable on his own authority, appears reasonable, and the offence be a felony, misdemeanor, or a case for a summary conviction, the charge is to be received and entered on the Charge Sheet, and submitted to the Magistrate; but if it should turn out upon the statement of the constable, or other person, that there are not reasonable grounds for suspecting that the offence has been committed, then the charge is not to be received, and the prisoner must be discharged.

9. The charge, as entered upon the Sheet, is always to be read over to the prisoner.

10. Whenever a person is apprehended under the Act 19 Victoria, clause 24, of unlawful possession of goods, and the case is to be taken before Magistrates in Petty Sessions assembled, the charge is to be entered on the Charge Sheet thus—"Having in his possession property suspected to be stolen."

11. When the charge has been received and entered on the Charge Sheet, the persons charged are to be detained until they can be taken before a Magistrate for examination, unless in cases in which bail may be taken.

12. Charges received during the day when the Police Courts are open are to be at once referred to the Police Court of the district.

13. Police officers taking charges at Stations are at all times to be properly dressed in uniform.

14. Persons who come to the Police Stations as witnesses, when a charge is being made, are not to be taken into custody and charged with being concerned in the offence. Such a practice may prevent persons from appearing who can give important evidence, and has the appearance of desire by the Police to suppress evidence in the case, especially when the charge is for an assault on the Police themselves, or for obstructing them in the performance of their duty, But in case of assault on the Police, obstruction in the performance of their duty, a rescue, or similar offence, where all the persons cannot be secured and kept in custody, the arrest should still be made, if possible, at the time, and the persons required to go to the station, and when such steps have been taken, then on their appearance at the station they may be arrested and detained upon the original charge.

15. The watchhouse-keeper or officer taking a charge which appears to rest on the evidence of one constable is always to make enquiry whether there is any other witness, in the Police or not, or other corroborative evidence, and if so, the additional witnesses are to attend before the Magistrate.

16. The watchhouse-keepers who enter the charges are to make such enquiries then, or previously to the case being sent before the Magistrate, from the constables or sergeants concerned in making the charge as will enable them to give proper directions that the requisite witnesses shall be in attendance at the Police Court when the case is heard, and also that all enquiries shall be duly made by the Police to support the charge, with a view to bringing forward any additional evidence that can be discovered.

Each constable concerned as witness or otherwise in a charge is to bring forward the necessary witnesses, and to use all exertions to have the circumstances of the case fully stated, and to afford every facility to the magistrate in carrying on the investigation at each hearing, if the case is remanded from time to time.

17. Constables coming off night duty who have charges of felony are not required to make enquiry as to prisoners previously to going before the Magistrate, unless immediate enquiry be necessary. In cases where the Magistrate thinks further inquiry by Police necessary, a remand may be applied for, for the purpose of making the enquiry. By this arrangement the constables will be enabled to take some rest in the morning previously to appearing at the Police Court.

18. A sub-inspector or sergeant is to attend at the Police Court in all cases when charges are heard by the Magistrates, to give necessary information.

CHILDREN.

1. When a child who is unable to tell where it lives, is found and brought to a Police Station, a description of it will be made out and posted outside the station door, and a copy is also to be sent to adjoining stations.

2. Necessary refreshment is to be given to a child when kept at a Police Station, and charged for.

3. When children are found, and able to state where they live, they are to be taken home by the police, or a message is to be sent to the parents.

CIVILITY.

1. All persons are to be treated with the utmost civility, forbearance, and good temper by the police.

2. They are to give the best answers they can to the numerous questions which will be put to them, and show at all times a readiness to do all in their power to oblige, consistently with the Rules of the Service; at the same time they are to avoid as much as possible entering into unnecessary conversation with any one.

CLERKS.

1. Each Inspector is allowed a sergeant or constable, as circumstances may require, to act as clerk in his office, but he will explain to such member of the Force that the occupation is of a very confidential nature, and that he will be held strictly responsible for his conduct in such office, as well as for a due observance of, and obedience to, the General Rules and Regulations of the Force.

2. No other officer will be allowed the services of a member of the Force as clerk, without express permission from the Commissioner.

CLOTHING.

1. All grades in the Police Force excepting native troopers, will have to supply themselves out of their pay, with uniform—which must be in accordance with the regulation pattern—excepting the following articles which will be supplied by the Government:—

   Cloaks for mounted constables
   Great coats for foot constables
   Oilskin capes for foot constables.

2. If any member of the Force appears dressed in any article of uniform not in exact accordance with the regulation pattern, such article will be condemned.

COMMENDATIONS.

Commendations of police are to be entered briefly in the Register of Good Conduct Book, in red ink, and copied on the printed form of defaulter sheet under the heading of "remarks," so as to be brought under the notice of the Commissioner, if a man is recommended for promotion, reported for misconduct, or for consideration in granting a certificate of conduct.

(*See Rewards.*)

COMMISSIONER.

1. The Commissioner is appointed under the authority of the Act of Parliament 27 Victoria, No. 11, to have the superintendence, under the direction of the Colonial

Secretary, of the Police Force of the whole colony, including the Native Police Force.

2. He will, from time to time, issue such Orders and Regulations as may be found expedient for the general management of the constabulary, as well as for the purpose of meeting any contingency which may arise, rendering the removal of portions of the Force from one district to another necessary. He will take every step in his power to cause all under his control to discharge their duties both to the public and the Government satisfactorily and efficiently.

3. All communications which the officers in charge of districts may wish to be made known to the Government, or to the head of any other department, should be forwarded through him, and they must look to him for advice in any case of difficulty that may occur.

4. He will furnish the Government with an annual report of the general state of the Police Force, as to the number of men, their distribution and general efficiency, the increase or diminution of crime, the number of new stations that may have been formed, with such other information as it may be necessary to afford.

COMMISSIONER'S OFFICE.

1. All persons coming to the office on business are to be treated with the utmost civility and attention.

2. Persons not in the police are not to be permitted to remain in any of the offices longer than is necessary for transacting the business upon which they come.

3. The Police are to observe strict order and discipline when attending for any purpose at the Commissioner's office.

4. Police bringing letters to the Commissioner's office are in all cases to enquire, and, if necessary, wait, for an answer.

5. Private letters addressed to Police cannot be taken in at the Commissioner's office.

6. Any reports against men for misconduct, requiring to be settled by the Commissioner, are to stand over until the following day, unless special circumstances render it desirable that they should be submitted immediately.

COMPLAINTS (BY POLICE).

1. Members of the Police Force can, at any time, make any representation they wish to the Commissioner, provided that the complaint be in writing, and be made in a respectful manner, and forwarded through their immediate superiors.

2. Any officer on receiving any complaint, will forward it to the officer in charge of the District, who, if it is intended for the Commissioner, will forward it accordingly.

3. While the officers are to consider it imperative on them to forward all such complaints, they should accompany them by such statements of their own, having reference to the subject of the complaint, as they may consider necessary.

4. Attention will be paid to the wants or wishes of the constables, but all combinations, and, as a general rule, any petition signed by numbers, for any purpose, will subject those who sign it, or join such combination, to punishment.

5. The means of redress are at all times open to any member of the Force who may think himself aggrieved; but it is to be understood that protection will be equally afforded to any person against whom frivolous or unfounded complaints may be made, and the person making such, more especially when against his own superiors, will himself be liable to a proportionate punishment.

6. Any member of the Force feeling himself injured or aggrieved, must bring the circumstances of the case under the notice of his superior officer at once.

7. Complaints by Police against each other are to be made in writing, and signed, and are to be submitted through the Inspector.

8. Grievances or causes of complaint by Police can at any time be laid before the Commissioner through the superior officers.

COMPLAINTS (BY PUBLIC).

1. The statement of any person making a complaint against the police, at a Police Station, is to be taken down in writing, and submitted to the Inspector in charge of the district. The complainant may be requested to sign the statement.

2. Persons wishing to make a complaint are not to be referred to any other station.

3. The complaint is to be sent, by the officer on duty, to the station to which the man belongs.

4. When a complaint is made against police, the Inspector is to ascertain from the person complaining previous to the case being brought before the Commissioner, whether he is willing to make his charge before a Magistrate, and if the case is to be sent for investigation by a Magistrate, the Commissioner will wait until the Magistrate shall have decided upon it, when further directions will be given by the Commissioner according to the nature of that decision.

5. Complaints against any of the police are to be personally investigated by the Inspector of the district when practicable.

6. Police complained of, and sent before a Magistrate for any offence less than felony, are not to be entered on Charge Sheets, but on special sheets for the purpose.

7. No member of the force, charged by another member with a breach of discipline, shall be brought before a Magistrate without permission from the Commissioner.

CONFESSIONS (BY PRISONERS).

1. Every confession, in order to be admissible, must be free and voluntary. And in case of a confession before a Magistrate or other person, unless it be shown affirmatively on the part of the prosecution that it was made without the defendant's being induced to make it by any promise of favor, or by menaces, or undue terror, it shall not be received in evidence against him.

2. If it be said to the defendant that it will be better or worse for him if he do or do not confess, or if a confession

is procured by a threat to take the defendant before a Magistrate if he do not give a more satisfactory account, or to send for a constable for that purpose, or " you had better tell all you know," or " I should be obliged to you if you would tell us what you know about it, if you will not of course we can do nothing," or, " it will be best for you if you tell how it was transacted," the confession will not be admissible.

3. Any statement made by an offender before his arrest can be made use of against him.

CONSTABLE.

1. Each constable will bear in mind the extreme importance of making himself perfectly acquainted with such parts of the law relating to his office, as may be necessary to enable him, with a due regard to his own safety, to act efficiently for the protection of the public.

2. It is specially necessary to take care that newly appointed constables do not form false notions of their duties and powers.

3. The powers of a constable, as will be shown, are, when properly understood, and duly executed, amply sufficient for their purpose.

4. He is regarded as the legitimate peace-officer of his district, and both by the common law and Acts of the Legislature, he is invested with considerable powers, and has imposed on him the discharge of many important duties.

5. The constable, though frequently acting on specific orders, applicable to the occasion, is very generally, in the execution of his duty as a peace-officer called upon to act on his own responsibility; he therefore requires discretion, intelligence, decision, and perfect command of temper.

6. It is of great importance that a constable should be respected by the public; he will, therefore, be extremely cautious in his demeanour, and by sober, orderly, and regular habits, and ready zeal to execute the lawful orders and commands of the Magistrates, endeavour to obtain the approbation of all classes.

7. The situation in which the constables are placed renders it of the highest importance that they should be on the most cordial terms with each other, and join in everything that can tend to the advantage of the Force. Any constable who is inclined to quarrel with his comrades is liable to be punished and dismissed as unfit for the service.

8. He must be scrupulously exact in the care of his arms, clothing, and appointments, and be perfectly clean and neat in his person, as a constable who is negligent in these respects must be looked upon as careless and slovenly in the execution of his official duties.

9. He must be active, energetic, and unimpeachably honest, and must discharge his duty independently, without fear or favor.

10. When called upon by a person to take another person into custody, he must be guided in a great measure by the circumstances of the case, but if he has any doubt as to how he ought to act, the safest course is to ask all the persons concerned to go with him to the Station, where the officer in charge will hear and determine whether the charge is to be entered or not, and the responsibility is then taken off the constable.

11. When a constable is called on, to act, he must do so with energy, promptness, and determination, for if he wavers or doubts, the thief may escape, or the opportunity to render assistance may be lost.

12. The duties of constables are defined under the different heads of Regulations, which can be seen on reference, it would therefore be superfluous to repeat them here.

(See "Civility," "Beats," "Reliefs," "Arrests," "Promotions," &c., &c.)

CONTAGIOUS DISEASES.

1. The Police are to carry out the provisions of "*The Contagious Diseases Act*" in all towns or places proclaimed in the *Government Gazette*.

2. The Police appointed under "*The Contagious Diseases Act*" will afford all the information in their power to the medical officer to facilitate the carrying out of his duties.

3. A general register of common women is to be kept by the Police officers in charge of the several Districts, and any changes recorded with as much accuracy as possible.

4. A list, copied from the register, is to be made out for the Visiting Surgeon, and corrected, at such times as may be found necessary.

5. Pocket registers for every sergeant and constable employed in charge of Districts under the Act are to be kept and used.

6. The pocket registers are to contain a complete list, corrected as necessary, of all common women in their Districts.

7. In districts where the periodical examinations require it, the Police are to take the directions of the medical officer as to the numbers of common women who are to attend periodically, and see that they are in attendance.

8. All common women informed against by brothel-keepers, or other individuals, are to be brought up for examination as soon as possible.

9. It is desirable that the whole of the common women should continue to be brought under the Act, as far as possible, without resorting to the penal clauses, and new comers should be carefully watched for, so that they may at once be made amenable to the Act.

10. Diseased women who travel from a distance to a place where the Act is in operation, in order to submit themselves to a periodical examination under the Act, are not to be refused admission into the lock wards (provided they acknowledge themselves to be prostitutes), on the ground that the women of the particular place must be first provided for.

11. The common women, under the Act, are to be examined periodically.

CONTINGENCIES.

1. Vouchers for allowances to constables when absent at night on duty are to be forwarded with the salary abstracts monthly, in duplicate, to the Commissioner's office.

2. All other vouchers, also in duplicate, are to be forwarded to the Commissioner's office about the first day in every month.

3. The allowance to a constable absent from his sub-district, or having by the force of circumstances to put up for a night at a public-house when actually on duty within his sub-district, is two (2) shillings per night.

4. This allowance is not made when a constable attends as a witness at the Supreme, Circuit, and District Courts, and his expenses paid as such, or is a passenger on board a steamer or other vessel, and his passage paid by the Government.

5. Members of the Force, in making claims for night allowance, must state the dates for which such claims are made inclusive—e.g., from 9th to 12th inclusive, four nights.

6. The allowances of fuel and light to court houses, watch houses, and police barracks throughout the colony vary according to locality; members of the Force in charge of stations will, therefore, be held strictly responsible that there is no unnecessary waste.

7. As a general rule, one load of wood and one gallon of kerosene oil is the allowance per month at stations where there are less than three men.

8. In places where wood can be procured without much difficulty, the police will provide themselves with the necessary fuel without charge.

9. Rules 8 and 9 do not apply to the City of Brisbane Police Station, and the Depôt there, where coals and gas are consumed.

10. Vouchers for fuel expended at Police Courts, will be made out by the Clerks of Petty Sessions, and certified to by the Police Magistrates as being correct, after which they will be forwarded direct to the Commis-

sioner's office, with the Police Magistrate and Clerk of Petty Sessions' salary abstracts. (See "Pay Abstracts.")

11. Great care should be taken in the preparation of vouchers for supplies to watch houses that the allowance is not exceeded, and that the contract price (if any) is adhered to.

12. Vouchers for fees to medical practitioners for evidence in cases of lunacy must, in addition to the usual certificate for services performed, contain a certificate of the adjudicating Justice or Justices that the examination was duly made, and evidence given in court. The fee for both must not exceed 21s. in each case.

13. A certificate of lunacy must be signed by two medical men; the names of both must appear on the face of each voucher submitted for payment to the Commissioner's office.

14. Police Surgeons having to visit members of the Force, or other persons at the request of Police, at a distance from their residences, may draw travelling allowance at the rate of 2s. 6d. per mile after the first mile from the boundary of the town in which they live.

15. The authorised fee for the visit of a medical man to prisoners or constables in districts where no medical man is appointed to the force, is in each case 5s. per visit, exclusive of medicines; for an operation, 21s.

16. In the case of the burial of paupers, or of bodies found drowned, or dead in the bush, and buried at the public expense, it should be stated on the voucher if any inquest or magisterial inquiry has been held, in which case the expense is chargeable to, and should be transmitted to, the Attorney-General's Department. When there is no inquest or inquiry, the expense will be defrayed by the Police Department.

17. The total expense of burials should rarely, if ever, exceed the sum of £2 10s., and in cases where this amount has been exceeded, the vouchers must be accompanied by a special report, which must show a valid reason for a larger amount being expended.

18. All vouchers for each district should be sent to the Commissioner of Police at one and the same time, and

D

accompanied by the printed letter of advice, stating the various items, and showing the gross amount of the vouchers.

19. In order to facilitate the payment of vouchers, copies of authorities for special payments or appointments should be forwarded in support of the vouchers for these services.

20. In case a receipted voucher is received at the Commissioner's office without a penny duty stamp being affixed, the member of the Force sending it will be charged with the postage fees of the correspondence arising out of such neglect.

21. In remote districts where receipt stamps are not procurable, a penny postage stamp will be forwarded with the voucher (but not affixed thereto), for which a receipt stamp will be substituted at the Commissioner's office.

22. In the case of one person signing a receipt on behalf of another, an order or authority, signed by the payee, and duly witnessed, must be attached to the abstract or voucher, and returned therewith to the Commissioner's office.

23. Envelopes or covers enclosing vouchers for payment should bear distinctly on the outside the words " Vouchers only." No letters or correspondence should be enclosed therewith. This may also apply to returned receipted vouchers.

CONTRABAND GOODS.

1. Every member of the Police Force should do all in his power to prevent fraud upon the revenue by persons evading the Acts for the regulation of Her Majesty's Customs, the Licensed Publicans, and Licensed Distilleries Acts, &c., for which purpose they will pay particular attention to the provisions of those Acts.

2. When the Police seize any contraband goods, every article, however trivial, is to be entered in the occurrence book at the Police Station, and stated to the Magistrate. If the goods are forfeited by the Magistrate's decision, they are to be sent to the Custom House, or elsewhere, as directed by the Magistrate.

CONVEYANCE (LETTERS AND DESPATCHES).

1. When it is absolutely necessary to send a letter or other document from one part of the country to another by despatch, it should be sent by a mounted constable to the next Police Station, to be given to the officer in charge there, when the constable will return to the station from which he started, and the officer to whom the letter was delivered will in like manner forward it to the next station, and it will thus be forwarded to its destination without any constable being taken further from his own station than to the next.

2. When despatches are thus forwarded from station to station, written instructions, called a "Route," will accompany the despatch, and in it should be stated the time of starting, the rate per mile at which it is to be carried, and whether it is to be conveyed during the night. The time of the receipt of the letter, and its despatch from each station, will be entered in the "Route" by the officer in charge of the station, who will also make such remarks as he may consider advisable as to the condition in which the man and horse arrived. This "Route" should be carefully preserved, in case of its being necessary to refer to it.

3. No officer is to forward a despatch by means of a mounted constable unless it is of so urgent a nature as to require a more speedy delivery than could otherwise be obtained; and every such letter should be endorsed "urgent," and have the name of the writer written on its cover, and every officer so forwarding a despatch will be held responsible that there was a sufficient case of urgency to justify his having done so; if the line of stations is not specified, the officer in charge of each station where the despatch arrives will use his discretion in forwarding it to the next, by the best line for its reaching its destination.

4. The weekly reports, returns, and other ordinary correspondence, can for the most part be forwarded to head quarters by the usual patrols, or by post, without the necessity of despatching a special messenger.

CORONER.

1. An inquest of death should be held in all cases of violent or sudden death, of casualties by which death ensues, of persons found dead, of persons dying in prison, and of *all* suicides.

2. When any sudden death or murder occurs, and becomes known to the Police, the sub-inspector or sergeant on duty at the station is to give notice to the Police or other Magistrate for the District. The entry in the Occurrence Book is to show the number of the police constable by whom the notice is forwarded and the hour at which it is sent.

3. A constable is to attend an inquest to preserve order and render assistance to the Coroner or Magistrate : he is to remain in attendance till the coroner or Magistrate leaves, and he is to to report the result of the inquiry.

4. Immediately at the conclusion of an inquest or magisterial inquiry that member of the force who was concerned in the inquiry will fill up a "Report of Inquest" form, and submit it, without delay, through the proper channel, to the inspector of the District.

5. The property found upon the body of any dead person, into the circumstances of whose death an inquiry has been held, shall be minutely entered under the proper heading, and if handed over to the Curator of Intestate Estates, his agent, or other person, a receipt for the same must be attached to the report of inquest when forwarded through the Inspector to the Commissioner's office.

CORRESPONDENCE.

1. All letters and reports from any district for transmission to the Commissioner's Office, should be forwarded through the Inspector of the district, except in case of outrage, serious breach of the public peace, or in any matter of an urgent nature, when officers in charge of stations or divisions are to report direct to the Commissioner.

2. All correspondence and reports must be expressed in clear and concise terms, and should be written in a neat and legible hand, on foolscap paper, with one third margin.

3. Reports from subordinate members of the Force should be drawn up in the third person, according to the following form:—

District,
Station,
1876.

"Constable [*or* sergeant, &c., *as the case may be*],
(Letter and number) reports &c."

4. With the exception of officers in charge of districts, who are each allowed the services of a member of the Force as clerk, it is expected that all members of the Force will make out their reports in their own handwriting.

5. Reports relating to outrage upon person or property, or to the peace of the country, although conveyed in concise terms, should embrace a full statement of facts, and of such other particulars as may enable the Government to form a correct opinion upon the case. In every instance of crime, the officer should state in his report whether any, and what clue has been obtained to the discovery of the perpetrators, and the steps which have been adopted to trace out the offenders, and should also inform the police of the neighboring district or station of the particulars of the offence.

6. Such occasions afford the head of the department a fair opportunity of judging of the zeal, intelligence, and ability of the members of the Force, who should bear in mind that in estimating their claims to promotion, due reference will be had to the manner in which they have been accustomed to acquit themselves of this immediate branch of their duties, as well as to the success which has attended their efforts to bring criminals to justice.

7. In referring to communications previously received from head quarters, officers are enjoined to quote, not only the date of such communications, but also the numbers and letters which they may have borne, if any; and when any communication is forwarded with a minute, the party receiving it will, after noting and attending to it, return it without delay, to the person by whom it was forwarded.

8. In forwarding the usual returns, or any returns which may be called for by the Commissioner, it is not required that they shall be accompanied by any communication, unless it may be necessary to give some explanation or information respecting such returns.

9. All correspondence with other Departments of the Public Service, as well as (generally) with persons not in the police, on any matter of police duty, is to be carried on through the Commissioner's Office.

10. Police may communicate with each other on matters of duty, and for the purpose of obtaining information.

11. Whenever a Magistrate or other authority desires the police to make a communication to the Commissioner on any subject, they are to be requested to make the communication in writing, to prevent any misapprehension or mistake in conveying the communication.

12. In cases where the Commissioner desires the police to acquaint persons with any matter, they will make such communication verbally, and not in writing.

13. Communications by telegraph with police of any other colony, are not to be made, except through the Commissioner's Office.

14. Anonymous correspondence by police is strictly prohibited.

15. All papers and correspondence are to be kept very carefully and clean.

16. Papers upon which inquiries are directed, are to be completed and forwarded to the Commissioner's Office with as little delay as possible.

COUNTERFEIT COIN.

1. In all charges relating to counterfeit coin the police are to search prisoners immediately in the place where they are taken into custody, and in the presence of the complainant, when the circumstances admit of its being done; or otherwise to take such precautions as will prevent the prisoners making away with false coin or other evidence of guilt.

2. There is no offence in passing counterfeit coin unless their is evidence of guilty knowledge, and it is an offence to bend or deface the current coin of the realm.

COURTS (POLICE).

1. The police are to observe the utmost attention and respect towards Police Magistrates at all times.

2. The police are not to enter into conversation with, or make statements when before, a Magistrate, except as evidence, or respecting a case under investigation.

3. Money or fees of any kind are not to be received by police at Police Courts; such monies are to be received only by the Magistrate's clerk.

4. The police concerned in cases for hearing at Police Courts are to be punctual in attendance at the hour for transacting business, properly dressed, clean, and neat in appearance.

5. They are to take with them from the station an attendance card to show the times of departure and arrival. After the duty is performed the cards are to be returned to the Sub-Inspector's office.

6. If a Magistrate wishes to communicate through the police to the Commissioner on any subject, he is to be requested to do so in writing. (See "Correspondence.")

7. If a prisoner through drunkenness or other cause cannot be taken before a Magistrate, the Charge Book, with a memorandum under the heading of "remarks," explaining the cause, is to be submitted to him. If a prosecutor or any witness is known by the police to be drunk, or not quite sober, a communication to that effect is to be made to the Magistrate before the individual appears in the court to give evidence.

The communication to the Magistrate is to be made by the Sub-Inspector, if one is present, if not, by the sergeant or constable engaged in the case.

8. A Sub-Inspector, sergeant, or senior constable is to be present at every Police Court for the better regulation of the police who attend, and to see that no waste of time takes place; also to mark up the cards of attendance of

the officers engaged, and to report any misconduct on the part of the police, or any remarks by the Magistrates affecting the police.

9. Strict order is to be observed at Police Courts, and the passages and approaches to the Courts are to be kept quite clear and free from obstructions.

10. The police are not to draw up summonses, that being the duty of the Magistrate's clerk. Any assistance, in statement of the circumstances of each case, is to be given by the officer charged with obtaining the summons.

11. Sergeants or constables will not sit down or lounge about the Court, during any portion of the time a Magistrate is sitting on the Bench.

COURTS (SUPREME AND DISTRICT).

1. A police sergeant or constable having to attend at Sessions is to parade at the Police Station on the morning of the day on which he is bound over to appear, sufficiently early to enable him to arrive at the Court at ten o'clock, and at the same hour on each subsequent day, so long as the trials last.

2. Before leaving the station, he is to be inspected by the Sub-Inspector or sergeant on duty, to see that he is clean and in proper uniform; also that he takes all property with him necessary to be produced in Court in the case in which he is concerned (see paragraph 7). The Sub-Inspector or sergeant is to give any instructions which the peculiar circumstances of a case may require.

3. On arrival at the Court the Sub-Inspector, sergeant, or constable who has charge of the case, is to endeavor to find the prosecutor and witnesses, and keep them together, to appear in Court at any moment the case may be called on: and the police are not to leave without permission from the proper officer of the Court, and the other witnesses are, as far as possible, to be prevented doing so.

4. Where a list of cases for trial is posted in the Court, it is to be frequently referred to for information; but the police and other witnesses are to bear in mind that cases may be called on out of their order on the list for trial.

5. Should any witness be absent when the case is called on for trial, the police are to inform the Crown Solicitor or Crown Prosecutor of such absence; and all witnesses are to be reminded that the Court will refuse expenses to any person improperly absent.

6. The whole of the property taken from the person or lodgings of a prisoner, or found anywhere, if it relates to any charge against him, is to be taken to the Court and held in readiness to be produced as soon as the case comes on; and if in parcels, to prevent delay, they are to be opened.

7. The Sub-Inspector or sergeant on duty at the station, when the case is disposed of by the Magistrate, may, when he thinks proper, direct a sergeant or constable to keep in his own custody all property relating to a case for trial, that such property may be more easily identified at the trial.

8. The sergeant on duty at the station is in every instance to keep an account of all articles left with a sergeant or constable, who is to secure and mark the property while in his possession, so as to be enabled to swear that each article is the same as that first received by him. The officers or sergeants in charge of stations will be held responsible should any man leave the service with any such property in his possession.

9. When bulky or weighty property is required to be produced in Court, it is not to be carried by police from place to place, but conveyed by cab or otherwise, and the cost is to be charged to Contingent Account.

10. The police, when giving evidence at Supreme, District, or Police Courts, are to stand in an upright, respectful manner, speaking calmly and explicitly in a clear, distinct, and audible tone, so that the court and jury may easily hear them. They are to confine themselves strictly to evidence in the case before the Court, and be prepared with any notes of the circumstances which they may have made at the time of their occurrence; keeping also constantly in mind the depositions which they signed before the Magistrate, with which their evidence at the trial should exactly agree. They are not to use any low o

cant expressions; they are not to refer to any former conviction against the prisoner, unless called on by the Judge or Magistrate to do so. When cross-examined by counsel for the prisoner, they are to answer with the same readiness and civility as when giving evidence in support of the charge, remembering that the manner or insinuations of counsel are not to affect them, and that the ends of justice will be best aided by their showing a desire simply to tell the whole truth, whether in favor of or against the prisoner.

11. The police are not to drink with, or provide or pay for, or in any way interfere with providing refreshment for witnesses, by whomsoever they may be requested to do so, unless in any special case previously authorised by the Commissioner.

12. No one in the Police is to recommend a prosecutor to employ legal aid in any case, or interfere in any way with procuring legal aid either for a prosecutor or a prisoner.

13. All property in the hands of the police, which belonged to a person convicted of felony, is to be delivered up immediately to the Inspector of the district.

14. If any question is raised, during or after a trial, as to whom any property in the hands of the police should be given up, application is to be made by the Police concerned at once to the Judge to make an order respecting the disposal of such property. If such order be not made, a full report of the circumstances, with names and account of any person claiming the property, is to be made to the Commissioner.

15. In all cases of property given up to any person by direction of the Judge, a receipt, enumerating each article, is to be taken by the police and handed to the sergeant on duty at the station on the return of the police from the Court, that it may be compared by the sergeant with the list of articles in the Charge Book.

16. The police are not to incur any expenses in conveying witnesses to any trial without the sanction of the Commissioner.

17. Any of the police being a witness in a case before a Magistrate, if he is under recognizance to attend to prosecute at the Sessions in another case, is to inform the Magistrate before whom he is giving evidence, and previous to the remand or committal of the prisoner, of the day or days on which he is already under recognizance to appear and give evidence in a previous case, in order that he may not be required to attend at different places on the same day.

18. If any of the police have to attend at a Police Court with a charge on the same day they are under recognizance to appear at any District or Supreme Court, they are to acquaint the sergeant on duty at the station, by whom a report is to be made to the Sub-inspector or officer on duty at the Supreme Court, in order that he may acquaint the Crown Solicitor or Crown Prosecutor with the cause of their absence. The police are to go first to the Police Court, and report to the Sub-Inspector or sergeant on duty, who is to apply to the Magistrate to have the case disposed of without delay to enable them to attend as soon as possible at the District or Supreme Court; and when the case at the Police Court is disposed of, they are to go at once to the District or Supreme Court.

19. Any of the police under recognizance to appear at the Supreme or District Court, or who have a case for hearing before a Magistrate, are not to be sent into the country on duty, or allowed leave-of-absence for any purpose so as to interfere with their attendance as witnesses.

20. If a case is disposed of without the police concerned being called as witnesses, the Sub-Inspector or sergeant is to acquaint them, so that they may not be unnecessarily detained at the Court.

11. The whole of the police attending Supreme or District Courts as prosecutors, witnesses, or on any other duty, are to appear in proper uniform, except those allowed to wear plain clothes.

CRIME (PREVENTION OF).

1. In performance of their duty as peace officers, the police are distinctly to understand that their efforts should be principally directed to the prevention of crime. The

security of person and property, the preservation of public tranquility, and all the other objects of a Police Force will thus be better effected than by the detection and punishment of offenders after they have succeeded in committing crime.

2. When in any district offences are frequently committed, there must be reason to suspect that the Police Force in that district is not properly conducted. The absence of crime will be considered the very best evidence that can be given of the complete efficiency of the police; and the officers and men of any district in which this security and good order have been attained may feel assured that such efficiency will be taken notice of.

CRIME REPORTS—THEIR PREPARATION.

1. It has been observed that there is not, on the part of members of the Police Force, that uniformity of action that there should be with regard to the course to be adopted in the preparation and transmission of reports of crime, and of other information connected with the criminal class generally. This absence of uniformity has been more particularly observed in the transmission of reports of matter for insertion in the *Police Gazette*.

2. In preparing and forwarding communications for insertion in the *Police Gazette*, too much attention cannot be paid to the following instructions :—

    (1.) *Police Gazette.*—Communications for this *Gazette* should be addressed to "The Commissioner of Police, Brisbane," prepaid; they must be of Police interest, or no notice will be taken of them. Officers in charge of stations are requested to report to the Commissioner of Police every instance of the non-delivery of the *Gazette*.

    (2.) *Report of offences committed.*—Every such report must be prepared on a criminal offence form, signed by the officer in charge of the District or station, and forwarded to the Commissioner's office, with the least possible delay, with duplicate of warrant if not executed.

(3.) *Warrants.*—Whenever it is desired that any individual whose name is given, shall be apprehended, it should be stated in the advertisement for the *Gazette* whether or not a warrant has been issued for the apprehension of the offender. When a warrant has not been issued in the first instance, any subsequent report, announcing the issue of a warrant, should repeat the offender's description, or refer to it in the *Police Gazette*.

(4.) *Names.*—It is particularly requested that in all informations the names of persons and places may be spelt correctly, and written legibly, the christian name being given with the surname whenever possible, and written in full to prevent mistakes.

(5.) *Stray Cattle.*—No advertisements of lost horses or cattle will be published in this *Gazette*, unless they be Government property, but notices of horses or cattle believed to be stolen will be inserted gratuitously.

(6.) *Property described.*—The brands of horses and cattle should be imitated as nearly as possible, and their exact positions given. In describing watches, it should be stated whether they are opened-faced, hunting, double-cased, or half-hunting—the term "double-cased" being reserved for those watches whose outer case is removed in order to wind, "half-hunting" implying a very small glass in the metal cover of the dial.

(7.) *Rewards.*—No notice of reward offered by any private party or parties will, for the future, be inserted in the *Police Gazette*, unless there be forwarded to the Commissioner of Police the guarantee of some responsible person that the reward shall be payable according to law, on the arrest or conviction of the offender, and not merely for the recovery of property. If such notice be communicated by telegraph, the addition of the words "guarantee received" will be sufficient. In such cases, however, the guarantee must be forwarded without delay.

(8.) *Previous references.*—It is requested that, in all reports respecting cases already *Gazetted*, officers in charge of police, or others concerned, will be good enough to quote the date and page of the *Police Gazette* in which the previous notice has appeared, and in reporting arrests, to state by whom effected. Supplementary reports of cases already reported, but not *Gazetted*, should contain such information as will clearly identify the case.

(9.) *Telegrams.*—In telegrams the use of figures must be avoided, and words at full length substituted. In forwarding the brands of horses and cattle per telegraph, it should be stated of what kind of letters the brands consist, whether of roman capitals, or in writing.

(10.) *Members of the Police Force* are directed to peruse the *Police Gazette* carefully, and to notify to the Commissioner any information in reference to anything therein inserted of which they may be possessed.

3. Care is to be taken to describe the offence as accurately as possible; the table of indictable offences (see appendix M.) will be of assistance in this matter, and is circulated among members of the force for the sole purpose of assisting them in describing offences in proper terms, and not to explain the state of the colonial law with regard to the offences named. If there be in any case a doubt on the latter point, reference must be made to the Acts of the Queensland Legislature, or other legal works of authority.

4. The distinction between ordinary larceny and robbery must be observed. Larceny or theft is the unlawful taking and carrying away of things personal, or of things which have been made the subject of larceny by statute, with intent to deprive the right owner of the same.

5. Robbery is open and violent larceny from the person, or the unlawful and forcible taking from the person of another, or in his presence, against his will, of goods or money to any value, by violence, or putting him in fear.

The previous violence or putting in fear is, therefore, the criterion that distinguishes robbery from other larcenies. A case of larceny should not be described as robbery, unless the act of stealing have been accompanied by violence, or putting in fear by force, or threatening by word or gesture, so as to create an apprehension of danger, and thereby induce the owner to part with his property without or against his consent.

6. The particular kind of larceny should be specified; as larceny from the person, larceny from a dwelling house, larceny by servants, larceny of letters containing money, or simple larceny, as the case may be; and if the amount stolen be less than 40s. the offence should be described as simple larceny under 40s.

7. So also in the case of robbery, or an attempt to rob; the particulars should be given as robbery under arms, highway robbery, assault and robbery, assault with intent to rob, &c.

8. Cases have occurred in which obtaining money under false pretences, misappropriation or fraud, have been improperly termed larceny, but attention to the foregoing remarks of the circumstances that constitute larceny or robbery should be sufficient to prevent the repetition of such an error.

9. Embezzlement is often confounded with larceny, on the one hand, and with breach of trust, on the other. Embezzlement is the act of appropriating to one's own use that which is received in trust for another. It is distinguished from larceny as being committed in respect of property which has come into the possession of the defendant by virtue of his employment, and has not since been in the possession of the owner. The offender must be a clerk, servant, agent, factor, &c., or he must be acting in some such capacity for another person.

10. A breach of trust, on the other hand, is merely a violation of duty by a trustee, executor, or other person in a fiduciary position, and it by no means necessarily implies that the person guilty of this breach of trust has applied the property to his own use. As previously stated, it does not form the subject of a criminal charge, and is

noticed in this place solely for the purpose of showing in what it differs from embezzlement.

11. The distinction between larceny, embezzlement, and breach of trust, are often so nice and subtle that it is difficult to say under which head an offence ranges. Where there is this doubt as to the description of an offence, the particulars of the offence should be given as fully as possible.

12. Breach of prison, or prison breaking, must be distinguished from escaping from legal custody. In the former there must have been an actual breaking, and the offence amounts to felony if the charge against the offender were treason or felony, but a misdemeanor only in other cases. The mere escape from legal custody without violence is never more than a misdemeanor. But neither breach of prison nor escape from custody will be an offence unless the imprisonment have been legal.

13. In giving the names of offenders and others, the christian name or names should stand before the surname, and all the names should be written at length. When it is advisable, as it generally will be, to state the trade or profession also, it should be written, so as to guard against its being misunderstood for a surname. If this be not attended to, the word "baker" or "tailor," and there are many other such, might be read as either a surname or as a trade.

14. In giving the date and hour of the offence, instead of "12 a.m." or "12 p.m.," say "noon" or "midnight" as the case may be, the midnight having the same date as the day preceding.

15. If information of the offence have been given to the police by letter, it should be so stated on the criminal offence form, under the head "date and hour reported to the police, and by whom." This will account for any incompleteness in the report, in consequence of the police not having had an opportunity of questioning the informant.

16. All the names or aliases of offenders or others named in the report should be given as fully as they are known to the police.

17. If the grounds for suspecting any person named would appear to justify the issue of a warrant for his arrest, and no warrant has been issued, the reason for there being no warrant should be given under the head " steps taken and whether warrant issued."

18. If a warrant has been issued, it should be stated under the same head by what Bench and how the warrant has been disposed of, that is, whether it has been filed in the office of the officer in charge, or forwarded elsewhere. If the Bench be at a place where there is no Police Station, the name of the nearest Police Station should be given. It is important that the *Police Gazette* notice should contain these particulars, in order that the police may not only be informed where to apply for particulars respecting the warrant or the offence, but that in case of the arrest of the offender, they may, in the absence of the warrant, be better able to obtain a remand of the prisoner on the production of the *Gazette* notice.

19. Where the warrant is one of *commitment in default of distress*, the amount of the judgment with costs should be given. A constable has no right to arrest in such a case, if the total amount with the cost is tendered to him, and if, therefore, he do not know that amount, he cannot be certain whether he should arrest or not. Nor should the constable arrest the defendant unless he have the warrant in his possession at the time, to be produced to the defendant if required. If he apprehend without the warrant, he will expose himself to risk; for his detention of the defendant will be illegal, whether he be required by the defendant to produce the warrant or not.

20. In addition to the brands of horses and cattle, their sex, colour, &c., should be given so far as they can be ascertained. (See " Burglary," " Warrants.")

CRIME REPORTS, THEIR TRANSMISSION, Etc.

1. All reports of offences committed, which reports are, as a rule, to be prepared on the Criminal Offence Form; supplementary reports relative to the same, reports of arrests, and generally reports of all matters connected with crime,

E

which it is desirable should be published in the *Police Gazette*, are, in the first instance, and with as little delay as possible, to be forwarded by officers in charge of districts, direct to the officer in charge of Detectives, Brisbane, who will enter, in red ink, on the upper portion of all such reports, the date on which he received them, and after noting such of the information contained therein, as may be of service to the Detective Police, will forward the reports to the Commissioner, with a view to such of the information as it may be deemed desirable to publish, being inserted in the *Police Gazette*.

2. The Officer in charge of Detectives must be careful to arrange that these reports are forwarded to the Commissioner's office with strict punctuality, so that matter for publication may not fail to appear in any number of the *Gazette*, through delay on the part of himself or any one under his command.

3. But cases will occasionally occur, in which the slight delay arising from such reports being forwarded through the Detective Office, in Brisbane, should be avoided, and the earliest possible information should be communicated to the Commissioner's office. In every such case, a duplicate of the report forwarded to the Officer in charge of Detectives, should be inclosed to the Commissioner direct, but such report, in addition to being marked "duplicate," should contain a remark that the original had, at the same time, been forwarded in the usual course to the Officer in charge of Detectives, and the original report should, in the same manner, contain a remark that a duplicate of it had been enclosed direct to the head of the department.

4. In urgent cases, members of the Force in charge of out stations, will forward reports direct to the Commissioner, instead of sending them in the ordinary course to their respective officers in charge. When a member of the Force adopts this course, he should, at the same time, send a *duplicate of the report* to the Officer in charge of the District.

5. It may be remarked, indeed, that in every case in which duplicate communications are forwarded, whether they be reports of crime or not, each report should contain a reference to the other. If this be not attended to, there is the danger that the two reports will be treated as if they referred to different cases, instead of being regarded as duplicate reports of but one case.

6. Officers in charge of police, will forward to the Commissioner's office, *at the earliest possible moment*, full particulars of any and every occurrence of more than ordinary interest, in the districts under their control, whether in the shape of disturbance, the discovery of new gold fields, or incidents of a like nature.

7. Officers in charge of Districts connected with Brisbane by means of the electric telegraph, have every facility for forwarding speedy and authentic reports on matters of the kind.

8. On the first day of each month, a return showing the cases of crime reported during the previous month in which no arrests have been made, and the steps taken by police, in each case, to arrest offenders, &c., will be forwarded by the members of the Force in charge of Stations, to the officers in charge of their respective Districts.

9. It is of importance that all information upon which it may be the duty of the Detective Police to take action, should reach the officer in charge of that body at the earliest possible date.

10. Any notice which an officer of police, or other person may wish to appear in the *Police Gazette*, should be forwarded direct to the Commissioner, if it is clear that it does not contain information of which the Detective Police should take cognizance.

CRIMINAL STATISTICS.

1. For the purpose of compiling annually the Police Criminal Statistics of the colony, it is necessary that for every person arrested by the police, the following parti-

culars, entered on a card for the purpose, should be forwarded to the Commissioner's office:—

District
Station
Date of arrest
Offence
Name
Sex
Age
Country
Religion
Education
Occupation
If previously convicted
How disposed of

2. As, with very few exceptions, every person arrested will be confined in some police watchhouse, and the charge against him or her will be entered in the Charge Book, the members of the Force in charge of lock-ups will be responsible for the preparation of the cards for all prisoners whose names appear in the Charge Book, and will hand them weekly, or as much oftener as may be required, to the officer in charge of the station.

3. In cases where persons arrested are not confined in any watchhouse, and whose names, consequently, do not appear in any watchhouse book—as, for instance, when a prisoner is arrested during the sitting of a Police Court, and is at once taken before it, or when a person is arrested for debt, and at once forwarded to some gaol—the arresting constable will be responsible for the preparation of the necessary card, and for handing it to the officer in charge of the station.

4. Unless particular attention be paid to this arrangement, it will often happen that debtors and others will be arrested, and the necessary information will not be sent to the Commissioner's office, simply because they have not been confined in any lock-up. For every person arrested, whether he be confined in a lock-up or not, a

card showing the necessary particulars must be prepared and forwarded.

5. These cards are to be enclosed by the sergeant or constable in the weekly duty reports, and forwarded to the Inspector or officer in charge of the district, who will be responsible for having the cards compared with the return of prisoners arrested, given in the duty reports, for the purpose of seeing that the proper number of cards have been prepared.

6. The sergeant or constable in charge of any station, and the officer in charge of the district, through his clerk, will thus be separately responsible, not only that a sufficient number of cards is forwarded for the prisoners arrested, but that duplicate cards are not forwarded for the same offence.

7. The cards are then to be forwarded with the duty reports to the Commissioner's office, and the cards for each station should be kept separate, so as to facilitate their being compared with the returns.

8. When a prisoner is remanded by the Bench, and the charge remains undecided when the returns for any week are sent in, the card for that case must be held over by the officer in charge of the station, until the case has been discharged, summarily disposed of, or committed for trial; the card must then be completed by the insertion of the necessary particulars, and forwarded to the headquarters of the district.

9. Should a prisoner be removed from one Police Station to another, under remand, to a different Bench, or for any other purpose, the card for that prisoner must be forwarded with him, and the sergeant in charge of that station to which the prisoner was forwarded will be responsible for its due completion and transmission. If a card has not been received with any prisoner, the sergeant should at once write for it, and not make out a fresh one.

10. The exceptions to this rule are remands of deserters to the military or naval authorities and remands to places out of the colony. So far as regards the preparation of

these cards; a remand under any of these heads may be considered as a final disposal of the case, and entered on the card accordingly.

11. Sometimes a prisoner is brought before a Bench on a charge which, on the production of evidence, has to be altered or changed to one altogether different. In that case, the charge to be entered on the card is not to be that, on which the prisoner was arrested, but that on which he is dealt with by the Bench. Thus a charge of horse-stealing, which the Bench would have no option but to discharge, or to commit for trial, may be changed to a charge of illegally using another person's horse, which the Bench has power to deal with summarily. Charges of burglary, or house-breaking, are often altered to cases of simple stealing from a dwelling; and attempts to commit rape become cases of common assault. Many other instances might be named.

12. When a prisoner is charged with two or more offences, such as drunkenness, and assaulting the police, and all the offences are proved, but one penalty only inflicted for the whole; the charge to be entered on the card is not necessarily to be that, which in a legal point of view is the most grave offence; but that which in the whole matter has assumed the most prominent and striking character. Thus in the case of the two offences here named; if the man were very drunk and the assault of but trifling consequence, the charge on the card should be that of drunkenness; but if the assault on the police was of an aggravated character, it is obvious that that should be the charge to be inserted. These cases are not of frequent occurrence, and when they do occur, the members of the force concerned, who have had the opportunity of hearing the cases in Court, will have little difficulty in deciding which offences are to be inserted in the cards; should they, however, be at a loss to decide, they had better meet the difficulty by inserting all the charges.

13. When, however, a separate penalty is inflicted for each offence charged against the prisoner, whether the offences have been committed at the same or on different occasions, a separate card is to be prepared for each

offence thus disposed of, in the same manner as if the prisoner had been arrested and punished for the several charges on different days.

14. When a penalty gives a prisoner the alternative between a fine and imprisonment, it must always be stated on the card, whether the prisoner paid the fine or chose the alternative of imprisonment.

15. When debtors are arrested, the term of imprisonment mentioned in the warrant of commitment must be stated.

16. When a prisoner is committed for trial, it should be stated whether the case is to be tried in Supreme or District Court, and the place and date of the sitting of the Court should be added. Unless this be done, there may be considerable difficulty and delay in the Commissioner's Office, in ascertaining the result of the trial; more particularly as prisoners are sometimes committed for trial in a part of the colony distant from that in which they were arrested.

17. To enable the Commissioner of Police to ascertain the result of all committals for trial, it is necessary he should be furnished, as soon as possible, after the sitting of each Court (either Supreme or District), with a return showing the disposal of all prisoners committed for trial at that Court. Every officer in charge, therefore, will be responsible for forwarding to the Commissioner's Office, immediately after the termination of every such Court in his district, a return in the form given in Appendix G, showing the names of prisoners committed for trial, date of committal, offence, and sentence. Such returns are to include all cases committed for trial, from whatever district they may have been committed, and whether the case has been tried or not. Cases, therefore, which the Crown Law Officers do not consider it necessary to allow to proceed to trial, or in which, as it is technically termed, a *nolle prosequi* is entered, must not be omitted.

18. There will seldom be any difficulty in ascertaining the particulars of such cases, but as a precautionary measure it will be found advisable that, in the office of

each officer in charge of a district, there be kept a return of all prisoners who, in that district, have been committed for trial, and the officer in charge, through his clerk, will be responsible that his returns for the Courts in his district give the result of every case committed for trial in the same district. When the result of any committal has been forwarded to the Commissioner's Office in the required form, the entry of the case in the return in the head-quarters office should be ticked off, as requiring no further attention.

19. But when cases are committed for trial at a Court in a different district, information of such cases should be communicated to the officer in charge of that district shortly before the trial, in order that he may not leave his returns incomplete, by omitting from it any case which has not been allowed to proceed to trial through a *nolle prosequi* having been entered.

20. Should any officer, however, be unable to ascertain with certainty the result of any such case, he should, nevertheless, include the case in his return, but should also state in it that he has been unable to learn the result, and the Commissioner will obtain the further particulars necessary by inquiring at the Law Offices.

21. In stating the date of arrest on the card, the name of the month is to be written in full.

22. As to the description of the offence, the instructions given under the head "Crime Reports, preparation of," apply also to the preparation of these cards. In addition, however, to the return of indictable offences therein referred to, a further table of offences, as classified for the Annual Police Statistics of Crime, is given in Appendix F. It is apprehended that with those two tables, the one of indictable offences only, the other of all offences for which arrests may be made, there will be little difficulty in describing an offence for either purpose; but should a member of the Force be at any time at a loss to know under what head to classify an offence, or should the offence be such as he considers cannot well be placed under any head in those lists, he should state the offence at length, giving, if possible, a reference to the Act under

which it was disposed of. If the space on the card be insufficient for this purpose, the necessary particulars can be continued on the back.

23. A distinction should always be made between the charges of " drunkenness" and " drunk and disorderly," which, it will be observed, are classified separately in the tables.

24. In the case of lunacy, the known, or supposed cause should be stated, as " lunacy from the effects of drink," &c.

25. When lunatics are remanded for medical examination, the final disposal of the case should be ascertained and entered, that is, whether they have been discharged, remanded to the asylum, or otherwise disposed of.

26. In the case of "assaults with intent, &c.," the nature of the intent must be stated, that is, whether it was to rob, to commit a rape, to kill, &c.

27. As with criminal offence reports, the christian name of the prisoner should precede the surname.

28. The age and country of the prisoners are to be ascertained as accurately as possible.

29. With respect to the head of religion, it will be sufficient if the prisoners be classed under one or other of the following heads :—

    Protestants
    Roman Catholics
    Jews
    Mahometans
    Pagans
    Unknown.

30. With respect to education, it will be sufficient to class them under the following heads :—

  (a) Neither read nor write
  (b) Read only, or read and write imperfectly
  (c) Read and write well
  (d) Superior instruction.

31. For the sake of convenience, the first four letters of the alphabet may be used for this purpose; that is, (a) for neither read nor write, and so on, as shown above.

32. Greater care must be observed in describing the occupations of prisoners. By occupation is meant the trade or calling the prisoner follows to earn a living ; "wife of," "housewife," "married woman," therefore, are objectionable entries; if married women follow occupations, the occupation, such as "laundress," "servant," &c., should be stated; if they follow no occupation the entry should be "none."

33. Prostitutes will seldom call themselves such, but will in preference term themselves laundresses, servants, or something of the kind ; but whatever they may term themselves they are to be entered as prostitutes, if it is known to the police that they gain their living by prostitution.

34. Offenders have in this colony so many inducements to go from place to place, that it is quite possible that any one may in succession become an inmate of every prison in the colony without its being known to the authorities of any one of them, or of the police, that he or she had ever been in custody before. It is not, therefore, to be expected that the police should always know whether a prisoner has been previously convicted or not, but when it is known to the police that a prisoner has been in confinement before, the card should state as fully as known to the police, on how many previous occasions, and with what results.

CRUELTY TO ANIMALS.

1. A constable on his own view, or on the complaint of a person stating his name and place of abode, may apprehend without warrant any person who shall cruelly beat, ill treat, overdrive, abuse, or torture any animal, or cause the like to be done.

2 The animal may be detained by the constable as security for penalty, and a Justice may, after conviction, order same to be sold.

3. Provision is made under the Act (14 Vic. No. 40) to compel the proprietor of any vehicle to produce the driver or conductor or servant by whom the offence was committed.

4. A summons to the offender is sufficiently served if served on him personally, or left at his usual or last known place of abode.

5. A warrant may issue in the first instance if good grounds for its issue be deposed to on oath.

6. The information must be laid within one calendar month after cause of complaint arose.

7. If one Justice hears the complaint he must sign the conviction and warrant of commitment, but if two Justices hear the complaint both must sign the conviction aud warrant of commitment.

8. A summons for an offence under 14 Vic. No. 40 sec. 1, is not to be applied for by police without the sanction of the officer in charge of the district in which the offence has been committed.

DEAD BODIES.

1. When the body of any deceased person is found by the police, or reported to them as having been found, it should be immediately removed to the Morgue, or the nearest public house in the neighbourhood, but when there are two or more public houses adjacent, they are to be used alternately.

2. It is not the duty of the police to remove dead bodies from any house where they may be lying.

3. When a dead body is conveyed to a Morgue or other place by the police, the face is to be covered.

4. When a body, apparently dead, is in the hands of the police, the instructions issued by the Royal Humane Society, and the National Life boat Institution, copies of which are distributed in every district, are to be immediately and strictly acted upon, but Medical aid is to be sent for as soon as possible; claims for Medical attendance in such cases will be approved according to the regulated scale. If, from the body being in a state of decomposition, or other cause, there can be no doubt that life is extinct, Medical aid is not to be sent for.

5. In all cases where persons are found dead, and are not immediately identified, a description of the body, dress, &c., is to be circulated immediately on receipt of the particulars.

6. When dead bodies are found, and not identified, and their features are not distorted, or the body decomposed, the Inspector may, if he considers it desirable, obtain a photograph, with a view to proving future identity, the cost to be charged in monthly contingent account.

7. Every circumstance connected with the appearance of the body, the position in which it was found, and the probable length of time dead, should be noted; the body should then be carefully searched, and the effects found thereon kept in the custody of the police, and produced at the inquest.

8. The circumstances of the finding of a body, or any case coming to the knowledge of the police where an inquest ought to be held, should be immediately reported to the Police Magistrate and to the senior officer of police in charge of the station.

9. Should the Police Magistrate be absent or unable to attend, a communication to that effect should be forthwith made to the nearest Magistrate, that he may hold an inquiry.

10. A constable is to remain in charge of the body until an inquest or inquiry has been held thereon.

11. On all occasions, a report should be made to the Police Magistrate of the following cases:—Persons found drowned, persons found dead, persons killed by accident or otherwise, persons dying suddenly, prisoners dying in any of Her Majesty's Gaols or other places of confinement, suicides, and all other cases where death is suspected to have occurred from foul play; and a similar report, together with the result of the magisterial inquiry, should be made to the Commissioner of Police.

12. In cases of suicide, murder, &c., the instrument by which death had been induced, such as a knife, razor, pistol, &c., or bottle or paper which contained poison, should be carefully preserved by the police, and produced at the inquest.

13. Immediately on any death occurring from any of the above causes, the police should endeavor to procure evidence of identity of the deceased, and secure the attendance at the magisterial inquiry of the persons who shall have found such body or witnessed the circumstance causing the death of the deceased, or who shall be able to give any necessary information on the subject.

14. When the place is remote, and no Police Magistrate is within a reasonable distance, the police should have the body examined by some medical gentleman if possible, but if not, they must then make the best examination they can themselves; the object being, in such cases, to ascertain if death has been caused by violence.

15. Should there be marks of violence on the body, it is of importance to ascertain the instrument, if any, with which the wounds have been inflicted.

16. If the wounds consist of a cut, the length, breadth, and depth should be ascertained as far as possible, together with the exact position and appearances. If firearms appear to have been used to cause death, it is desirable to find the bullet or any other matter which may have entered the body; but in all cases, before the body or any weapon or other article which could in any way be connected with the case is moved, or its position altered, care should be taken that every particular is noted in writing.

17. Every exertion should also be made to find the particular weapon supposed to have been used, and if found, its state when first seen by the police should be carefully noted, with all the other particulars.

18. The constable should then wait upon the nearest Magistrate and give his deposition, forwarding a copy immediately to head-quarters, with a full statement of all particulars which may enable the Commissioner of Police to judge if the matter has been properly inquired into by the police.

19. Where a suspicion of felony attaches, the most careful inquiry should be made of the names, both christian and surname, of all persons who may be supposed to know any circumstance connected with the

death. Above all things, every person without exception present at the time of death should be examined before the Magistrate.

20. Police should not take on themselves to bury the body, unless on the receipt of a certificate in the form for the purpose from the Justice of the Peace.

21. In inquiries into violent deaths, the police officer in charge of the station at the time must consider himself as the person whose special duty it is to get up the case for the Magistrate.

DEBTS.

Members of the Force must not contract debts to publicans and others, or incur obligations of any kind, nor place themselves in a position calculated to in any degree shackle their exertions or impair their efficiency in discharging the duties of their office. (See "Money.")

DEFAULTER'S SHEET.

1. On a constable's misconducting himself, the particulars of the case are entered in a Defaulter's Sheet, which must accompany him should he be transferred to any other district. On a constable who has never committed himself being transferred a Defaulter's Sheet containing his name and date of appointment only, must be forwarded with him.

2. For the accuracy of these sheets the officers in charge of districts will be held responsible, retaining them in their own possession, at the head quarters of their districts.

3. On the discharge or dismissal of any man from the Force, his Defaulter's Sheet must be forwarded to the office of the Commissioner, to be there filed for reference, and on the application, written or personal, of anyone who has been discharged, a printed certificate of character will be made out in accordance with his sheet, signed by the Commissioner, and furnished to him, and no other certificates of character or service are to be given to the parties leaving the Force.

4. No certificates of character are given to those who have been dismissed.

5. The Defaulter's Sheet is not to be produced in any Court, unless by special order of the Commissioner. No person is entitled to require the sheet to be produced.

6. When any of the police appear before the Commissioner for misconduct, an Inspector or Sub-inspector is to attend, that the Commissioner may be informed as to the general character of the individual reported, and to carry out any directions given by the Commissioner.

7. In cases where men rejoin the service, the reports against them for misconduct (if any), which are attached to their papers in the Commissioner's office, are to be sent to the districts to which they are transferred; and these are to be submitted, with any later reports that there may be, in every case where these men are brought before the Commissioner, or upon their leaving the service, in which latter case the former certificate is to be permanently retained in this office, and a new certificate for the full period given according to their conduct in the service.

8. No member of the Force excepting the officer in charge of a district will make any entry whatever in a constable's Defaulter's Sheet.

DEPOSITIONS.

1. The police are not to sign depositions at a Police Court, unless previously read over to them, and known to be an accurate statement of their evidence.

2. When police are concerned in cases sent for trial, notes of evidence given by them in their depositions before the Committing Magistrate are to be made and kept, in order that they may refresh their memory before being called upon to give evidence at the trial, and so prevent any discrepancy occurring.

DEPÔT.

1. All candidates for admission into the Police Force are to attend, with an application in their own handwriting, and such testimonials as they may have, at the

Police Depôt in Brisbane, at 9 a.m. on Wednesdays, where, if they are considered suitable, they are engaged. As no exception can be made to this rule, no candidate need, under any circumstances, apply elsewhere.

2. It is to be understood that the Depôt is the headquarters of the whole Force, and, as such, it is under the immediate supervision of the Commissioner himself.

3. All members of the Force, of whatever rank, on visiting Brisbane, whether on duty or leave-of-absence, will report themselves there. If on duty, they will be expected to reside on the premises, for which purpose quarters and accommodation are provided; but should they particularly wish to reside out of the Depôt during their stay in Brisbane, an application to that effect must be made to the officer in charge, who will lay the same before the Commissioner. If on leave-of-absence, it is only necessary that they report themselves both on their arrival, leaving their address, and again on the expiration of their leave.

4. It may happen that the officers reporting themselves will be senior to the officer in charge of the Depôt. In this case they are not to consider that their reporting themselves implies any superiority on the part of that officer, but that, as a matter of discipline, it is incumbent on them so to report themselves, whoever and of whatever rank the officer in charge may be. Nor will they take upon themselves any command, nor interfere with any of the internal arrangements of the Depôt.

DESERTING FAMILIES.

For the offence of deserting families an apprehension is not legal unless a warrant is obtained from a Magistrate; and the police are not to apprehend any person charged with the offence without a warrant.

DETECTIVES.

1. The Detectives, although subject to the same discipline are in most other respects a distinct body of the Force, their duties being to detect rather than to prevent crime.

2. They are under the control of an officer whose office is at Brisbane, and who receives his orders direct from the Commissioner, and as being dressed in plain clothes they may occasionally be required to produce the authority under which they are acting, each of them is furnished with a "warrant card" for the purpose, signed by the head of the department.

3. One Detective is stationed in each of the more important districts, while occasionally a mounted party is employed in various districts, removing from one to another as circumstances may require.

4. They all, however, correspond direct with the Chief Officer in Brisbane; but although they look to him for orders, they will be under the control of the officer in charge of the district in which they may be stationed, so far as his orders do not clash with those they receive from the Detective Office at Brisbane.

5. If this system is properly carried out with a view to the interests of the public, there should generally be no difficulty in detecting crime and tracing out offenders, who, to escape detection have fled from town to country, or from one gold-field to another; and it is expected that the preventive police will consider it imperative upon them to afford every information in their power to the detective police, and to facilitate, in every possible way the proper discharge of their particular duties.

6. The Detective Force is formed by selecting from the preventive police such persons as may be considered suitable for detective duty; they are employed on trial as supernumeraries, during which time they receive the pay of ordinary constables, and if reported favorably of by the officer in charge of that body, they are promoted to the rank and pay of a second-class detective constable, and in due course, if recommended for zeal and efficiency, will be further advanced to the pay of a first-class detective. There are no other grades in the detective body, and the rank of a first-class detective is to be considered as equivalent to that of a sergeant in the preventive force.

7. Although this is a general rule, candidates, who from previous habits, experience, or other reasons may appear

to be particularly adapted for detective duties, may be taken on as supernumeraries without having served in the preventive force, and if after due trial they are approved of, are promoted in the usual manner.

8. One of the principal duties of the Detectives is to make themselves well acquainted with all the criminals in their districts—their associates, habits, and residences.

9. A Register is to be kept at each station, in which all particulars of known criminals are to be entered—especial attention being paid to men againt whom convictions are recorded, in order that proof may be forthcoming if required.

10. It must be understood clearly that it will depend on the skill and vigilance shown by each man in the Detective Force; and, above all, by his success in following up crime and criminals, whether he is allowed to remain in it.

11. A printed Duty Register is to be kept at each station to which Detectives are attached. Each Detective is to enter daily, under the proper headings, the duties upon which he is actually engaged; and the officer in charge is to inspect the Register daily, or as often as he may visit the station, and give necessary directions, or initial each entry, to show that he is cognizant of, or satisfied with, the duties performed.

12. If an inquiry extends over several days, it will not be necessary to re-enter the offence or duty every day, but only the current name and date, and simply refer to the original entry thus: (*See* entry dated   ).

13. A quarterly report is to be made to the Commissioner, on the proper printed form, of the cases undertaken by each Detective, and the results.

14. Brass truncheons of a particular pattern, suitable for being carried in the coat pocket, are to be supplied for the use of Detectives and police specially employed in plain clothes. When called upon to act, and there is any doubt as to their office, the police are to draw the truncheon, which will be readily distinguished as a distinctive mark or badge of office by the persons doubting or resisting their lawful authority.

15. The truncheon is to be shown to the senior officer on duty at the station by Detectives when parading for duty.

16. When changes are made from Detective to uniform duty, the truncheons are to be handed to the Inspector, who is to deliver them to the police who are to be employed as Detectives.

17. The police employed on Detective duties are not to interfere in making private inquiries (not in the pursuit or detection of criminals), at the request of individuals, or to induce payment of money claimed, Such inquiries or interference do not come within the duties of police, and are exceedingly improper and dangerous; any one who does so will be dismissed, or otherwise severely punished.

18. If application is received for inquiry to be made by Detectives on any matter which appears to be forbidden by the above rule, a report of the circumstances of the case is to be made to the Commissioner, who will give directions as to whether the inquiries are to be made.

DISCIPLINE.

1. Dicipline, which implies authority, and its proper exercise on the one hand, and respect and obedience on the other, is essential to the practical direction, action, and efficiency of the Force.

2. As authority necessarily becomes divided, gradations of rank must be established, the holders of each which, while exercising command over subordinates, must pay respect to superiors; this principle holds throughout, until we reach that grade whose simple duty is proper respect to all in command, and prompt and unvarying obedience to their orders.

3. As responsibility for the full discharge of his own peculiar duties at all times attaches to every member of a disciplined force, it is necessary that each should know, as precisely as it is possible to define them, what those duties are, in order to insure a correct and cheerful discharge of them, but, further, as the responsibility

attaching to a superior *may*, at any time devolve on the next in rank, it is essential that the members of each grade shall be acquainted with the duties that circumstances may call on them to discharge.

4. Every inferior, whether officer or otherwise, is to receive the commands of his superior with deference and respect, and to execute them without question or comment to the best of his power; and every superior in his turn, whether officer or otherwise, is to give his orders in the language of moderation, and of regard to the feelings of the individual under his command.

5. The obedience and respect which are here required must be observed throughout the force generally, and not be understood in any partial or confined sense; real discipline, as has been already observed, implies obedience and respect wherever it is due on one hand, and on the other, a just, but energetic use of command and responsibility.

6. Every officer and constable must understand that it is an invariable rule in discipline, that in the absence of a superior, the whole of the duty or charge which was intrusted to that superior devolves upon the next in rank, so that the chain of responsibility may continue unbroken.

DISMISSALS.

1. Any man dismissed from the Police is not to be re-appointed.

2. Except under very particular circumstances, a police constable convicted of any offence before a Magistrate is to be dismissed from the Police Force in consequence of that conviction.

3. If there are any circumstances in a case which the Commissioner can take into consideration, and deem sufficient to justify him in making a recommendation to the Colonial Secretary that the constable should be retained in the service, he will do so, and suspend the constable until the result is known.

4. All pay due to a man dismissed may be forfeited by direction of the Commissioner.

6. Any constable is liable to be discharged for unfitness, or dismissed for negligence or misconduct, independently of any other punishment to which he may by law be subject. The Commissioner may also, if he think fit, dismiss him without assigning any reason.

DISTRAINT OF GOODS, &c.

1. In cases where a distraint is made for non-payment of rent or for any other cause, or disputes arise between persons as to ownership of property seized under legal process, a police sergeant or constable is not to give assistance to either, or interfere between them on any pretence whatever: he is not to enter the house, or the premises, unless it is necessary to prevent an immediate breach of the peace, or to quell a disturbance that has actually arisen, and he is on such occasions merely to take offenders into custody as he is authorised by law to do.

2. When it becomes necessary to sell goods seized under a distress warrant, if it be executed by any of the police, the officer in charge of the station will be held responsible that a respectable licensed auctioneer is employed, and that the charges are usual and reasonable.

3. When application is made by a bailiff of any Court within the colony for the aid of the police in executing a warrant for the apprehension of a party or seizing the goods, it is the duty of the police to aid in the execution of such warrant. (See "Sheriff.")

4. Constables are not, however, to leave their beats, but are to explain to the bailiff that they cannot do so, and refer him to the nearest station.

5. The officer on duty at the station is, when satisfied that the aid of the police is required, to grant such as appears necessary, *but it is the duty of the bailiff to execute the warrant*, and the police are only to act as circumstances make proper in his aid.

6. If application is made at stations for police aid to prevent a breach of the peace when an entry is to be made into any premises, directions are to be given that force used is a breach of the peace, and police are imme-

diately to interfere to prevent it, and apprehend persons committing such violence, though no charge be made by others.

7. Officers of the Courts of Law in the proper execution of their duty on legal process are to be assisted by the police, if required to act in preventing a breach of the peace, or carrying out the law.

8. When goods are fraudulently removed, and placed in any house, or place locked up, or otherwise secured, the landlord or his agent may with the assistance of a police constable (and in the case of a dwelling house after oath having been made before a Magistrate of a reasonable ground to suspect that the goods are in it) break open the house, &c., in the day time and distrain the goods as if they had been in any open place.

DISTRIBUTION OF THE FORCE.

1. The Force is divided into Mounted, Foot, Water Police, and Detectives.

2. The mounted and foot police are distributed among the various districts in such strength and manner as the requirements of the country may demand, and no change whatever is to be made in the location of the Force; without express authority from the Commissioner, except in case of extreme urgency, such as when the officer in charge of the district is convinced that the removal of men from one station to another, or the formation of a new station is absolutely necessary, or when the local authorities make an urgent demand for additional police protection; but in all such cases a full statement of the particulars, and necessity for the alteration must be forwarded to the Commissioner's office without delay.

3. When a number of the residents of any particular locality apply for police protection, the officer in charge of the district will forward the same, with such remarks of his own respecting the necessity of the case, the facilities that may exist for forming a police station, the population, whether scattered or not, the amount and nature

of crime in the neighborhood, whether frequent or occasional daily or nightly patrols would be sufficient, &c., &c., as he may think fit.

4. The principal portion of men in the districts of Brisbane and other large towns, are selected for what may be denominated, city police duty, the particulars of which will require to be given somewhat in detail. (See "Brisbane," "Beats," "Reliefs," &c.)

DISTRICTS.

1. The colony is divided into a certain number of districts, each district into sub-districts or divisions, and these again are divided into patrols or beats.

2. At one of the stations are the head-quarters of the officer in charge of the district, which is in most cases designated by the name of that station. The sub-districts are called by the names of the police stations situated within each respectively. The sub-districts, or stations, with the exception of the head-quarters station, are placed in charge of subordinate officers, and where the station is of minor importance, in charge of a sergeant or senior constable. In either case the party in charge is responsible to the Inspector of the district, for the locality over which he is placed.

3. From the auriferous nature of the colony, and the migratory character of a great portion of the population, consequent on the extension of established gold fields, or the discovery of new ones, it is not possible to decide what shall be, for any lengthened period, the number of sub-districts or stations in each particular district. The numbers and boundaries of districts must necessarily be varied from time to time as circumstances require, it often happening that a district of no great importance becomes, in a very short time, from an increase of population, far more than one officer can control.

4. For the better management of the internal details of the various districts, and in order to protect the public against misconduct on the part of subordinate members of the Force, all members of the Force below the rank of

Sub-Inspector will, in each district, be provided with a letter and number, the letter being general, and indicating the particular district, and the number particular, that is, confined to the sergeant or constable wearing it.

DIVINE SERVICE.

1. The Police are as much as possible to be encouraged to attend Divine service, both by precept and example of the superior officers.

2. Police constables are not to be sent on duty at churches, chapels, or other places of worship, unless specially sanctioned by the Commissioner; but an Inspector may, when he considers it necessary, shorten the beat in the neighborhood of any church or chapel, &c., during Divine service.

3. Should application be made for police at any other place of worship, report is to be made to the Commissioner.

DOGS.

1. Stray dogs, whether muzzled or unmuzzled, seen in the streets, and not under the control of any person, are to be seized by the police, and conveyed to the Police Station, where the sergeant on duty is to take a description, which will be entered in a book kept for that purpose, and circulate to other stations, printed informations.

2. If a stray dog is seized, and wears a collar with the address of any person inscribed thereon, information of the fact is to be sent to the address inscribed on the collar, and the dog is to be detained at the Police Station for forty-eight hours, after which, if not claimed, it will be destroyed.

3. A monthly return is to be made and sent in of the numbers seized, restored to owners, and destroyed.

4. When it becomes necessary for the police to kill a dog, it is to be done as speedily and privately as possible.

5. No officer of the Police Force can be allowed to keep a dog, unless safely fastened up so as to prevent its biting any person, or causing annoyance in any way.

6. The police are to do all in their power to become acquainted with the persons of dog stealers, their several residences, and places for concealing dogs, and endeavor by every means in their power to check the offenders.

7. No member of the Police is allowed to receive any money as a reward or gratuity for finding and restoring a dog.

DRILL.

1. As the Police Force is at all times liable to be called upon, in case of internal disturbances or from other causes, to act in concert as an armed body, and from the nature of many of their duties, such as escorting and guarding treasure and prisoners, and other similar duties, it is necessary that they should receive instructions in the use of such arms as may be furnished to them, and that they should acquire such a knowledge of drill as will enable them, if required, to act with precision as a body.

2. For this purpose, every constable who has been sworn in will, if circumstances permit, be instructed at the Depôt, in marching, file movements, fours, &c., and the manual and platoon exercises.

3. Those selected for mounted duty will, in addition to these instructions, be taught riding and the sword exercise.

4. All officers, whether in charge of districts or stations, will take occasional opportunities to exercise their men in these movements; but it is to be understood that such exercises are not in any way to interfere with the discharge of their regular police duties.

5. The Commissioner would here impress upon all members of the Police Force that they belong, not to a military, but to a civil force, and that he altogether discountenances all unnecessary military parade and show, as well as the frequent and unnecessary parade of firearms or other weapons. The principal object to be kept in view, in all exercises, in drill, and the use of arms, is to make the Force effective, and not to make it approximate in its character to a military body, further than by introducing the promptness and uniformity of action attained in such bodies.

DUTY RETURNS.

1. It has been noticed that the duty returns from many of the out-stations in the colony are improperly made out, so far as the correct entering of each man's duty is concerned.

2. The great fault in them is indefiniteness; for instance—a sergeant or constable is returned as being on duty from 8 a.m. till midnight. No one believes that the member of the Force who made such an entry intended the statement should be taken literally, and that during all that time the person had been continuously on duty.

3. As these returns are intended to show what each man does each day, so as to give those in authority an idea of the manner in which the duties are performed, only the hours that each man is actually on duty will be entered.

4. Beat duty will be entered as usual; but where mounted men are stationed, the words "F. Patrol" or "M. Patrol" will be entered, according to the nature of the duty performed by them.

5. Two hours are allowed to every mounted man, each day, for stable duty, and every man, whether mounted or foot, must perform eight hours duty out of the twenty-four.

6. Wherever there are two mounted constables, one mounted patrol at least must be performed every day, and when circumstances prevent this being done, an entry to that effect will be made in the Occurrence Book, and the corresponding column of remarks, in the Duty Reports.

7. A list of duties, which may be largely increased, is herewith set forth as a specimen of what should be entered, viz.:—"Office duty," "Court duty," "Attending calls on station," "Parading and drilling men," "F. Patrol," "M. Patrol along road (name of road being given), from   to   (time being set down),   miles." "M. Patrol to   (place) to execute warrant against (name of the offender), or to serve summonses" "M. Patrol in pursuit of offender (name to be given)," &c., &c.

8. The police at every station will be paraded and drilled every Monday, and an entry to that effect made in the column of remarks of the Occurrence Book.

9. It has been found in many instances that the duty of a constable recently transferred to a station has been entered in the duty returns without a remark as to where he came from.

10. When a member of the force, therefore, arrives at a station on transfer, an entry will be made under the proper day's heading—" Arrived at   (station), to be stationed   at (hour)." When leaving—" Left at (hour), transferred to   (station)."

11. Whenever an officer visits a station, the entry he makes in the Occurrence Book should be copied into the Return for that week.

12. The greatest care must be taken in entering the forage issued to police horses in the duty returns, as the rations, whether whole, half, or one-third, appearing as issued upon the face of the return, must fully agree in every particular with the rations shown to be issued in the forage return.

13. To make this plain, when checking one return with the other, the member of the force making them out will enter, in red ink, over the duty of each horse each day the figures 1, $\frac{1}{2}$, or $\frac{1}{3}$, as the case may be. This will mean that one ration, or a half-ration, or one-third of a ration, has been issued to the police or other horse that day.

14. It will not be necessary to enter the brands or duties of other station horses arriving on patrol, &c., for a night or so, in the station duty returns, this being shown in the forage returns. All that need be done is to note the arrival and state of horse and rider in the column of remarks in the Occurrence Book; and when the rations issued to the station horses are added up in the proper column, the number of rations or portions of rations issued to other station horses will be added, when the total will be given. The entry will be made thus :—

Rations issued to other station horses ...
                    Total   ...   .

15. All fuel, light, and water (chargeable to Government) received at the out-station of a district during each week will be entered in the Occurrence Book and the column for remarks in the weekly duty returns.

16. The duty, and where there are horses, the forage returns, will be forwarded every Monday to the office of the Inspector in charge of the district, and when checked and countersigned by him, will be transmitted to the Commissioner's office.

DRILL INSTRUCTOR.

1. The duties of a drill instructor are far too comprehensive to be detailed at length.

2. He must, of course, be thoroughly conversant with every part of the drill which it is his duty to instruct the recruits in—whether mounted or foot.

3. His demeanor and personal appearance are at all times to be such as to win the confidence and respect of his officers, and be an example and pattern to the recruits whom he is training.

4. He is carefully to avoid any undue familiarity with the recruits; for unless he has a proper sense of his own consequence he cannot enforce obedience, or ensure the respect necessary for the due performance of his duties.

DRINKING.

1. The police are not on any account to receive drink from anyone while on duty or in uniform.

2. The police are particularly cautioned against drinking with persons or witnesses engaged in any Court. Should any of the police be found guilty of such misconduct they will be considered wholly unfit for the Service.

3. The Commissioner will not receive as an excuse for drinking or intoxication that only a small quantity had been drunk, or that the liquor had been drugged, or that the police were off duty.

4. The keepers of houses who allow police to remain and drink while on duty are to be proceeded against in every case.

5. Police found drinking, or under the influence of drink, are to be reported. If drunk on duty, they are not to be permitted to remain on duty, arrangements are to be made to supply their places.

6. Superior officers are not to enter into conversation with constables who are under the influence of drink.

7. Superior officers are to do all in their power, by example, admonition, and precautionary measures, to prevent the evils of drinking among the police.

DRUNKEN PERSONS.

1. When the interference of the police becomes necessary a drunken person may be taken into custody, and charged at a Police Station; and under no circumstances is a police constable to leave his beat to conduct such a person to his home or elsewhere.

2. Persons are frequently found insensible in the streets, in reality suffering from apoplexy, or other natural cause, the symptoms of which give them much the appearance of persons under the influence of drink. In all such cases the first thing to do is to try and arouse them by a gentle shake; if that fails, the neck-cloth and collar are to be loosened, and the head raised a little, by which means breathing is made easier.

3. The police are strictly cautioned to be very careful in conveying persons apparently drunk or insensible to the stations.

4. When being conveyed on a stretcher, or placed in the cell, the head is to be kept slightly raised by a canvas pillow underneath it.

5. In every case where a person is brought to a station in a state of insensibility, whether supposed from drink, or any other cause, the officer on duty at the station is to send for medical advice as soon as possible.

6. Drunken persons are to be visited and spoken to in the cells every half-hour, and if they become insensible, and cannot be roused, medical advice is to be sent for at once.

ELECTIONS.

1. The attention of the police is directed to the statute 35 Vic. No. 5 sec. 7, that no person belonging to the Police Force shall be capable of giving his vote for the election of a member to serve in Parliament, nor shall any member of the Police Force by word, message, writing, or in any other manner endeavor to persuade any elector from giving his vote to any candidate, and any person so offending against this Act shall forfeit the sum of one hundred pounds.

2. On the occasion of an election, the Inspectors, Sub-Inspectors, or sergeants concerned are to have a sufficient number of police to keep the approaches to the polling places open to the electors, to protect them from outrage, and to preserve the peace.

3. A personal communication is to be made by the Inspector, Sub-Inspector, or sergeant, with the Returning Officer at each voting place in the morning, as early as possible, before the opening for polling.

4. The sergeant or senior constable in charge of the men at each booth is to keep himself in communication with the Returning Officer during the day, with reference to any alteration of arrangement that may become necessary, and he is held responsible for the strict performance by the police of all the duties with which they are charged.

5. A sufficient number of police to preserve order is also to be present on the days of the nomination, and the declaration of the poll, should polling take place.

ERASURES.

1. No erasures are to be made in any of the books or documents connected with the police duties.

2. If any error be discovered in such books or documents it is to be altered and corrected by drawing the pen neatly across the entry, and substituting the correction in red ink above it.

ESCORT (GOLD).

1. On the regular lines of road, or on other lines where the amount of gold or treasure is large, the escort will be composed of one officer, one sergeant, and four constables; but should a conveyance with prisoners accompany the escort, one, or if the number of prisoners be large, two additional mounted constables will be added to the strength of the escort. These additional men will, under such circumstances, ride close behind the vehicle in which the prisoners are being conveyed; but when no prisoners are being conveyed in the escort waggon, the presence of the sergeant close to it will be sufficient.

2. One mounted constable will form the advance guard, riding from one hundred to one hundred and fifty yards in front of the conveyance, according to the nature of the country through which the treasure is in transit. One mounted constable will march on the right, and another on the left flank, keeping as nearly as possible parallel with the conveyance, and at such a distance from it, not exceeding one hundred yards, as the nature of the country will permit. The other constable will follow in rear, at about the same distance behind the conveyance as the one in front is before, all keeping constantly in view of the officer in charge.

3. The sergeant will march immediately behind the conveyance, except when ordered by the officer in charge to see that the men are performing their duty properly; under which circumstances the officer will take the sergeant's place, so that at all times during the march, either the officer or the sergeant may be immediately behind the conveyance.

4. The duty of the officer is to supervise generally the manner in which the sergeant and men perform their duty, occasionally proceeding to the front, flanks, and rear, but travelling for the most part between the sergeant and the rear file; the motive for proceeding out of this position being to satisfy himself as to the vigilance of the men and the security of everything connected with the treasure and the conveyance.

5. The driver will regulate the pace according to the orders he may receive from the officer in charge; but the management and control of the draught horses should, as far as possible, be left entirely to the driver, who, in case of inefficiency, should be reported by the officer.

6. In the event of an attack being made, or any extraordinary circumstances occurring, such as to lead the man in advance to suppose that an attack or obstruction is probable, it is his duty at once to fall back on the escort, and apprise the officer in charge, who should immediately halt the escort; and in case of a probable attack, bring the men together, and place them at such a distance from the supposed assailants as to be out of shot, but within sight and range of the treasure, protecting themselves by trees or such other natural defences as the nature of the place will admit, and prepare to take advantage of any opportunity that may offer for using their firearms against the attacking party; the officer taking up his position in rear of the men, and having the sergeant close at hand to act upon his orders, or, in the event of anything happening to the officer, to be ready to take his place.

7. The officer would thus be enabled to make deliberate arrangements for defending his charge; and upon his subsequent coolness and judgment, the safety of the treasure will mainly depend; it being too generally the case that, in a surprise of the kind, the party attacked, by hurriedly returning the fire, does so at random, and without effect, thereby throwing away its means of defence, and exposing itself to the reserve fire of the assailants. In case of obstruction, he should either go himself or send the sergeant to examine it, and then act as he deems necessary.

8. The arms of the men composing the escort will consist of a rifle and a revolver, the latter to be carried in a belt around the waist, and the rifle to be carried in the bucket, with the hammer at half-cock.

9. Prior to starting, the escort officer will minutely examine the arms, and see that they are clean and properly loaded, so as to be ready for instant use.

10. The officer, on taking charge of the treasure, should be extremely particular to examine the seals of the boxes and feel the red tape, so as to ascertain whether or not the former are complete, and the latter attached in such a manner as not to be easily removed without seriously damaging the seal; also to obtain a proper entry of the treasure in the way-bill.

11. When the escort is relieved, the same attention must be given to the seals, &c., as before specified.

12. On the escort halting, either from accident to the conveyance, or any other cause, a sentry must always be placed over the treasure, and the sergeant or officer must remain in sight of it. If the halt is for the night, the treasure must immediately be conveyed into the place where it is to remain; and the officer should examine the seals to see that all is correct, and should he absent himself from the room in which the treasure is, his place must be kept by the sergeant. A sentry is to be kept outside the room during the night, and one or two men should sleep close at hand, so as to be available at a moment's notice.

13. Men composing the escort should not be allowed to absent themselves from their quarters while the treasure is at the station, except in cases of necessity, when only one man may be permitted to leave at a time.

14. On the arrival of the treasure at its destination, the same precaution must be observed with regard to the examination of the packages, whether containing treasure, or anything else entrusted to the charge of the escort, and a receipt for the same obtained on the way-bill, which will be filed. It should also be stated on the way-bill in what condition the packages are delivered over from the custody of the escort.

15. In the case of branch escorts, these receipts will be filed and carefully preserved with the others in the office of the Inspector, or other officer in charge of the district.

16. The pace at which the escort will travel is a smart walk, or very slow jog, not at any time exceeding four and a-half miles per hour.

17. The escort must start punctually at six o'clock a.m. in the summer, and at seven o'clock a.m. in the winter.

The hour of arrival is to be as uniform as possible, the pace being such as to render this practicable either in summer or winter.

18. The treasure is to be handed over immediately on arrival to the gold receiver in attendance. Should there not be any authorised person ready to receive it, the officer in charge of the escort is to report at once to head quarters the length of time he was kept waiting, but is in no case to take the treasure to any other place.

19. In the event of any accident occurring either to the horses, conveyance, or harness, the officer must attach a memorandum to the way-bill explanatory of the circumstances, and stating whether any blame is attributable to the driver, or any other person on account of carelessness. Should the conveyance break down, or should the horses, from the state of the roads, be unable to draw the conveyance, the officer must use his discretion in procuring the requisite aid, and carry out the service as economically as possible.

20. No passengers whatever can be allowed on the escort conveyance, with the exception of prisoners, or members of the Police Force in the performance of their duty; nor must packages be carried, except when forwarded by the proper authorities, and on the Public Service. In all cases these parcels must be included in the way-bill, and should any legitimate passengers be sent as above, their names and other particulars must be entered in the column of " Remarks" on the way-bill.

21. When the distance to be travelled exceeds thirty miles, the escort should, if possible, halt for a couple of hours in the middle of the day, so as to allow of the horses receiving a feed; during this time the bridles should be removed and the girths slackened.

22. Officers in charge of districts in which escorts are run will be responsible that the officers and men composing such escorts are made fully acquainted with these Regulations.

ESCORTS (PRISONERS).

1. Escorts form a very important part of the duties of the constabulary. In many instances, where stations are far apart and remote from main roads, it forms a very onerous and even harassing part of that duty; for this reason every means that experience can devise must be brought to bear upon it, in order to render it as light as the necessities of the service will allow.

2. The first consideration of escorts is the security of the prisoners or commodities placed in their charge; to this all else must be secondary and subordinate; they will, therefore, see that the prisoners or property to be escorted are delivered to them with due precautions for safe custody, and this they are to state in the receipt they give on taking them over.

3. The authority that in the first instance delivers to any escort, prisoners or property, should prescribe the nature and degree of personal restraint to be imposed on prisoners, and the fastenings securing property, and neither should be deviated from, or in any way altered by the escort or successive escorts in whose charge they are placed, unless under such circumstances of necessity as will fully justify the act. In all such cases the person in charge of the escort, making the alteration, will report clearly and at length upon the matter.

4. Having thus received their charge properly secured, it will be their duty to guard against that state of security being diminished or impaired; for this purpose they will frequently and closely inspect the handcuffs, chains, &c., placed on the prisoners, and the fastenings of doors, windows, &c., of any place of confinement; in like manner as regards property, they will inspect the locks, seals, or other means by which the packages are secured. Neither by day nor by night must their charge be separate from or lost sight of by an escort.

5. There may be occasions for escorts to stop during the night at public houses; this, however, must never be done when it can be possibly avoided, but when such a step is absolutely necessary, the cost of meals supplied to

prisoners must never exceed one shilling per head, and an agreement must be made with the proprietor of the house for the use of a room on the most moderate terms.

6. In such cases they are not to drink nor allow the prisoners in their charge to drink any fermented or spirituous liquors whatever; they are to place the prisoners in the most secure and private room obtainable, and are to adopt all proper and necessary precautions against escape.

7. Escorts with prisoners or property in charge are not to call or halt at public houses during the day, the necessary provisions and refreshments can be procured at, and be conveyed with them from, the place they have stopped at on the previous night.

8. On the march they will keep the prisoners in the centre of the party, and will not allow them to separate or straggle, and therefore the rate of marching must be regulated according to the powers of the prisoners if on foot, and if in carts according to the pace at which the vehicles can conveniently proceed. Neither acquaintances of the prisoners nor other persons are to be allowed to mix with or accompany the prisoners and escort.

9. The arms of an escort are invariably to be loaded, and ready for instant use. This of course applies more particularly to cases where treasure, or prisoners in custody on a charge of felony are being escorted, but in escorting females, lunatics, or persons charged with some trifling misdemeanor it will not for the most part be necessary that the escort be provided with firearms.

10. It must, however, be clearly understood, and constantly borne in mind, that nothing short of absolute and inevitable necessity can justify the constabulary in firing upon prisoners endeavoring to escape, or upon other parties attempting to rescue.

11. As prisoners are not on any account to be left in the possession of money, or other property, when under escort, any belonging to them is to be made up into separate sealed packages, marked with the name of the prisoner, and the amount, and these separate parcels—together with a list in triplicate made out on the authorised form, and signed by the authority delivering the prisoner.

the officer in charge of escort, and the prisoner himself—are to be enclosed in a strong sealed cover. A memorandum is to be delivered with this sealed parcel to the officer in charge, (his acknowledgement and signature being taken to a duplicate retained); this memorandum, and the sealed parcel, he is to hand, with the seal unbroken, to the person into whose charge he delivers the prisoners, taking his receipt for it.

12. The officer in charge of a party on escort duty should always march in the rear of such escort, and enforce a strict attention to the duty on the part of the men, who should not be allowed to straggle under any pretence.

13. Before taking charge of prisoners, for the purpose of conveying them from one place to another, the officer in charge of the escort will be particular that they are searched in his presence, and that he receives the proper authority for their custody, whether they may be remanded from one Bench to another, or under sentence. In every case the officer in charge will examine the warrants, or other authority, to see that they are signed and correspond with the prisoners handed over to their charge.

14. In cases where a prisoner is being escorted by one constable, the latter will on no account remove the handcuffs while on the line of route, and members of the force in charge of stations and lock-ups will point out to the escorting constable, especially if he be a man of short service, that prisoners so situated will make any number of excuses to induce him to remove the handcuffs, and that experience has shown that in many instances where constables have been thus induced to disobey positive orders, prisoners have escaped.

15. When a prisoner is being conveyed on horseback he will not be allowed to have the reins, these must be retained by the escorting constable, who will invariably keep the prisoner and his horse on his right hand.

16. Where practicable, after having given up charge of property or prisoners entrusted to them, the parties composing the escort will return to their stations by twos,

starting at different hours, and where convenient by different roads, the officer in charge of the escort forming one of the last party, so that he may be able to check any irregularity that may take place. In this manner they will form an efficient patrol.

17. Any constable accompanying a Judge when on circuit, or any other Government officer, as an orderly, should be relieved at each station, so as to avoid as much as possible taking any man to a distance from his station, or into another district.

18. No officer of the Force is under any circumstances to be accompanied by a constable as orderly. When an officer has to perform any duty in which his personal safety is endangered, he may take with him one or more constables, as the necessity of the case may require, but under such circumstances the constable or constables will precede instead of following him, as the attendance of constables on officers as a mark of honor is strictly forbidden.

EVIDENCE.

1. The police are to give evidence with the strictest accuracy; questions of the highest interest are decided by, and the administration of justice must in a great measure depend on the trustworthiness of, their evidence.

2. They are habitually to make accurate observation of all matters relating to duty, that they may be able if required, to state all the circumstances.

3. Notes should be made by them at the time of the particulars of a case, to refresh the memory, if called on to give evidence.

4. They are not to suppress or overstate the slightest circumstance, with a view to favor any person, or from ill will to either side.

5. They are to endeavour, as far as possible to feel indifferent as to the results of cases, and they perform their duty best by stating accurately, and without malice or favor, all the particulars they know.

6. When the police are sufferers from injuries received, and are giving evidence against those whom they believe

to be guilty, it is especially necessary that they should not allow any feelings or wishes as to the decision of the case to influence them.

7. Greater weight will always be given to the evidence of police if they state fully, and without passion, all they know, and make it evident that they are speaking the whole truth.

8. They are to be especially careful to state all they know upon the first occcasion, for if they afterwards add to their evidence in any material point, it is naturally looked on with mistrust, and is open to suspicion either as to accuracy or veracity.

9. Any of the police who wilfully depart from the truth are utterly unfit for the service, and will be immediately dismissed.

10. The police are not to enter into conversations or statements when before a Magistrate, upon any matters except such as the charge under investigation makes it their duty to mention.

11. If the police give improper or unsatisfactory evidence, or any remarks are made respecting the evidence of police by Judges, Magistrates, or Juries, the Sub-Inspector or sergeant present is to report through his Inspector full particulars to the Commissioner of Police on the following morning.

12. The Inspector or officer taking a charge, or the particulars of a case for summons, which appears to rest on the evidence of one constable, is always to make enquiry whether there is any other witness in the police or not, or other corroborative evidence; and if so, the additional witnesses are to attend before the Magistrate.

EXAMPLE OF OFFICERS.

1. It cannot be too strongly impressed upon the officers generally that the example on their part of strict attention to their own duties, combined with a uniformly steady and watchful demeanor towards the men under their command, not allowing any neglect of duty or mis-

conduct to pass unnoticed, together with the prospect of future advancement, will do more to induce the men to conduct themselves well than the fear of any amount of punishment.

2. On their capacity, discretion, and good management, the discipline and efficiency of the Force mainly depend; for it is only by their example as regards business habits and knowledge of police duties, as well as their private deportment, that they can gain that respect which it should be the desire, as it is the duty, of the men to evince towards them.

FEMALES.

1. The police are not to idle or gossip with females in the streets, or at the doors of houses.
2. The police are not to interfere with persons speaking to females in the streets, unless annoyance or obstruction is caused.

FINES.

1. A return showing all fines and other punishments inflicted during the previous month, on members of the Force, shall be forwarded to the Commissioner's office, on the first day of each month, by the Inspector in charge of each District. (See Appendix I.)
2. In cases where *prisoners* are fined, the watchhouse-keeper will be held responsible that all such fines are paid over *each day* to the Clerk of Petty Sessions, who will give a receipt, in each case, by writing his name across the decision in the Watchhouse Charge Book, after which he will insert the date of payment.
3. When a prisoner does not pay the fine inflicted, but goes to gaol instead, the letter I, in red ink, will be entered opposite the decision in the Watchhouse Charge Book, the date prisoner was sent to gaol being also given.
4. Before forwarding the weekly copy of the Watchhouse Charge Book to the Inspector's office, the watchhouse-keeper will enter the letter P, in red ink, in

the margin, where the copy of each decision is given, in all cases where the fine has been paid, and will also give the date of such payment.

5. If the prisoner be sent to gaol, the letter I, in red ink, will be written in the margin, where the copy of each decision is given, and also the date when such prisoner left the watchhouse for gaol.

FIRES.

1. Upon any alarm of fire being given, it becomes the duty of the Inspector, Sub-inspector, or sergeant in charge of a station immediately to repair to the spot, render all the assistance in his power, and take the entire control of the Police Force assembled. If the fire is in Brisbane, and a serious one, he is also to send notice to the Commissioner.

2. It is impossible to lay down any precise rules as to the special manner in which the police who first arrive at a fire are to be most usefully employed; but the great and principal object to be attained is the saving of life which may be in danger through the fire, and to effect this object, the constable is to give immediate alarm, and arouse the inmates and neighbors.

3. The next steps to be taken are to give or send notice of the fire to the Fire Brigade Station (in places where a fire brigade is established), and the Police Station.

4. Until the arrival of the firemen, the police are to exert themselves in every possible way for the rescue of persons in danger, and the protection of property.

5. The Inspector or other officer in charge of police, will clear the street or ground in the vicinity of the fire, of all persons not usefully employed, taking care that all the adjoining streets, as far as practicable, are kept clear of obstructions by crowds or vehicles, &c., so that the arrival of the engines may not be delayed, or those on business obstructed.

6. The police are not, on any account, to endeavor to control or direct the firemen, who are responsible to their own officers for the measures they adopt.

7. Special attention must be directed to the thieves and pickpockets, who are usually in the crowd.

8. If desired, property may be conveyed to the nearest Police Station, to be placed under the care of the police. Much loss is sustained at fires by the unnecessary removal of furniture, especially from houses not actually on fire. The firemen will be best able to judge whether danger is to be apprehended for the adjoining houses.

9. It frequently happens that in the confusion consequent on a fire, persons enter a house and leave open the doors, which causes an increased current of air to add greater fury to the flames. The Police are to prevent this as much as possible, but they are to use their discretion in allowing respectable persons to enter, whose sole object is the saving of life, or to assist the owner in the removal of articles of value. Improper characters, whose object is plunder, are to be prevented from entering a house under any circumstances.

10. If requested by the chief or other officer of the fire brigade to remove any persons who interfere by their presence with the operations of the brigade, the officer in command of police, if he is satisfied that by their presence they do so interfere, is civilly to ask them to remove, telling them at whose request he does so, and, if necessary, he is after that to direct the police to remove them.

11. The police may also clear any street in or near where a fire is burning. The officer in command of the police is to act on his own discretion in giving directions for the purpose.

12. Police, as may be necessary, are to remain at the scene of a fire until it is extinguished, and all danger to the public over, and the traffic has resumed its ordinary course.

13. The Inspector, or in his absence the Sub-inspector, or next in command, is to collect upon the spot all the information he can obtain relative to the cause of the fire, which, together with the circumstances attending it, the conduct of the police under his orders, the time they were employed, by whom the engines were called, whether by police or others, the duties actually performed, whether in

calling the engines, or other special matter, and the time they were withdrawn, are to be fully and carefully reported to the Commissioner.

14. Whenever constables are called away from their beats on any sudden emergency, the utmost exertion is to be made to supply their place from the reserve, and to prevent the commission of any offence during the temporary absence of the constable.

15. Chimneys on fire which required an engine to extinguish the fire are to be reported; trifling cases, where the fire was extinguished without the aid of an engine, are not to be reported.

16. Each police constable is to be made acquainted with the situation of the Fire Brigade Station, and the Sub-inspectors and sergeants are frequently to question the constables to ascertain that they know it.

17. It is supposed that fires have been caused by persons carelessly or wilfully throwing lighted matches or paper through openings in trap-doors, shutters, &c., of premises where straw, wood, or other inflammable articles are stored, and so setting fire to the stock, and causing great damage. The police are to notice any openings or defective doors, fanlights, &c., through which lights may be thrown, and draw the attention of the occupants thereto, and are also to be on the alert to detect and apprehend any persons seen throwing any lights into premises with a supposed wilful intent.

18. This order is to be frequently read to the men, especially to those who have recently joined.

FLYING KITES.

The police are to prevent boys flying kites in the streets, parks, or public places, where danger or annoyance is caused.

FOOTMARKS.

1. In some cases the proof of comparison of footmarks has failed from the shoe, &c., being put on the mark, which was thus effaced, and the comparison inaccurately made.

2. When it is desirable to ascertain whether the footmarks left at any place correspond with those of a person suspected, the shoe or boot, &c., used to compare, should not be laid upon the footmark, but a separate impression is to be made with the shoe or boot, which may be compared with the footmark.

3. Care must be taken not to obliterate by walking over or near them, the footmarks required for comparison.

FORAGE.

1. Contracts are as a rule taken annually by the Government, for the supply of forage to every Police Station throughout the colony, where there are police horses.

2. Members of the Force in charge of stations, are expected to give due notice to local contractors, if any, stating the supplies of forage needed, in accordance with the terms of contract.

3. When forage is delivered at any station by a contractor, the net weight must be ascertained, and the receipt signed for that quantity, for which in issuing, the officer having charge, and who signs the receipt, will be held responsible.

4. If a station be under the charge of a subordinate member of the Force, he should permit no one but himself to issue forage; at large stations one constable only must be authorised to issue.

5. When a fresh supply of forage is received at a station, it must not be issued until the old stock is consumed.

6. The police at every station are to exert themselves to ensure the supplies being stored in such a manner, as to prevent any injury through the effects of weather or other causes, as should any damage or loss occur, the strictest investigation will be made, and the party who, from negligence or culpability, allowed the same to take place, will be held personally liable for it.

7. The regulation scale of a ration is forage is :—
   14 lbs. oaten hay.
   8 lbs. maize, or oats.
   1 lb. bran.
   4 lbs. bush hay or straw, for bedding.

8. At out stations, where the stores are kept in a tent, or any insecure building, the police on the station must erect a strong fence round the same, to prevent any damage by cattle, &c.

9. Whenever forage is issued at police stations to any horses, &c., "for other than police service," and entered under that head in weekly forage returns, whether for stolen, stray, disputed horses, &c., or belonging to other departments, and merely accommodated at police stations, requisitions must be obtained from the person at whose request the forage is supplied, for the purpose of being forwarded to the Commissioner's office, attached to the weekly forage returns in which the issues are shown. In the case of a prisoner's horse, or a horse the subject of a criminal prosecution, the member of the Force having it in charge must draw the requisitions on the person in charge of forage, even if that be himself.

10. No forage is, on any account, to be issued from the police stores to any Government officer or other person whatever, without special authority, and in every instance where forage is issued for any other service than the police, a requisition must be obtained from the party requiring the same, which order must be attached to the weekly forage return, in which also, care must be taken to insert the particulars of the amount of forage drawn, the officer's name, and on what duty engaged; and the police are never to receive food for their horses at any private house without paying for the same.

11. No horse that is not the property of the department, or that has not been temporarily hired for some special duty, is to be taken into use by any member of the Force, and foraged and stabled in police stables, unless the permission of the head of the department has been obtained.

12. If possible, in districts where there is good grass, the horses should be kept without any forage whatever.

13. When forage is issued to any horses other than those actually belonging to the Police Department, or engaged on police duty, including unclaimed or disputed horses, or horses found in the possession of prisoners who are not charged with having stolen them, the sum of two

shillings and sixpence per ration must be charged for the same. Where prisoners are simply charged with drunkenness or other slight offences, horses found in their possession at the time of arrest, should, as a rule, and where practicable, be sent to the pound.

14. The expense of forage, for horses and cattle detained by the police as the subject of criminal prosecutions should be defrayed out of the public revenue; in such cases therefore, sufficient forage is to be issued free of charge, or the animals may be turned into a paddock, provided it is not considered that there is any risk of their being abstracted therefrom by the friends of the accused.

15. No disputed horses or cattle are to be foraged by police, unless the parties claiming are able beforehand to pay the regulation amount for the forage, otherwise the cattle or horses must be turned into a paddock or handed over to one of the claimants on his giving a sufficient guarantee for the animal's production when required. But in the event of its being necessary to retain an animal in the possession of the police, as ordered in a case of felony, and when, if turned into a paddock, it would probably be abstracted by the friends of the accused, such animal can be allowed half the usual ration of forage, and, if possible, the cost must be recovered from the owner.

16. At every station where there is grass in the neighborhood, officers in charge will, when it is advisable, turn out the duty horses to graze, issuing to them only half rations or such other allowance as may be deemed necessary, due regard being had to their being kept in a serviceable condition.

17. As soon after the termination of each month as possible, a return, in the form given in Appendix D., must be forwarded of all forage issued during the month to any horses, cattle, &c., on other than police service, and where any of the forage so issued has been charged for, the amount so received must be enclosed to the Commissioner's office, with the return.

18. In many Police Districts the practice has prevailed of feeding police horses only twice in the day. This practice is objectionable, and there is little doubt that it

has been the cause of many of the cases of colic, inflammation, and other sickness which has occurred. The ration of corn and bran should be divided into thirds, one third being given in the morning, another at noon, and the last in the evening; the hay being given, one moiety in the morning, and the other in the evening, and the straw being of course issued in the evening only.

19. The mid-day feed will thus be far more beneficial. It will, of course, have frequently to be given at other stations than that to which the horse belongs, and must be entered accordingly, in the returns for such stations.

20. In cases where no other station can be reached for a noon feed, it should be carried from the station from which the horse started in the morning (and entered in the returns for that station), unless urgent reasons exist to prevent such a course.

21. A sample return, showing the entries of issues by thirds, instead of halves, is given in Appendix E.

22. Officers in charge are not to understand this order as directing that forage is to be issued from stock exclusively in thirds of rations. Whether the day ration for each horse should be issued from stock in the morning, or in thirds at intervals during the day, is a question of convenience, to be decided by each officer in charge, according to the circumstances and requirements of the Stations in his district. All that is required is, that as a rule, the horses receive their rations at proper intervals. Where the forage is issued each morning in whole rations, it will be the duty of those in charge of the horses to see that it is divided, and is given to the horses as above directed.

23. When horses are sick the daily ration is to be:—

    14 lbs. Hay.
    12 lbs. Bran.
    4 lbs. Straw.

or such lesser quantity as may be considered desirable.

24. Horses being led or driven from one station to another, to be condemned or otherwise, are to receive 21 lbs. of hay per diem, half to be issued in the morning, and the other half at night.

25. A Forage Book will be kept at each station, where there are police horses. This book must be entered up day by day, showing the receipts and issues. A weekly return, copied from these books, will be forwarded to the head-quarters of the district. and from thence, after examination, forwarded to the Commissioner's office, by the officer in charge, along with the weekly duty reports.

26. Should any errors appear in the returns on examination, whereby the Government might be losers, the responsibility will rest with the officer certifying to their correctness, he having recourse to the subordinate by whom the return was compiled.

27. Police horses are not to be foraged or stabled at hotels oftener than is absolutely necessary. In cases where it is unavoidable, a requisition, in the printed form for the purpose, must be given by the officer in charge of the station to which the party belongs; and each horse must be groomed by its rider (and not by servants of the inn), in the same manner as if at a police station.

28. On the charge of any station being given over from one member of the Force to another, the forage in the store must be weighed, and receipts given for the actual weight, and any deficiency or surplus noted in the weekly forage returns.

29. If any constable absent from his station draws more than one ration per diem for his horse *en route*, he will be charged for the amount overdrawn.

30. At each station a copy of the conditions of contract upon which forage is supplied will be kept for reference, and the members of the Force in charge will be responsible that the conditions are faithfully observed.

31. In the event of having to purchase forage at the contractor's risk (see conditions of contract), officers in charge must send in the accounts to the Commissioner of Police, as soon after the purchase as possible, in order that the extra cost (if any) may be deducted from the first account sent in by the contractor.

32. Officers in charge of districts will use their best endeavors to induce contractors to render their accounts for forage supplied with as little delay as possible.

33. All forage accounts, after due examination, and being certified by the officer in charge of the district, will be immediately forwarded to the Commissioners' office for payment.

34. As all accounts for forage are checked in the Commissioners' office by the weekly returns, the greatest care must be taken to prevent errors, as such, however trifling, cause delay in the payment of the accounts.

35. On the first day of January and the first day of July in each year, and oftener if considered necessary, the stock of forage in hand must be ascertained by members of the Force in charge of stations by actual tally and inspection, and must be compared with the balance as shown in the Forage Book. Any surplus there may be must be taken into stock, and if there be a deficiency, it must, after due inquiry, be either made good or written off, as the circumstances of the case may require.

FORGERY.

1. Forgery is defined to be the fraudulent making or alteration of a writing or a seal, to the prejudice of another's right. The following are some of the principles applicable to it :—

(1.) An *intent* to serve the party forging, or to injure another person, is of the very essence of the crime. It is not necessary that the other person be *actually* injured; it is enough that he *may* be injured thereby.

(2.) Any fraudulent insertion, alteration, or erasure in a material part of a true instrument, whereby a new operation is given to it, is forgery,—as altering the figure 2 (in a cheque for £20) into 3, thus making it appear a cheque for £30.

H

(3.) In such a case the false instrument must carry on the face of it the *semblance* of that for which it was counterfeited; but it is not necessary that the resemblance be a perfect one, it is enough that it is calculated to impose on persons in general.

(4.) The false instrument must puport to be a valid one, and hence the false making of a promissory note, *without a signature to it*, would not be a forgery.

(5.) To constitute forgery, it matters not if the name forged, be the name of a fictitious or non-existent person.

(6.) The most usual cases of forgery, are those in which the prisoner assumes the name and character of a person really in existence. Forgery is in itself a crime, *although the forged instrument has never been uttered*.

(7.) It is forgery to draw and sign forged certificates or letters of character, or to fill in a blank signed cheque, with an amount different from what the signer authorised.

2. When an offender is arrested on a charge of forgery, as a general rule it is the duty of the constable having charge of the case, to visit the house or lodgings of the accused person, and make a thorough search for papers, as it frequently happens that the offender, before committing the actual forgery had been practising himself in writing the name intended to be forged, on one or more sheets of paper.

3. A clue to a well masked forgery was once obtained by a detective, by the finding of a sheet of blotting paper that had been used by the forger to dry the signature to a cheque.

FORMATION.

1. The Police Force of Queensland consists of the following ranks, viz. :—

        Commissioner
        Inspectors (First-class)
           „   (Second-class)

Sub-Inspectors (First-class)
„   (Second-class)
Senior Sergeants
Sergeants
Senior Constables
Constables (First-class)
„   (Second-class)
„   (Third-class.)

2. The head-quarters of the whole Force shall be in Brisbane, under the immediate supervision of the Commissioner of Police.

FOUNTAINS.

The police are to prevent, as far as possible, any damage being done to public drinking fountains ; and if necessary, to apprehend persons wilfully offending.

GAMBLING.

1. Attention is directed to the provisions of "*The Vagrant Act,*" which are to be enforced by the police.
2. This Act (15 Vic. No. 4) says, among other things, that "every person playing or betting at any unlawful game, every person playing or betting in any street, road, highway, or other open and public place, at or with any table or instrument of gaming at any game or pretended game of chance shall be deemed a rogue and a vagabond, and be liable, on conviction before a justice, to six months' imprisonment, with hard labor."

GAMING HOUSES.

1. The owner or keeper of any gaming house, or other person having the care or management thereof, and also every banker, croupier, or other person acting in any manner in conducting any common gaming house, room, premises, or place, is liable to a penalty not exceeding £100, or imprisonment not exceeding six months.
2. Any person found in such house, room, premises, or place, without lawful excuse, is liable to a penalty not exceeding £5.

3. Where there are grounds for believing that any place is used as a common gaming house, the Sub-inspector, sergeant, or constable is to state the same in writing to the Inspector in charge of the district, who will take steps to obtain authority to enter such place, by force if necessary, and take into custody all persons found therein, and seize all instruments of gaming found therein.

4. There must be an information to ground the proceedings, and under section 7 the indictment need not state to whom the money belonged, but a conviction must state the particular game.

5. A tent, or part of one, erected on or near a race-course, and kept only during the races, may be a common gambling house.

6. It is lawful for all constables and officers of police to enter into any house, room, premises, or place where any public table or board is kept for playing at billiards, bagatelle, bowls, rackets, quoits, skittles, nine-pins, or any game of the like kind, when and so often as such constable and officer shall think proper. (*Vide* 14 Vic. No. 9.)

GRATUITIES.

1. No gratuity is to be received by any of the police without the express permission of the Commissioner.

2. The Commissioner will allow gratuities to be received upon all proper occasions, upon the circumstances being reported to him.

3. A gratuity offered at the time by a person to whom special services are rendered upon any sudden emergency may be taken, subject to the decision of the Commissioner as to its being retained or returned to the person giving it; in such a case the name and address of the person giving the gratuity is to be procured, and the sum received handed over as soon as possible to the Inspector of the district.

4. A report of the circumstances will be laid by the Inspector before the Commissioner for his decision.

5. The Inspectors, before they submit to the Commissioner their recommendations that gratuities should be allowed, are to make such inquiry as to satisfy themselves that no solicitations, direct or indirect, have been made to the persons by whom the gratuities are given, and if there is reason to suppose that solicitation has been made, or that there are any other circumstances which make it improper for the gratuities to be received, all the particulars are to be reported to the Commissioner.

6. After the distribution of an amount is approved by the Commissioner, no alteration is to be made in the amounts handed to each individual, without the express sanction of the Commissioner.

7. No application is to be made for any reward arising out of convictions under the revenue laws, unless the approval of the Commissioner is previously obtained.

8. When any sum is left with a subpœna for police to attend at any Court, the amount is to be reported in the same manner as any other gratuity.

9. Gratuities are not permitted to be received by police for restoring dogs, discovering or assisting at fires, or for calling up persons in the morning. (See " Pensions.")

HANDCUFFS.

1. Handcuffs are supplied to each Police Station. The police on ordinary day duty in cities or towns are not to carry handcuffs; handcuffs are not to be used except in cases of necessity, when a prisoner is desperate, or likely to attempt to escape when being conveyed, and on the authority of the officer on duty at a station.

2. One pair of handcuffs are supplied to each constable —mounted and foot—for which they are responsible, and which must be returned into store on their being discharged, or transferred to another district.

3. Any constable striking a prisoner, or other person, with his handcuffs is liable to be dismissed, and may be sent before the Bench for an assault.

4. Constables performing night duty, and constables when on patrol in the bush, must carry handcuffs. (See " Appointments.")

HAWKERS.

1. Any person, without having first obtained a license, carrying on the business of a hawker or pedlar in any place within the colony, is to be seized and detained by any constable, until the day next after the day on which he shall have been so seized, for the purpose of being proceeded against for such offence.

2. A licensed hawker or pedlar must have the words "Licensed Hawker" painted or printed in large legible letters on every pack, bag, box, trunk, case, cart, dray, waggon, boat, or other conveyance; as also his name in full, and the number of his license, under a penalty not exceeding ten pounds.

3. An unlicensed person writing, painting, or printing the same words is liable to a like penalty.

4. Any licensed person must produce or show on demand his license to a Justice, constable, or to any person to whom he sold, or offered for sale, goods within twenty-four hours previously.

5. A licensed person having in his possession, or on his cart, any fermented or spirituous liquors, is liable to a penalty of twenty pounds.

6. Any licensed hawker or pedlar carrying fermented or spirituous liquors contrary to the provisions of the Act, may be arrested by any police constable, and the liquor may be seized by him and detained.

7. Printed books, pamphlets, periodicals, or other printed publications are exempted. And by 13 Vic., No. 36, s. 23 (which defines the meaning of a hawker or pedlar), printed newspapers, fish, fruit, water, fuel, milk, vegetables, victuals of any description and agricultural produce are exempted also.

8. A person sending his own goods to a town, not his residence, and there selling them, would be trading as a hawker.

HOOPS.

1. The attention of the Police is directed to boys trundling hoops in the streets or thoroughfares, where accidents or danger to passengers may be caused.

2. All children trundling hoops in the streets are to be cautioned against doing so, and informed that they are liable to have their hoops taken away from them.

3. The hoops may be taken from the boys if they persist in rolling them after caution being given ; and if the parents complain, they are to be referred to the Police Magistrate, when the Police concerned are to attend.

HORSES, CARE OF.

1. Each member of the Mounted Police Force will be furnished with a horse, which will be branded with a broad-arrow over Q G on the near shoulder; and the officer or constable taking charge of it will be held strictly accountable for the manner in which it is treated, and the general condition in which it is kept. Should it be found that any member of the Force either ill-treats or permits to be ill-treated or neglected the horse told off to him, or any other horse in his charge, he will, in addition to such other punishment as may be inflicted on him, be dismounted, and ordered to return to foot police duty, provided he is retained in the Force.

2. It is expected that the officers in charge of districts will see that every horse under them, as well as its rider, shall have a fair share of work to be done, and that they will not allow some horses to be petted and kept idle in the stables, while others are being injured by severe usage or neglect; nor are any of the horses to be kept clothed in the stables, unless sick, or by permission of the Commissioner.

3. Officers in charge of districts will hold the men accountable for the horses in their charge having sore backs or saddle-galls (which in most cases are caused by hard riding or inattention in not seeing that the saddles are properly fitted), as well as for any other diseases which could have been prevented by attention. No excuse will be received for a horse being rendered unserviceable from the above causes, unless it can be satisfactorily proved that some accidental and unlooked-for circumstance has rendered it necessary that the horse should be so used ;

and unless the cause can be traced to some other source than neglect, the member of the Force to whom the horse was told off, will be charge for the forage of the animal while unfit for use, in addition to such other punishment as may be awarded.

HORSES, CAST.

1. When police horses are cast they will be branded with the broad-arrow alone, on the near jaw.

2. In the event of any horse being sold from the Force, it will be disposed of at public auction, in such manner as the Commissioner may direct.

HORSES, DUTIES OF THE OFFICER IN CHARGE OF DEPOT WITH REGARD TO.

1. The officer in charge of the Police Depôt at Brisbane is responsible for the general management of all horses at the Depôt, and in the police paddock, or any other reserve attached to the Depôt.

2. The arrival of all horses, either from the districts or from the police paddock, or other reserve attached to the Depôt, will be at once reported by the sergeant in charge to the depôt farrier, who will examine them minutely, and note any particulars respecting them, as to condition, injuries (if any), &c., and report the circumstance as soon as possible to the officer in charge; the animals are to be placed in the stockyard, school, or stable, until orders have been given for their disposal.

3. Before transferring to duty such unbroken horses as may from time to time be purchased, he will cause them to be properly broken-in, and trained to stand fire when mounted, and to carry the sword.

4. He will also cause them to be branded with the Government brand.

5. He will occasionally inspect the horses spelling at the police paddock, and take notes of those which may be fit for duty, or which may require treatment, &c. He will cause horses to be brought from the police paddock from time to time, and examine them as to their fitness to be put to work; he will cause those intended for troop

purposes to be ridden daily, prior to being sent to the duty for which they may be selected, and those intended for draught purposes to be tried in single and double harness, as may be necessary.

6. He will keep in a book, termed the Stud Book, and in the form given in Appendix A, a record of all the horses of the Force; he will enter in this book the description of all all horses purchased for the service from time to time, the particulars of purchase, with the police brand, and will record all transfers of horses from one district to another, all sales, deaths, losses from straying, &c., of police horses with full particulars, so that on reference to the book at any time, he may be able to state where any particular horse should be, or if it has been disposed of, in what manner, and on what date.

7. He will, not less frequently than once a-day, go round the stables, and see that the horses are properly attended to, and will cause them to be examined by the depôt farrier, to see that none of them are suffering from sore backs, or disease of any kind, in order that the attention of the veterinary surgeon may be at once called to any case requiring treatment.

8. He will cause to be furnished to him daily by the farrier, a return, in the form given in Appendix B, of all horses under medical treatment, which return he will submit to the Commissioner on his visiting the Depôt.

9. He will from time to time, report to the Commissioner, in the form for the purpose (*vide* Appendix H), all horses which he may consider unfit for further service. In examining horses for this purpose, he should be assisted by the veterinary surgeon, or some other officer of police, who should also sign the report, wherein the condition of the animal, and the causes of its unfitness for further duty, so far as they are known, should be fully detailed.

10. The officer in charge of the Depôt will carefully file, for reference, all papers, correspondence, and returns he may receive, relative to police horses; but if any file referred to him from this office deals with other matters than the management, treatment, or condition of police

horses; it must be returned to the Commissioner's office. In such case he may make a copy of such portion of the file as he may require.

11. A horse is to be referred to by its number in all reports and documents respecting it or relating to it.

HORSES, PURCHASE OF.

1. Horses are to be purchased for the Force, when required, by direction of the Commissioner, who will either purchase them himself, with the assistance of an officer of police, or will appoint some person to make the purchase; and the horses so procured, must, in all cases where practicable, be examined by a veterinary surgeon in conjunction with the officer of police, so appointed, and must be certified by the head of the department as being suitable for the Force, as to soundness, age, and general fitness for service before payment is made.

2. In the event of authority being given for the purchase of horses in remote districts, the certificate must be signed by two officers.

3. No pecuniary or other advantage whatever from such purchase is to accrue to any member of the Police Force.

HORSES, SHOEING OF.

1. The following rules are to be observed by the farriers employed to shoe the police horses :—
- (1.) The shoe to be levelled off so as to leave space and prevent pressure to the sole.
- (2.) Caulking is to be applied to the hind shoe only, and is to be confined to the outside heel, the inside heel to be thickened in proportion.
- (3.) The weight of the shoe to be from 14 to 16 oz. A variation may occur to either side when requisite, but 16 oz. is quite heavy enough for any horse in the patrol service.
- (4.) As a general principle, horses are to be shod with not less than six nails in the fore, and seven in the hind shoe, nor is it considered that a shoe requires more than six or seven nails to fasten it to the foot.

(5.) The nails should be kept as far as possible from the heels, and particularly in the inside quarter.

(6.) The nails used need never exceed in size what are termed the 8-lb. nails. A fore and hind pattern shoe is issued to the Inspectors of the exterior districts as a guide for the shoeing of the patrol horses, and whenever a deviation is made from this pattern, a report is to be made, stating the case.

2. Attention is directed to the follwing points regarding the shoeing of the horses:—

(1.) The bad manner in which many shoes are applied is productive of most serious consequences; the hoof is broken or chopped away at the edges, the sole, frog, and bars are cut away to make the foot look neat; the results are thrush, corns, scratchy heels, broken hoofs, sand crack, fever, and tenderness; these also lead frequently to broken knees, and cut or tender mouths.

(2). The manner in which the hoof is rasped above the clutches, and the hoof covered with grease, &c. These practices are most injurious in their consequences.

(3.) The shoe should be as light and as narrow as possible, and, where required, the toe should be steeled; the inside of the shoe should be as thin as possible, the sole and frog should not be cut, only the shells and rags should be removed, the crust reduced by flat rasping or paring, and no foot to be rasped above the clutches of the nails; the frog be allowed to reach the ground, and no caulkings be allowed on the fore shoes, and if possible, none on the hind shoes.

(4.) No horse to be shod with leather, or to have a bar or round shoe without special instruction.

(5.) The farriers are to be informed of the above.

3. The Inspectors are to select competent farriers, convenient to the several stables.

4. The horses supplied to officers of the Police Force are for the performance of police duties only, and are not

to be used on any other occasion, or in any other way than may be required and beneficial for the service.

5. The horses supplied to sergeants or constables are not to be used by a superior officer, unless some special occasion arise, which renders it important for the benefit of the service. Whenever such a case occurs a report is to be made to the Commissioner on the following morning.

HORSES, TREATMENT OF SICK.

1. At nearly every station in the colony it is stipulated that the person who contracts for the police farriery shall also furnish, without charge, all necessary veterinary attendance upon police horses in cases of foot lameness and such other diseases as may be treated without consulting a veterinary surgeon. Medicines supplied by his directions are, of course paid for by the department.

2. In all serious cases of sickness of, or injury to, horses, a report should be immediately forwarded to the officer in charge of the district, who will forward it without delay, with his own comments, to the Commissioner's office; and if the case be of such a nature as to require immediate attention, application should be made to a graduated veterinary surgeon, if one should be practising within a reasonable distance.

3. If the attendance of a veterinary surgeon cannot be obtained, the contractor, if competent to treat diseases, should at once be requested to take charge of the case; but should he be incompetent, application should be made to the nearest competent practitioner for the like purpose. pending instructions from the officer in charge, who will in like manner receive his instructions from the Commissioner.

4. Economy must be practised in incurring such expenditure as is implied in the preceding, and all accounts must be submitted to the Commissioner's office for approval, previous to payment.

5. In no case may recourse be had to blistering or firing without special permission from the Commissioner's office.

6. As among horses colic or gripes is a common and frequently severe disease, requiring prompt treatment, and may occur where there is no contractor for farriery available, or where the contractor is incompetent to act, a supply of suitable medicines is to be kept at each station for use when required, and can be obtained from the Depôt in the usual manner. Should however any horse fail in such cases to recover speedily, the instructions contained in the paragraphs 2 and 3 should be at once acted on.

7. When it is not considered necessary in the first instance to submit cases of this description to a veterinary surgeon, the following symptoms appertaining to different diseases, which may be mistaken for each other, should be well considered:—

8. *Symptoms of gripes or spasms of the bowels.*—The horse often manifests, during the paroxysms of pain, impatience, and sometimes violence of manner; the pulse is increased in frequency of action, and is small and thready in character; the animal stamps, or paws, or strikes at its belly, looks round to its side, lies down suddenly and rolls, and after a time rises, and perhaps remains quiet for a time, the pulse subsiding in its number of beats, and generally, but not always, acquiring its usual character. After a short time the above symptoms recur at intervals, generally shorter in duration as the disease proceeds, until ultimately there is perhaps no interval of ease whatever, the pulse participating in the general excitement. The bowels are occasionally relaxed; the urine is often withheld until the spasms cease. If the disease does not yield with the first bottle of the medicine the horse should have another two hours afterwards, and at the same time a dose of physic; three or four hours after which, if the disease still resists treatment, a veterinary surgeon should be consulted.

9. In addition to the medicine, injections should be freely used in these cases.

10. *Symptoms of inflammation of the bowels or Enteritis.*—A dull appearance, hot mouth, the animal occasionally looking round at its side, and lying down

without being seemingly in much pain; remaining down sometimes half-an-hour or more, it then gets up, and perhaps eats a little, and may remain apparently easy for some time, when it again evinces the same pains; paws the ground, looks back, twists its tail, and lies down again; the pulse is generally accelerated, is mostly hard and full, and maintains a uniformity of number of beats per minute. Whereas, in gripes, it varies according to the paroxysms; the bowels are usually confined, or the horse passes hard dry fœces only, and often in single balls; the mouth is hot, sometimes dry. If the horse is not relieved, the respiration becomes quickened and the animal breaks out into a sweat and shows anxiety of countenance, lies down and rolls more frequently, in bad cases incessantly; has a tucked-up appearance, paws repeatedly, and walks round and round in his box until all the symptoms become aggravated.

11. A strong purgative dose of physic should be administered in the first instance, but the subsequent treatment is the proper department of the veterinary surgeon.

12. Injections, as in gripes.

13. Other diseases which the police might venture to treat, are:—

14. *Simple Catarrh.*—Requiring merely rest, mash diet, or green food, an appropriate application to be rubbed into the throat, and fever medicine.

15.—*Strangles.*—When the swelling takes place between the jaws, the rubbing in of the like application should be resorted to until the tumor points, when it is to be freely opened. If the tumor points at the junction of the head and neck, near the root of the ear, a professional man should be called in as soon as the tumor is sufficiently developed to be opened. A professional man should also be consulted when the breathing is stertorous, and the tumor is blocking up the air passages.

16. *Wounds of an ordinary description, and when not extensive.*—Though they may be small in extent, yet if they are in the vicinity of the points or sheaths of tendons, and accompanied with much pain and lameness,

they should be regarded as serious cases, and the directions in paragraphs 2 and 3 should be followed with regard to them.

17. If a young horse persistently refuses to eat its food, or eats it seemingly with but little inclination, it is occasionally caused by the tushes not having come through the gums. When this is the case, the mouth and gums look red, and the horse flinches on pressure with the thumb upon the hidden tush. Cutting the gums with a sharp knife, immediately over the point of the tush, so as to liberate it, will effect a cure.

18. In every case in which the treatment is likely to be protracted, a detailed report should, as before mentioned, be forwarded, stating full particulars, &c., so that instructions may be issued from the Commissioner's office as to whether the case should be treated in the district, or forwarded to the Depôt.

19. Urgent cases may occur in which the horse may be hopelessly injured, and it may be necessary to destroy it at once, before instructions can be received hence, even by telegraph. In such cases the officer in charge must use his discretion, and report all the circumstances in detail immediately. If he think proper to have the animal destroyed, it should be by shooting.

20. Ointments, purging balls, and other medicines for treatment of colic, sore back, greasy heels, &c., will be supplied from the Depôt as required, so as to avoid the expense of purchasing them at country stations.

21. It should be borne in mind, in making application for medicines, that, as they are liable to deteriorate, it is not advisable that too large a stock be kept on hand.

22. *Pleuro-pneumonia.* — With regard to cases of *pleuro-pneumonia*, more specific directions seem to be necessary, and the following instructions have accordingly been compiled from a standard work on veterinary surgery.

23. All that is intended by these instructions is to put the officers of police in a position to decide promptly, on the first appearance of the symptoms of this disease, as to the treatment which should be had recourse to, pending

the receipt in any particular case of more full instructions, which, in the case of horses suffering from this disease, can be obtained by applying direct to the officer in charge of the Depôt.

24. The earliest and most remarkable symptoms of the disease are loss of spirits and animal power, accompanied by a dejected appearance, and pulse feeble in character, beating from 65 to 70 or 80 per minute. The breathing is accelerated, and the appetite generally more or less suffers, though in some instances the animal feeds moderately well. There is sometimes discharge from the eyes and nostrils; in other cases these symptoms are absent. The same remarks may be made with regard to cough; in the early stages it is not invariably present, but when it is, the cough is usually feeble in character, increasing gradually as the disease advances, and after the lapse of a few days it becomes hard and sonorous. The lungs and pleura will then in most cases be found affected, and perhaps a deposit of scrum commencing in the cavity of the chest, the breathing being performed with some difficulty. The membrane lining the mouth is often of a yellowish hue, and the horse seldom lies down for any length of time together. In cases that end favorably, the above symptoms remit within ten days or a fortnight.

25. The medicines proper for this disease consist of horse balls and liniment; of the latter, a supply will be forwarded from the Depôt, and should be kept in store ready for use. The balls must be prepared, and forwarded as required; and on the appearance of the symptoms of this disease, no time should be lost in applying to the officer in charge of the Depôt for the necessary supply.

26. Pending the receipt of this medicine, a ball should be administered to the animal, morning and evening, composed of the following ingredients:—Camphor pulverized, one drachm; nitre, three drachms; tartarized antimony, half a drachm; resin, three drachms.

27. The animal should be fed with mashes and hay, or what is still better, with green fodder; and it should be allowed to take as much water with the chill taken off, as it chooses to take. If it be winter, the body should be

warmly clad with a rug, and the legs bandaged with dry flannel bandages.

28. The disease being of a debilitating nature, it is not advisable to weaken the system by bleeding, resort to that remedy can only be justified in the earliest stage of the disease, where the pulse warrants its necessity, that is where it is full and strong, or oppressed and full, a condition rarely exhibited in the malady under consideration.

29. If there should not be a supply of the appropriate liniment at hand, and that there should be a prospect of some delay in obtaining it; a liquid blister is to be well rubbed into the neck along the windpipe down to the breast; and if there be a difficulty of breathing caused by congestion, or a deposit of fluid in the cavity of the chest, it is to be also well rubbed in upon the ribs on each side, immediately behind the elbows, half way up towards the wither, covering a space over the lungs equal in extent to the size of a large dinner plate. If, however, the appropriate liniment is at hand, it is to be used instead of the liquid blister, as its action is much more beneficial. It is to be well rubbed in daily as directed for the blister until the external surface feels hot, and there is some swelling also between the fore-legs, which is usually the case after four or five applications. In the secondary and later stages of the complaint, the liniment is indispensable.

30. Of the balls which should be administered concurrently with the application of the liniment, one may be given morning and evening. In severe cases they may be administered at intervals of eight hours. When the pulse abates or intermits in its action, or the disease appears to be subdued, the medicine is to be administered less frequently.

31. The balls referred to, might be kept stored in the different districts ready for use in the same way as the liniment; were it not for the fact that they will not keep without rapidly deteriorating, and must therfore be prepared and forwarded as required.

I

32. Any expense incurred for veterinary attendance or medicine for police horses, otherwise than as herein provided for, or any loss accruing to the Government through neglect of any part of this order; will be charged to the member of the Force, who is responsible for the non-observance of these instructions.

INDECENT OFFENCES.

1. The police are not to conceal themselves for the purpose of watching persons supposed to be about to commit indecent offences, but are to interfere immediately in any case in which an act is done, to justify it without waiting for a more serious offence to be committed.

2. Charges of indecently exposing the person are not to be lightly made, especially if it is supposed that there is no improper intention.

INSANE PERSONS.

(See "Lunatics.")

INSPECTOR, TRAVELLING.

1. He is in immediate connection with the Commissioner, from whom he will receive his orders relative to the duties he may be required to perform.

2. He will from time to time in accordance with such instructions as he may receive, proceed from district to district, for the purpose of minutely inspecting the internal economy and discipline of the Force. He will be particular in inspecting the appointments, horses, Government stores (including forage), &c., and will see that they are kept in proper order; he will observe whether the officers and men are properly dressed, in strict conformity with the regulated pattern; that the quarters and stables are kept clean and in order, and will forward a report of the state of each station he visits, calling the attention of the Commissioner to any matters that require alteration.

3. He will make himself acquainted with the manner in which the police duties are performed by all grades of the Force, both towards the Magistracy and the public, and

the general estimation in which the police, both officers and men, at the different stations, are held, for which purpose he will, where practicable, obtain the opinion of the local benches as to the manner in which the police duties are carried on. He will take every opportunity where trifling irregularities exist, to point out the proper method of conducting matters, and will be particular in carefully examining all books and returns of the district he may be inspecting, to see that they are kept on a uniform principle.

4. He will, when it may appear advisable, afford to the officers of police such assistance, either by his advice, or otherwise, as they may require.

5. On his judgment, and the strictly impartial discharge of his duties, much will depend, for the force being scattered over such a wide extent of country, it is only by a constant supervision that it can be maintained in a state of thorough efficiency and uniformity.

INSPECTOR.

1. The duties of the Inspector are those of direction, of constant and active supervision and inspection, requiring his movements to be rapid and uncertain, and his vigilance unrelaxing. He is responsible for the prevention of crime, the detection of criminals, and the general preservation of peace within his district, of which it is expected he will acquire a knowledge, and of its inhabitants generally.

2. On his capacity, discretion, and good management the discipline and efficiency of the officers and men in the district almost wholly depend; for it is only by his example as regards business habits, and knowledge of police duties, as well as his private deportment, that he can gain that respect which it should be their desire as it is their duty to evince towards him.

3. It is not possible exactly to define his responsibility, but he is bound to see that all under his control discharge their respective duties towards the public with zeal, fidelity, and efficiency; and it is expected he will be at all times ready and able to afford advice and information on any matter relating to their public duties.

4. As the advancement in the service of those under his command will very much depend on his recommendation, he will be particular to know what are their relative merits, and the qualifications that fit them for promotion.

5. His residence will be at the Principal Station in the district, and he is not to leave his district without permission from the Commissioner, and will as far as possible confine the working of the Police Force under his command to the limits of their own district.

6. As he is responsible for the general conduct and good order of the officers and constables under his command, he should make himself well acquainted by frequent personal intercourse with the Sub-Inspectors and sergeants, and through them with the characters, temper, and conduct of each constable; he will be firm and just, and at the same time kind and conciliating towards them in his behaviour on all occasions.

7. He is to see that each member of the Force is well acquainted with the contents of the "Manual of Instructions," and that such parts as may be necessary are read and explained to the men from time to time. He will also expect of all under his command that they regularly peruse and make themselves acquainted with the contents of the *Police Gazette*.

8. All orders, as they are issued, are to be carefully read and explained to the men, great care being taken that each individual understands them. He will also take care that all instructions and orders that are given from time to time are promptly and strictly obeyed.

9. Much must be done by himself and under his own immediate inspection. As he is held responsible for the general performance of police duties within his own district, he must give clear and precise instructions to the officers under him, and report every instance of neglect to the Commissioner.

10. He will feel the importance of visiting the stations, watch-houses, &c., in his district at uncertain times, and as often as possible, when he will see that they are kept

clean and in proper order, and will inspect the books, and see that they are kept in a neat, correct, and regular manner.

11. He will also strictly examine the mess quarters, the barrack bedding and furniture, inserting his opinion of the whole in the Station Occurrence Book, and reporting every irregularity or neglect of the barrack regulations or discipline which may appear to him on such inspection.

12. He must see that the men are acquainted with the use and management of their arms and appointments, and with their general duties, and that the constabulary at the several stations are well acquainted with the roads and the bush, so as to enable them to move by the shortest line to any required point.

13. He will strictly examine the roster of duties, to see that they have been arranged with perfect impartiality.; he will also enquire of the men whether they have any complaints, and will at once investigate them, if preferred.

14. He will see that at the various stations a proper system of patrols is established, so that as far as possible the whole of the district may be properly guarded.

15. He will strictly satisfy himself that officers and constables have not, by contracting debts to publicans and others, or by incurring obligations of any kind, placed themselves in a position calculated in any degree to shackle their exertions, or to impair their efficiency in discharging the duties of their office.

16. Property that may come into the possession of the police, he will cause to be entered in a book for the purpose, in order to its being disposed of as may be directed by the Commissioner, or other competent authority.

17. He is not himself to frequent, nor allow his subordinates to frequent, public-houses; in fact, he will best consult his own character and respectability by never even entering them, except on necessary duty.

18. The consideration that his example will do much to regulate the official deportment and conduct of those placed under him, should never allow him to appear

apathetic in the discharge of his own duties; but, on the contrary, should urge him to a prompt and anxious execution of all he may be called on to perform or to superintend, without regard to individual interests, time, or his own personal convenience.

19. He is to pay strict and constant attention to economy, and whenever he sees any means of reducing the expense and promoting the utility of the Force in the locality within his charge, he should not fail to communicate his views to the head of his department, whom he will always find ready to adopt any suggestion that may tend to advance the public service.

20. He will be held responsible for a careful scrutiny of all estimates, accounts, and vouchers connected with the Force under him, which are to be supported and authenticated by his certificates of approval; and that all accounts, returns, reports, and other official documents are drawn up and perfected with the greatest accuracy, precision, and neatness, and transmitted punctually at the proper periods.

21. On the transference, retirement, or removal from the service of any officer under him, he will cause all public records, books, including files of the *Police Gazette*, or other documents the property of the public in that officer's possession, to be handed by him to his successor; and on the Inspector himself giving up the charge of a district from any of the above causes, he will in like manner hand all public records, books, and documents to the officer relieving him.

22. On the receipt of an order for the discharge or dismissal of any member of the Force, he will order the party into head-quarters, when he will see that all his arms, accoutrements, &c., are given into store complete, and in good condition. He will then issue an order for the payment of such salary as may still be due.

23. On the transference of any sergeant or constable from one district to another, he will send, under cover, to the officer in charge of the district to which the party is transferred, his defaulters' sheet, together with his

register, in proper form, detailing his name, description, amount due for clothing, date up to which paid, &c , &c.

24. When the Inspector leaves his quarters on any duty which may detain him from them for a day or longer, he is to direct that all official documents or letters which may reach his office during his absence shall be handed to the sub-inspector or other officer in charge at head-quarters, who is hereby empowered and directed to act upon them to the best of his judgment if it appears to him that the public service could not admit of the delay consequent upon their being forwarded to the Inspector, or stand over until his return to head-quarters.

25. Should it be necessary for the Inspector to leave the District, the senior Sub-inspector of the district will take charge, until the return of the Inspector, or the appointment of some other officer to it. Also, when the Inspector is absent from head-quarters, inspecting the stations in the district, or on other duty, the same officer will assume charge; so that, as a rule, either the Inspector or the senior Sub-inspector will always be in charge at head-quarters.

26. He is to superintend the discipline, inspect the officers and constables, the barracks or quarters, the stables, paddocks, horses, arms, clothing, appointments, and equipments of the Force committed to his charge.

27. He, or in his absence the officer acting in his place, will attend at his office every morning at 9 o'clock, or as soon after as possible, to hear and decide on complaints made against any of the men of his district.

28. He may settle complaints against any of the men under him of such lighter description as he is allowed according to the Regulations under the head of " Punishments ;" the facts of each case, with his decision thereon, are to be stated in the regular reports.

29. If a constable is not satisfied with his Inspector's decision, he may have the case brought before the head of the Department, when, if the objection prove to be frivolous, he will be liable to a more severe punishment than that he objected to.

30. He will make a report in writing as early as possible of any complaint of misconduct on the part of any member of the Force which it has been considered necessary to refer to a Bench of Magistrates for adjudication.

31. He will be at all times prepared to hear and investigate any charge which may be brought by the public against any member of the force, and should such offence be of a serious nature, or the complainant desires that it should be decided by the magistracy, he will at once bring the party before the Bench, forwarding a report of the particulars and the decision of the bench to the Commissioner's office. He may also if he considers it advisable suspend the individual from duty, awaiting the decision of the Commissioner, but in no case will he dismiss or discharge any member of the force without the necessary authority to do so.

32. Should the party who has misconducted himself be of a higher rank than a constable, the Inspector will at once suspend him from duty, and forward to the office of the Commissioner a report of the matter, with the evidence given, and stating his view of the case, with the previous character of the party complained of. He will not himself inflict on any member of the force, above the rank of constable, any punishment greater than a reprimand, but in cases which require a more severe punishment, will await the decision of the Commissioner.

33. Should the offence be committed against the public, he will, unless the case be very gross, and will not admit of delay, mention the matter to the local Bench, and request that it may stand over until the head of the Department has been communicated with, in order that if it may be necessary that the party should be brought before the Bench, he may be first reduced to the rank of constable, it being considered that as his position is superior to that of a constable, he should be reduced to that rank before receiving any punishment greater than a reprimand.

34. Any member of the Force suspended from duty, although not performing any Police duty, will remain within the limits of the station to which he belongs, unless under orders to the contrary, and will not be

entitled to salary for the time he remains suspended, unless by special authority from the Commissioner.

35. He will make himself acquainted with the various stations in the district, and their requirements generally, and will from time to time, according to his discretion, grant immediate police protection to any locality that may require it, if it is apparent that the peace of the locality would be endangered by the delay consequent upon his referring the matter to head-quarters for instructions.

36. It is of great importance that Government should receive immediate intelligence of every occurrence involving the safety of persons or property, or the maintenance of the public peace.

37. If, therefore, any newspaper or other account of an outrage shall precede the police report of it, the Inspector in whose district such outrage shall have occurred will be deemed guilty of neglect of an important duty, unless he can satisfactorily explain the delay on his part, and show to whom the blame of it should attach; and if any loss of time shall occur between the commission of an outrage and the necessary report of it, the cause of such delay must be explained in the report, for the accuracy of which explanation the officer will be held strictly responsible.

38. He will arrange for some trustworthy member of the Force, where possible an officer, to attend all meetings of a political nature, in the district, for the purpose of reporting any seditions or exciting language made use of by the speakers, or any circumstance tending in any way to endanger the peace of the District.

39. He will see that the members of the Force under his command exert themselves to the utmost, not only in the prevention of crime, which is their principal duty, but also in its detection, and will be answerable for their general conduct and good order.

40. He will cause the men to be instructed when they have cases to bring before the Bench, how to obtain evidence and conduct the cases, so as to present the particulars to the Magistrates as clearly and intelligibly as

possible. He will not only give directions to this effect to the constables, but will also see the necessity of attending the Police Court himself, as frequently as possible, to see that his instructions are carried into effect.

41. He will, as far as lies in his power, act in accordance with the wishes of the Bench, for which purpose he will frequently communicate personally with the Magistrates to ascertain whether their lawful orders are duly carried out by the members of the Force, and whether they are active, diligent, and efficient in the prevention of crime or the pursuit of criminals, and respectful, orderly, and steady in their conduct.

42. The Inspectors in whose jurisdiction are cities or towns, if resident therein, are to make a proper division thereof into walks or beats, according to the necessities, local circumstances, and strength of the Force allocated to such cities or towns respectively, adhering to the system pursued in Brisbane, as far as the circumstances in each case will permit.

43. Each Inspector will see that the following Books are properly kept by the Sub-inspector :—

    General Order Book, to contain copies of all General Orders that may from time to time be received from the Commissioner's office.
    District Order Book, to contain copies of all other orders
    Letter and Minute Book
    Warrant Book
    Registry of Horses
    Miscellaneous Property Book
    Store Book.

44. He will also make the following periodical returns :—

    Weekly Return of Duty performed by men and horses, and persons apprehended at each station
    Weekly Forage Return
    Monthly General Report, to be furnished on the first of each month

Monthly Return of Strength and Distribution of the District

Monthly Return of Postage Stamps used in the Public Service

Quarterly Return of Police Horses.

45. The duty and forage returns will be kept by the officers or sergeants in charge of the stations, and all must be examined and certified by the Inspector.

46. Copies or duplicates of all returns made by the Inspectors are to be kept by them.

47. Each Inspector is allowed a sergeant or constable, as circumstances may require, to act as clerk in his office, but he will explain to such member of the Force that the occupation is of a very confidential nature, and that he will be held strictly responsible for his conduct in such office as well as for a due observance of, and obedience to, the General Rules and Regulations of the establishment.

48. No other officer will be allowed the services of a member of the Force as clerk without express permission from the Commissioner.

49. In order to maintain, as nearly as practicable, one uniform and complete system throughout the establishment, the Inspectors are to refrain from making any regulations, or issuing any orders which may be calculated to produce alterations, or cause innovations in the Standing Orders of the Force.

50. Whenever in the opinion of the Inspector it may be expedient to introduce any new regulation, or to alter an old one, he should submit his ideas on the subject for the consideration of the head of the Department, who, should he deem the proposition advisable, will carry it into effect by a General Order. This, however, is not to be understood as extending to an order of a temporary nature; but a copy of any such temporary order is to be sent to the Commissioner's office.

INSTRUCTION BOOKS.

1. An Instruction Book is supplied to every man in the service.
2. The Instruction Books are to be numbered, and produced with other appointments, for the inspection of the Inspector, and are to be given up by men who leave the service.

INTERPRETERS.

1. When an interpreter is required in any police case, the officer in charge is responsible that a competent and trustworthy person is employed; such officer should inquire beforehand to know who is properly qualified.
2. If there are competent interpreters in the police, and they are available, they may be employed.

KEYS OF PREMISES.

1. The police are forbidden to receive from any inhabitant or other person, or have in their possession, any skeleton or other key, without the permission of the Inspector of the district.
2. Every constable who has charge of keys for his admission into private grounds for the better protection of property is, when he comes off duty, to deliver the keys to the sergeant on duty at the station, at the time he is relieved, and the officer on duty will be held responsible that the keys are handed to the constable going on duty in the evening.

LAMPS.

1. The sergeants and constables on beats are to notice and report when coming off duty, the state of the public street lamps, and if any are out of repair, or are not properly lighted and cleaned, the situation and particulars are to be stated.
2. Information is to be given to the proper authorities who have control of the street lamps.

LANTERNS.

1. A lantern is supplied to every sergeant and constable on night duty in Brisbane, or other large towns.

2. The lanterns are to be deposited at a police station, and they are to be cleaned and trimmed ready for use, before the tour of duty commences.

3. Accidents are liable to occur to persons travelling by night, on horseback, or in carriages, in streets where there are no lights, by constables suddenly turning the light of their lanterns full on the persons approaching them, and thus frightening the horses; this is to be avoided, unless in case of accident, or when desired by the persons concerned.

4. Should the light be turned on previous to any persons, as above stated, coming near, the constable is to let it remain so until they have passed some distance, as turning it off too suddenly, near a horse, may produce the same effect as if it were suddenly turned on.

LEAVE OF ABSENCE.

1. No officer is to absent himself from his district or station except on duty, without permission from the Commissioner. Every officer who shall obtain leave of absence, is to return to his quarters on the evening of the day on which the period of such leave shall terminate, and is to report his return accordingly on the following day in the usual manner to the Commissioner.

2. When an officer applies for leave of absence, he is to submit the name of the member of the Force who is to act for him, and such member of the Force will be held responsible for the correct discharge of that officer's duties during his absence.

3. Leave of absence granted to an officer of the Force will not be renewed or extended, except in cases of urgent necessity, which must be clearly shown by the officer applying for extension, and in the event of illness being the plea for an extension of leave, a medical certificate of such illness must accompany the application.

4. When sergeants and constables are allowed leave of absence, it will be according to the following scale :—

    For any period not exceeding 14 days, on full pay.
    Above 14 days, and not exceeding one month, on half pay.
    For any period exceeding one month, without pay.

5. Officers in charge of districts may occasionally grant leave of absence for periods not exceeding three days, but not beyond the boundary of their respective districts; and in every case they will give to the party obtaining leave a certificate of the fact, on one of the printed forms supplied for the purpose, carefully preserving the counterfoil for reference.

6. Applications for leave of absence for more than three days, must in every case be submitted for the approval of the Commissioner.

7. Men going on leave are not to take any part of their arms or appointments, or any Government horse with them, and are to report themselves to the senior officer of the Force at or near whose station they may be residing while on leave.

8. In all applications for leave of absence, it must be stated at what periods, and for what length of time, the applicant had been absent during the year previous to the date of application.

9. Members of the Force when on leave, are to consider themselves subject to every Order, Rule, and Regulation of the Force, and as liable to be called on to act as constables, and to the consequences of any breach of discipline or good order, as if they were serving at their proper stations; and all members of the Force, whether officers or otherwise, are required to report all cases of misconduct on the part of men on leave of absence, whether such misconduct may have been witnessed by them or reported to them by others.

10. Leave may be granted to every man one Sunday in each month.

11. Annual leave may be allowed to each rank as follows :—

Inspectors, one month.
Sub-Inspectors, 21 days.
Sergeants, 14 days.
Constables, 7 days.

12. All applications for leave are to be submitted through the Inspector of the district.

13. A Sub-Inspector may grant 24 hours' leave.

14. " Sick leave " is granted on the recommendation of the Police Surgeon.

15. Before the Inspector recommends a man for leave, he is to ascertain whether there is any case in the Courts, District or Supreme, or in the Police Court, or any other duty, which should prevent the man leaving his district, and if so, the leave is not to be recommended.

16. The Inspectors are not to recommend a larger number of police of any rank for leave at one time than can be spared, due provision being made for carrying on the duties effectively.

LEGAL PROCEEDINGS.

1. Legal proceedings are not to be taken by police without the Commissioner's sanction being first obtained.

2. If police are proceeded against in respect of matters connected with public duty, and it is subsequently satisfactorily proved that no blame attached to them, the Commissioner may, if he thinks fit, pay the legal costs of defence out of the Police Contingent Fund.

3. It is to be understood that no request for payment of *Counsel* in defending constables before a Police Magistrate will be entertained. In the event of the acquittal of a constable upon charges made against him in the execution of his duty, the Commissioner will decide on the merits of each case, whether payment of the solicitor's fee will be made.

LIBRARY.

1. A library is established at the Depôt, and the books will be apportioned to different stations in Brisbane, and changed as occasion requires.

2. The object in founding this library is to encourage the police to employ their leisure hours in a manner that shall combine amusement with the attainment of useful knowledge, and to teach them the value of sober, regular, and moral habits.

3. The books are for the use of the police only, and the property in them is vested in the Commissioner of Police.

4. No books are to be purchased, nor any received as a donation, until approved by the Commissioner.

5. Each member of the force stationed in Brisbane is to subscribe threepence per month for the purchase and repair of books, which will be deducted from their pay at the termination of each month.

6. One volume at a time may be issued to each person, who may retain it for fourteen days, and on returning it, may have it re-issued to him, if not required by another person.

7. The library is to be open for the issue of books for at least one hour every day. The officer in charge of the Depôt will arrange for the most convenient time.

8. A sergeant is always to be present when the library is open, to keep a register of books taken out or returned.

9. Books lost or damaged are to be paid for by the person to whom they were lent. Maps, busts, &c., are to be kept in proper repair.

10. Any one who feels aggrieved in any matter connected with the library may appeal from the decision of the officer in charge of the Depôt to the Commissioner.

11. No outlay for books, &c., is to be made without the Commissioner's sanction; and when this is obtained the officer in charge of the Depôt will pay the amount of approved vouchers to the tradesmen supplying the books, &c., if the vouchers when presented are properly receipted.

12. The library is to be inspected at the termination of every year, and a report made, on the 1st January

in each year, of all the additions or alterations that have been made during the previous year in the catalogues of books in the library, and as to the condition the books are then in.

13. The district library catalogues are not to be altered, or any book re-numbered without the previous knowledge and consent of the officer in charge of the Depôt.

14. When any books are purchased, they are to be numbered, and a report of the titles and catalogue numbers they will bear is to be sent to the Commissioner.

15. The room at the Depôt appropriated as a Library Room is set apart for the use and convenience of the police, and it is desirable that it should be made as comfortable and as nearly assimilated to a private room as possible.

LUNATICS.

1. The police are to apprehend, and charge before a Magistrate, any person who is evidently insane, who is found wandering about, and not under proper control, whether such person be a pauper or not.

2. If the police are called on to take into custody an insane person, under control of friends, they are not to do so, but are to refer the person applying to a Magistrate.

3. If an insane person becomes violent, and likely to injure himself or his friends, the police may assist in restraining him, until the Police Magistrate can be communicated with.

4. When an insane person, whose name or address is not known, is apprehended, a full description of dress, &c., is to be circulated in printed informations.

5. In the absence of the Police Magistrate it is necessary to have two Justices to hear a lunacy case, and before any person charged with lunacy can be sent to a gaol, reception house, &c., two legally qualified medical practitioners for the colony must make affidavit that the person so charged is a dangerous lunatic, and unfit to be at large.

6. In places where there is a gaol or reception house, it will be the duty of the police immediately upon the re-

K

ceipt of the warrant of commitment, and other necessary documents, to remove the lunatic to such gaol or reception house without delay.

7. When a person of unsound mind is confined in a watch-house, the keeper will use every precaution to prevent the lunatic from doing himself or other person any harm, and everything in the cell which might be used by him to commit suicide will be removed.

8. It frequently happens that lunatics are sly and crafty in carrying out intentions of self-destruction, lockup keepers will therefore be watchful of their movements, and visit them frequently in their cells.

9. Lunatics should be treated with the greatest kindness, and any unnecessary roughness in dealing with them carefully avoided.

MAGISTRATES.

1. The police are required to obey all Magistrates in the execution of their judicial duties, by serving all legal processes, such as warrants, summonses, orders of Court, &c.

2. When a command, which may appear to be unlawful, or not in agreement with the Regulations, is given by a Magistrate to a constable, it should be received with respectful attention, and on no pretext whatever will the constable answer back in a pert or disrespectful tone of voice, and where there is a reasonable doubt as to his duty, he will refer the matter to his superior officer for solution.

3. The Magistrates are not vested with any powers of interference with the interior executive arrangements of the Police Force, but should they at any time suspect any felonious attempt upon life or property, of a nature so serious as to render it necessary for the public safety that they should act personally, then they are empowered to call for the attendance of such of the police constables as they may deem necessary; and all constables so called upon shall act under the Magistrate's orders, so long as he is personally present, and during the time necessary for the suppression of such attempt.

MEDICAL AID (FOR PRISONERS).

1. In case of casualties occurring to persons in the streets, such as accidents or sudden illness, the police are to take the persons to the nearest surgeon, apothecary, or hospital.

2. Persons brought to a Police Station charged with offences and suffering from injuries, or those who are in custody, and are taken ill, are to be visited by the surgeon appointed for the purpose.

3. When a surgeon is called by police to a station, or attends elsewhere, to visit a person suffering from injuries or severe illness, he is to be asked by the officer on duty at the station, or by the constable present, for directions as to the necessity for removing the individual to a hospital, or other place.

4. Only one attendance is allowed at the station, unless the urgency of the case makes others absolutely necessary to the safety of a prisoner.

5. When expense has been incurred in consequence of medical aid being required for a prisoner whose illness or injury has resulted from his own misconduct, or who appears to be able to defray the cost, the member of the Force who is in attendance at the Police Court is to acquaint the Magistrate who investigates the case, with the amount which has been so expended on his account.

6. In cases of accident (brought to a Police Station) to persons apparently in a position to pay the surgeon, they are to be requested to do so, if circumstances admit of it before the surgeon leaves.

MEETINGS.

1. The Police are not to interfere with persons attending political meetings, unless specially ordered by the Commissioner.

2. If it come to the knowledge of the police that a political meeting is to be held at any place, or that disorder or a breach of the peace is likely to occur, a full report of all information obtained is to be made to the Commissioner.

3. The following extracts from a charge of the Lord Chief Justice Tindal to the Grand Jury (on the occasion of trials at Bristol, England, under a special commission, in 1832), contain valuable information relative to the provisions of the law, and the duty of the subject, in regard to unlawful and riotous assemblies.

4. The Lord Chief Justice, on that occasion, after stating that it was unnecessary to consider whether the acts of outrage and rapine (which were the offences to be tried) were caused by the riotous proceedings which occurred at an earlier period of the same day, or whether wicked and designing persons, taking advantage of the state of excitement in which the people already were, availed themselves of it, to effect their own purposes of destruction and plunder, observed to the Grand Jury:—

It might be safely concluded, that if the excitement which led to the defiance of the law at the earlier part of the day had not existed, the weightier crimes, subsequently committed by the populace, would not have taken place; and that it is precisely for this reason that the law of England has at all times held in the greatest abhorrence riotous and tumultuary assemblages of the people. No man, said the Lord Chief Justice, can foresee at the commencement what course they will take, or what consequences will ensue. Though cases may occur in which the object of such assemblies is at first defined and moderate, they rapidly enlarge their powers of mischief; and from the natural effect of the excitement and ferment inseparable from the collection of multitudes in one mass, the original design is quickly lost sight of, and men hurry on to the commission of crimes which, at their first meeting, they had never contemplated. The beginning of tumult is like the letting out of water; if not stopped at first, it becomes difficult to do so afterwards; it rises and increases, until it overwhelms the fairest and the most valuable works of man.

5. It has been well said that the use of the law consists first in preserving men's persons from death and violence, next in securing to them the free enjoyment of their property. And although every single act of violence, and each individual breach of the law, tends to counteract and destroy this its primary use and object, yet do general

risings and tumultuary meetings of the people, in a more especial and particular manner, produce this effect, not only removing all security both from the person and property of men, but for the time putting down the law itself, and daring to usurp its place.

6. The law of England has accordingly, in proportion to the danger which it attaches to riotous and disorderly meetings of the people, made ample provision for preventing such offences, and for the prompt and effectual suppression of them whenever they arise.

7. In the first place, by the common law, every private person may lawfully endeavor, of his own authority, and without any warrant or sanction of the Magistrate, to suppress a riot by every means in his power. He may disperse, or assist in dispersing, those who are assembled; he may stay those who are engaged in it from executing their purpose; he may stop and prevent others whom he shall see coming up from joining the rest; and not only has he the authority, but it is his bounden duty, as a good subject to the Queen, to perform this to the utmost of his ability.

8. If the occasion demands immediate action, and no opportunity is given for procuring the advice or sanction of a Magistrate, it is the duty of every subject to act for himself, and upon his own responsibility, in suppressing a riotous and tumultuous assembly; and he may be assured that whatever is honestly done by him in the execution of that object will be supported and justified by the common law.

9. In stating the obligation imposed by the law on every subject of the realm, the Lord Chief Justice observed :—

The law acknowledges no distinction in this respect between the soldier and the private individual. The soldier is still a citizen, lying under the same obligation, and invested with the same authority to preserve the peace of the King, as any other subject. If the one is bound to attend the call of the Civil Magistrate, so also is the other; if the one may interfere for that purpose, when the occasion demands it, without the requisition of the Magistrate, so may the other also. If the one may employ arms for that purpose, when arms are necessary, the soldier may do the same. Undoubtedly, the same exercise of discretion which requires the private subject to act in subordination to, and in aid of, the Magistrate, rather than upon his own authority, before recourse is had to arms, ought to operate in a still stronger degree with a military force. But where the danger is pressing and immediate, where a felony has actually been committed, or cannot otherwise be prevented, and from the circumstances of the case no opportunity is offered of obtaining a requisition from the proper authorities, the military subjects of the King, like his civil subjects, not only may, but are bound to do their utmost, of their own authority, to prevent the perpetration of outrage, to put down riot and tumult, and to preserve the lives and property of the people.

10. Still further by the common law, not only is each private subject bound to exert himself to the utmost, but every Sheriff, constable, and other peace officer is called upon to do all that in them lies for the suppression of riot, and each has authority to command all other subjects of the Queen to assist them in that undertaking.

11. By an early statute, which is still in force, any two justices, together with the Sheriff or Under-Sheriff of the county, shall come with the power of the county, if need be, to arrest any rioters, and shall arrest them.

12. It is not left to the choice or will of the subject, as some have erroneously supposed, to attend or not to the call of the Magistrate as they think proper; but every man is bound when called upon, under pain of fine and imprisonment, to yield a ready and implicit obedience to the call of the Magistrate, and to do his utmost in assisting him to suppress any tumultuous assembly. Magistrates have full power to command assistance by way of precaution; the Act of 1 and 2 Will. IV., c. 41, having invested the Magistrate with that power in direct and express terms, when tumult, riot, or felony is only likely to take place, or may reasonably be apprehended.

13. Again, that this call of the Magistrate is compulsory, and not left to the choice of the person to obey or not, appears from the express enactment in the last-

mentioned Act, that if he disobeys, unless legally exempted, he is liable to the penalties and punishments therein specified.

14. The most important provision of the law for the suppression of riots is to be found in the statute 1 Geo. I. statute 2, c. 5, by which it is enacted :—

That if any persons to the number of twelve or more, being unlawfully, riotously, and tumultuously assembled together, to the disturbance of the public peace, and being required or commanded by any one or more justice or justices or by the Sheriff of the county, or his under sheriff, or by the Mayor, bailiff or bailiffs, or other head officer, or justice of the peace, of any city or town corporate, by proclamation to be made in the King's name, and in the form stated in the Act, to disperse themselves, and peaceably to depart to their habitations, or to their lawful business, shall to the number of twelve or more, notwithstanding such proclamation, unlawfully, riotously, and tumultuously remain or continue together by the space of one hour after such command or request made by proclamation, then such continuing together shall be adjudged felony.

15. Such are the different provisions of the law of England for the putting down of tumultuary meetings; and it is not too much to affirm, that if the means provided by the law are promptly and judiciously enforced by the Magistrate, and honestly seconded by the co operation of his fellow subjects, very few and rare would be the instances in which tumultuous assemblages of the people would be able to hold defiance to the laws.

16. Let me impress on the attention of all those who, from idleness, curiosity, or mere thoughtlessness, suffer themselves to form a part of a riotous and disorderly meeting, that they subject themselves, unconsciously, to the danger of punishment for crimes which they never contemplated; for where many are collected together in the prosecution of an illegal object, it is often impossible to discriminate between the active and unoffending part of the mob. It requires evidence on the part of the accused, which they may not be able to produce, in order to defend themselves against the charge of participation

in the guilt of others. The only safe course for the peaceable and well-disposed on all occasions of popular tumult is this—to lend their ready aid to assist the Magistrates in suppressing it; or, at all events, forthwith to separate themselves from the others.

MESSES.

1. Messes are to be established and kept up at every station, where there are more than two unmarried constables.

2. The sergeants and constables only are to belong to a mess.

3. No member of the Force is to supply any article for a mess, nor is he to have any profit or interest in the supplies.

4. The members of each mess may appoint any one of their number to act as caterer.

5. The mess money is to be collected from each member on pay-day, and entered in an account-book, with the name and number of the constable.

6. The caterer of the mess—where there is no contract for messing the police—is to enter all the payments for supplies, and the cook's salary, on the Cr. side of the account-book, and keep the vouchers, which are not to be destroyed for one month; and at the close of each month's account he is to sign the following certificate at the foot of the Dr. side of the book, viz. :—

"I certify that I have collected the mess money, and paid all the mess bills, as entered above, for the month ended   187   ."

7. Each member of a mess is to be permitted to see the account-book upon application to the caterer.

8. An entrance fee of five shillings, and a subscription of sixpence per month, or such greater sum as the members of the mess agree to pay, is to be paid by each member, to form a fund for the supply of mess utensils, viz., plates, knives and forks, table cloths, &c., to remain the property of the mess for the time being; and when a member quits a mess he ceases to have any property in

the utensils, or claim for money he has paid on such account. The necessary cooking apparatus is provided at the cost of the Government.

9. The supplies are to be ordered from respectable tradesmen, who will be required to charge the lowest price, the object being stated, and the payments assured monthly.

10. The meals are to be so arranged (if practicable), that the men of each relief shall be able to sit down at the same hour, clean and neatly dressed, and if any man be unavoidably absent on duty for one night, the meals from which he is absent will not be charged to him.

11. The senior member present, of each mess, is responsible to the Inspector for reporting, in the absence of a sergeant, any impropriety of language or behaviour by any constable at the mess.

12. The mess regulations are printed on a separate sheet, and a copy hung up in each station.

13. To prevent fraud, small memorandum books are to be used, in which each tradesman is to be requested to enter the supplies, and acknowledge payment for them by giving receipts in the books, which will enable the officer who examines the mess accounts to ascertain if the preceding month's accounts have been paid, and are properly receipted.

14. Police are not to be employed as cooks to a mess at any station, unless arrangements are made so that such employment in no way interferes with the performance of the full regular period of police duty.

15. In stations where there are a great number of men in mess, it will be found more convenient to have a providor, who then assumes the whole responsibility of paying the tradesmen, &c., charging for meals at a certain price, fixed by mutual agreement.

16. A committee will be formed, of three, four, or more members of the Force, one of whom must be a sergeant, to regulate mess affairs, one of the number acting as secretary, and another as treasurer.

MONEY.

Any one in the police borrowing money from a publican or beer-shop keeper is liable to be dismissed. (See "Debts.")

NEWSPAPERS.

1. The police are not to give any information whatever to persons connected with the Press relative to duties to be performed, or orders received, or communicate in any manner with the editors of newspapers on police matters, without the consent of the Commissioner.

2. The Inspectors, or officers in charge of districts, are to search all newspapers, and cut out and submit to the Commissioner any extracts bearing upon the police, or the conduct of any individuals in it.

3. The members of the Police Force should bear in mind, that, although they are the servants of the public, they are accountable for their conduct while in the performance of their duty, to the Government, and to those who are especially appointed to the Department to which they belong. It is therefore not only inexpedient and unnecessary, but directly opposed to orders, that individuals in the employment of the Government should have recourse to public journals, in order to defend themselves against any reflections cast upon them from other sources; it is sufficient for every Government servant that he merits and retains the approbation of the Government that employs him.

NUISANCES.

1. Attention is to be directed to the streets and byeways, in all places which come under the provisions of "*The Towns Police Act*," where the drainage is neglected, where dead animals are found lying, or where an accumulation of decayed vegetable matter, offal, or filth, is collected or laid.

2. Persons offending, whose residences are known, are to be cautioned that proceedings will be taken if they continue to act against the provisions of the Act.

3. Reports of nuisances of the above description, which may require application to other authorities, are to made at once to the officer in charge of the station, who will communicate the particulars to the proper authorities.

NUMBERS.

The numbers on helmets are not to be concealed in any way; they are worn by police for the purpose of reference and identification, and persons wishing to take or ascertain the number of any man are not to be obstructed; but if the number is properly asked for, it is to be given immediately.

OATH, NATURE OF.

The following extracts from a pamphlet by the Hon. and Revd. S. G. Osborne, and reprinted in the "London Metropolitan Police Regulations," are here inserted for the information and guidance of the police, and their serious attention is called to them :—

1. It appears somewhat extraordinary that the teaching "the nature of an oath" forms no part of the general system of education; but a little experience in our courts of justice will convince any careful observer that whilst it is acknowledged to be highly important that men should understand what they really do when they are sworn to their evidence, there is nothing more common than to find the grossest ignorance on the subject.
2. It is your duty, when called on by a magistrate or anyone in authority over you, to give evidence for or against a fellow creature, whether it be to clear the innocent or to convict the guilty.
3. A person about to be sworn, if a Protestant or Roman Catholic, takes the Bible or Testament in his right hand, and attentively listens to the terms of the oath he is about to take; he then shows his willingness to fulfil them by pressing the book to his lips, having first repeated the words "So help me God."
4. Jews are sworn on a Hebrew Bible, according to the formula of their faith.

5. The person addressed is called on to swear "That, in the matter in question, he will speak the truth, the whole truth, and nothing but the truth—So help him God."
6. By saying "So help me God," I solemnly declare that as I stand before God, and rely on Him in all things, I will endeavor to speak that only which is true.
7. I press the book to my lips, or kiss it, to show my love for it, and my desire that every word that passes my lips may be as true as that book is true.
8. By speaking "The truth," I am required to state what I really saw, heard, or did, in the matter upon which I am being examined.
9. By speaking "The whole truth," it means that I am to keep nothing back of that which I am called on to prove; I am to state all I saw, heard, or did, in the matter upon which I am examined, without any concealment, and without any regard to the effect my so speaking may have on any person concerned in it.
10. By speaking "Nothing but the truth," it means that I am not to add anything to that which I state to be the fact, because I may have reason to think it true when I do not actually know it to be so. I am equally bound to speak the truth at all times, whether I am sworn or not.
11. Men are required to swear to the evidence they give in a court of justice, because it is thought right to remind them thus solemnly that they are about to speak in the presence of God, that they may be more cautious, lest their feelings lead them to say that which is untrue, or to keep back any part of the truth.
12. Because justice seems to require, in matters in which the lives, character, or property of our fellow creatures may depend upon the truth of the evidence given, that every allowable means should be used to remind the witness that though he may deceive an earthly magistrate or judge, he will one day have to answer to the Great Judge of Heaven and earth as to the truth of what he has deliberately called on him to witness.

13. Man could not dwell in any safety from the malice or violence of the wicked, if the guilty, when detected, were not proved to be so ; the innocent, when wrongly accused, acquitted of the guilt imputed to them. In either case, if I give false evidence, I sin against my fellow creatures, for I either try to protect the guilty from the punishment they deserve, or allow the innocent to suffer wrongfully when I am giving evidence on which may depend the proof of the guilt or innocence of a fellow creature ; that I may be enabled to speak without malice, and without deceit, the truth, the whole truth, and nothing but the truth.

14. That you may give your evidence with perfect truth, and with satisfaction to yourself, you should endeavour, before you go into Court, to bring clearly to your recollection all the circumstances of the case in which you are about to be examined, so far as you were or are any way concerned in it. When you are sworn, think well on each question before you commence answering it. If you do not clearly understand a question say so at once, and the Judge or Magistrate will cause it to be explained to you. Never be in a hurry to answer, but take time to consider what is the real truth in the matter required of you. When you feel you have spoken the truth, adhere to it ; do not be induced to go back from it. Every witness is liable to be what is called cross-examined—that is, to have questions put to him calculated to draw answers which may contradict, or qualify, more or less of what he stated on his first examination. In a cross-examination it is customary seriously to remind the witness that he is on his oath ; it is urged on him that he may have been mistaken in what he said, or that he may have misunderstood the questions put to him on his former examination. Great pains and skill are (strange to say) often used to confuse a witness, particularly as to points of time, or the identity of persons he may have sworn to.

15. Now, let me advise you to look at this species of examination in its true light ; consider it as a means taken under the sanction of the laws of your country

to ascertain, as far as possible, the real weight to be attached to the evidence of a witness under examination. Some men, it is known, do not sufficiently regard the sanctity of an oath, and others, through malice, or for the sake of gain, will purposely give false evidence; or to gain some end they have in view, they will withhold some part of what they know. This has made it expedient that a witness, after having stated the facts to which he is on his first examination called on to swear, should then have his knowledge of every such fact and his motives in giving evidence thoroughly sifted; and this is generally done by counsel, persons skilled from practice in discovering where a witness may be supposed to speak from actual knowledge, and where he may be suspected to speak that which is false, from some improper motive, or where, from carelessness or misunderstanding, he may have stated that which, on further consideration, he will acknowledge not to be the fact.

16. Now, if you are really desirous to speak only the plain truth, and if you will determine to weigh well each answer before you give it, being cautious never to speak positively to dates or persons unless you are positive of them, if you have well considered how solemn a thing an oath is, and are resolved to give your evidence without any malice against others, or desire to screen or benefit yourself, you have nothing to fear in a cross-examination, for it will only prove your former evidence to have been truly and carefully given, and from no other motive than a desire honestly to do your duty before God and before man.

A person who wilfully says upon oath that which is untrue commits perjury, and is liable to severe punishment on indictment.

OBSCENE WORDS, BOOKS, &c.

1. Obscene words or figures written, painted, or chalked on walls, doors, &c., are to be defaced by police during the night.

2. Such offences are to be prevented as far as possible, and the offenders are to be charged if detected.

3. Observation is to be kept upon shops where obscene books, prints, stereoscopic slides, &c., are exposed for sale, or where it is supposed they are sold; and, if necessary, authority is to be obtained, for a warrant to be applied for, to seize the articles.

4. If supposed obscene or immoral bills or pamphlets are distributed or offered for sale in the streets, copies are to be obtained, which, together with the names and addresses of persons selling the same, and of their employers, are to be submitted to the Commissioner for directions.

5. If the matter or pictures be grossly obscene, persons offering them for sale or distribution may be apprehended and charged with the offence.

OBTAINING MONEY OR GOODS BY FALSE PRETENCES.

1. Any person charged (under "*The Vagrancy Act*") with obtaining money or goods by false pretences is to be apprehended by a constable or officer of police if the offence be committed in his presence.

2. Any person finding another person committing the offence of obtaining money or goods by false pretences may himself immediately apprehend such person for the purpose of taking him before a Magistrate, to be dealt with according to law; and a constable is to assist, if required to do so, in apprehending the person and taking him before a Magistrate, and in detaining him at the Station (where the charge is to be entered, and signed by the person preferring it) until the prisoner can be taken before a Magistrate.

OCCURRENCE BOOK.

1. An Occurrence Book is to be kept at each Police Station, in which the full particulars of every occurrence are to be entered by the officer on duty immediately it is reported, under the proper heading of the day of the week and the date.

2. From these entries the Weekly Report is made by the member of the Force in charge of the Station.

OCCURRENCES.

Any occurrence of an unusual nature is to be immediately reported to the Commissioner by telegraph, and a detailed report is to follow as quickly as possible.

ORANGE PEEL.

The police are to remove pieces of orange peel whenever seen on the pavement. Frequent accidents have occurred through persons slipping down from stepping upon orange peel.

PARLIAMENT HOUSES.

1. The police on duty at the Houses of Parliament are to be strictly attentive to their duties, and very respectful in their manner and conduct towards Members of Both Houses.
2. The police are not to address Members except upon police matters or duty which may occur at the time.
3. The constable on duty at the Members' entrance to the Legislative Assembly is to be provided with a book of cab fares, which he is always to carry with him for reference.
4. See printed instructions issued by order of the Speaker, and hung up in the Parliamentary Buildings, for the guidance of those constables on duty.

PATROLS.

1. The duties of a district cannot be performed efficiently without the establishment of a proper system of patrolling, which should be carried out under the general instructions of the Inspector, so that the patrols from the different stations may be regulated with a view to general co-operation.
2. The particulars of every patrol made from a Station will be entered in the "Occurrence Book" of the Station—the hours at which patrols have been made from each Station, the places visited, and the incidents which have occurred to the patrols—so that the officers in charge may be enabled to form a return of the patrolling which has

taken place at Stations. He can then regulate it with a due regard to the requirements of the service, and the extent of duty which the men are called on to perform.

3. This duty, to be performed efficiently, must be performed silently, and without any sign of preparation which can attract attention and put ill-disposed persons upon their guard.

4. Patrols are not to go out on stated nights or at particular hours, but at irregular periods, and are always to visit suspected places and observe suspicious houses and persons.

5. They will not confine their attention to the main lines of road only, but will occasionally proceed through the bush, calling at the houses of the settlers to find out what is going on, to ascertain if their assistance is required, or to obtain any information they can relative to horse and cattle stealers or any other offenders.

6. If disorderly and suspicious persons are met by patrols at unseasonable hours, they are to be apprehended and brought before a Magistrate for examination.

7. In certain cases it may be more conducive to the objects of patrols to conceal themselves near suspected passes or places than to prolong their march along a public road; when so concealed the strictest silence must be observed.

8. When on patrol duty, constables are not to smoke, to separate, nor talk loudly, or enter public houses except in the performance of their duty.

PAWNBROKERS.

1. A "Pawnbroker's List" of all articles lost or stolen, which bear a distinctive mark, or are of some particular pattern by which they can be identified, is to be distributed immediately after report of a robbery is received by the police—one copy to each pawnbroker and dealer.

2. Where stolen property is found to be pledged, and the owner of the property makes application to the pawnbroker for its restoration, the Police are not in any case to interfere or accompany the owner to the pawnbroker, with a view to getting the property restored.

PAY ABSTRACTS.

1. The pay of Inspectors, Sub-Inspectors, sergeants, and constables is drawn monthly, on an abstract prepared by the Inspectors of each district, and sent to the Commissioner's office on or about the 24th day of each month.

2. The amount of each abstract (excepting those forwarded to Sub-Collectors of Customs) is paid by cheque from the Commissioner's office to the Inspectors, who obtain cash from the bank, and pay the police as soon after as possible.

3. Where the Sub-collectors of Customs pay the police direct from revenue received at the different ports, the abstracts will be made out in the usual form, and when fully completed (with the members of the Forces' signatures, &c.) they will be forwarded to the Treasury, and duplicate copies to the Commissioner's office.

4. Each man is to sign the pay-sheet at the time he receives his pay, and if there is any doubt as to the correct amount he is entitled to, he is to mention it at the time he discovers the apparent error, which will be rectified or explained.

5. Any complaint respecting counterfeit coin will not be entertained unless made at the time, and prior to the money being placed in the man's pocket.

6. Deductions are made from the pay of police, and are shown on the pay sheets, for sickness and fines, and the police sign for and receive only the nett amount of pay, with any allowance they may be entitled to for the performance of special duties.

7. Pay drawn on abstract for any man who is subsequently suspended before being paid, is to be retained by the Inspectors, unless the case is decided in the meantime, and Commissioner's directions received.

8. Cash not called for, or in hand from any other cause, is to be refunded to the Commissioner's office.

9. Pay is not to be drawn for police suspended, or on leave without pay.

10. The pay abstract must be an exact copy of the Pay Ledger, which will be signed simultaneously with the acquittance.

11. Should any alteration be made in the pay abstract either by the Commissioner, the Treasury, or the Audit Department, a corresponding alteration will be made in the Pay Ledger in red ink.

12. Erasures are not to be made either in the Ledger or in the pay abstract. Corrections must be made in red ink, and initialed by the Inspector.

13. The pay abstracts are to be kept clean and neat, and if any man wilfully or carelessly signs in the wrong place, he is to be reported to the Inspector.

14. If from sickness or any other cause a man is unable to sign the acquittance, the Inspector will sign for him, with red ink, which will mean that the man, or his representative, has received the correct amount of pay due to him.

15. All abstracts of the salaries of Police Magistrates, and Clerks of Petty Sessions, are to be transmitted monthly in duplicate to the Commissioner of Police, after examination by the Clerk of Petty Sessions, and the certificate of a Magistrate thereto.

PENSIONS AND GRATUITIES.

1. Gratuities may be granted of one month's pay for each year's service to any officer of police, who shall be duly certified to be unfit for service; and to have served with diligence and fidelity for any number of years not exceeding ten, and a further gratuity of two month's pay for each year he shall have so served, exceeding ten years, and not exceeding fifteen.

2. When any person applying for remuneration or superannuation, shall be *under sixty years of age*, it shall not be lawful to grant any such remuneration or superannuation unless upon certificate from two legally qualified medical practitioners duly appointed in that behalf by the Governor; that such person is incapable from infirmity of mind or body, to discharge the duties of his office; in which case, if it shall be certified by the Commissioner that such person has served with zeal and fidelity for

fifteen years and less than twenty years, it shall be lawful to grant him by way of superannuation, an annual sum not exceeding one-half the salary of his office.

3. If above twenty years, and less than twenty-five years, an annual sum not exceeding two-thirds of such salary.

4. If above twenty-five years, and less than thirty years, an annual sum not exceeding three-fourths of such salary.

5. If above thirty years, an annual sum not exceeding the whole of such salary.

6. And if such person shall be *above sixty years of age*, and shall have served fifteen years, and less than twenty years, it shall be lawful, although there shall be no certificate of incapacity from infirmity or injury of body or mind, to grant him by way of superannuation, any annual sum not exceeding one-half of the salary of his office; and if such person shall have served over twenty years, he shall come under the provisions of the rules 3, 4, and 5.

7. For injuries received at any time in the actual performance of duty, a pension for life may be granted of an amount in proportion to the resulting disability, but not exceeding the full pay; the grounds of disability are to be carefully investigated and fully set forth.

8. If a man's conduct has not been uniformly good, or his incapacity has been brought about by irregular or vicious habits; the Commissioner will recommend that a lower scale of pension or gratuity may be granted to him, if he is certified as unfit for further service, and he has served the necessary time to entitle him to pension or gratuity.

9. When a man is granted a pension, and all the necessary forms have been complied with, he will be paid in advance the amount calculated to the end of the current quarter, and subsequent payments will be made in advance at the commencement of each quarter.

10. When any married member of the Force (who has served with zeal and fidelity) dies, the gratuity to which

he may have been entitled at the date of his death, may be paid to his widow, subject to the approval of the Governor.

11. A pension or retiring allowance is granted only upon the condition that it becomes forfeited, and may be withdrawn by the Governor in any of the following cases :—

    (1.) On conviction of the grantee for any indictable offence.

    (2.) On his knowingly associating with thieves or suspected persons.

    (3.) On his refusing to give information and assistance to the police, whenever in his power, for the detection and apprehension of criminals, and for the suppression of any disturbance of the public peace.

    (4.) If he enter into, or continue to carry on, any business occupation, or employment, which shall be, in the opinion of the Governor, disgraceful itself, or injurious to the public; or in which he shall make use of the fact of his former employment in the police in a manner which the Governor considers to be discreditable and improper.

12. Any man who resigns, and is allowed again to enter the Force, forfeits all claim to have the time of service previous to his resignation reckoned as part of the period for which a pension or gratuity may be granted on his being certified unfit for further service.

13. When pensioners from the police are taken into custody for any offence, a full report is to be made to the Commissioner of the particulars of the case, and a further report is also to be made of the result before the Magistrate, or at the trial.

14. A deduction of 2 per cent., calculated on the gross amount, is made from the pay of each member of the Police Force, on account of the Superannuation Fund.

PICKPOCKETS.

1. The police are to make themselves acquainted with the persons of pickpockets, and wherever they are seen loitering about, they are to be watched, and prevented from committing crime, or detected if they make the attempt.

2. Pickpockets who are known, and who travel in omnibuses for the purpose of committing crime, are to be pointed out to the conductors, if seen to loiter about the starting places for omnibuses, or to travel in omnibuses.

3. Picpockets resort to various expedients to attract a crowd, to enable them to make a rush, or attempts at persons' pockets.

4. When pickpockets are apprehended, the police are to inquire and ascertain their former course of living, and if they can be identified, and former convictions proved, the police who can give evidence, are to be in attendance at the Police Court for that purpose.

POLICE ABSENT.

When any of the Police are absent more than 24 hours from their Stations without leave, they are to be suspended, and a description of their persons and dress is to be circulated in the printed informations in the usual manner adopted when any other persons are missing.

POLICE MAGISTRATES.

See "Courts—Police," and "Magistrates."

POST OFFICE.

1. The attention of police is directed to the various attempts that have been made to intercept letters posted in pillar letter boxes. Constables are carefully and frequently, especially at night, to examine the apertures of the boxes on their beats, by running their fingers, as far as possible round the inside, and should they discover that any device, trap, or sticky substance has been inserted, they are *not* to remove it, but keep quiet and

careful watch to endeavour to discover the offender, until visited by the sergeant, who will send immediate information to the Station.

2. The officer in charge, upon receiving such information, either through the police, Post Office authorities, or others, is at once to direct a plain-clothes constable to proceed to the spot, and keep observation until the arrival of the postman to empty the box, who is then to be made acquainted with the attempt.

3. A report, stating what description of trap was laid, is to be made in every case to the Inspector, who will forward the same to the Commissioner.

4. When a constable is on duty at the General Post Office and Telegraph Office, he will be careful to act with the utmost civility to all classes of persons, and be ever ready to answer such questions as may be put to him by persons seeking information respecting matters within his knowledge, having reference to the different places where letters may be posted or received, telegrams sent or received, money orders, &c.

PRISONERS.

1. In apprehending a person, or making him or her a prisoner, no more violence is to be used than is absolutely necessary for the safe custody of the prisoner.

2. The usual plan is to seize the arm, and keep hold until the prisoner is in the Station, to prevent the possibility of escape. When a prisoner is once in custody, he is not to be released except by direction of a Magistrate, or on the responsibility of an officer in charge of a Police Station.

3. If a prisoner resists, the constable is bound to struggle with him, and overpower him, but not injure him unnecessarily.

4. If the constable is likely to be overpowered, he may draw his baton, and use it, taking care to avoid striking any one on the head. The arms and legs should be aimed at to disable a prisoner, at parts of the frame least likely to suffer serious injury.

5. The constable may also blow his whistle, which will bring assistance, but these extreme measures are not to be resorted to, except in urgent cases, where all other attempts have failed, and a prisoner is likely to escape through the constable being ill-used or overpowered.

6. Prisoners who are very violent, or who are charged with very serious offences, are, if necessary, to be hand-cuffed, to prevent danger, or the possibility of escape.

7. Prisoners under remand, are not to be confined at a Police Station where there is a Gaol. Should a Magistrate or other person in authority, desire a prisoner to be remanded to a Police Station, he is to be informed that the cells are unsuitable for prolonged confinement of prisoners.

8. Prisoners are to be made as little uncomfortable as possible; safe keeping, and not punishment, being the object during the time they are in custody of the police.

9. No conversation is to be held in the hearing of prisoners, nor is improper language, or taunting remarks to be used towards them.

10. Prisoners, if not in an unfit state from drunkenness or other cause, are to be at once taken before the Magistrate, if the Police Court is open, but if not open, then at the earliest subsequent opportunity.

11. When Petty Sessions are held at public houses in outlying districts, special care is to be taken to prevent prisoners obtaining drink.

12. Bail may be accepted for the appearance of prisoners, for which see "Bail."

13. Prisoners are to be supplied with clear water to drink. Tin pint cans, supplied on requisition, are to be kept for the purpose.

14. A pewter basin and sponge are supplied at each Police Station, where charges are taken solely for medical purposes, and for use of the Police Surgeon.

15. One basin and two towels are supplied for use of prisoners, who may be confined for several hours, and who may desire to wash themselves.

16. Officers in charge of Stations are responsible for the proper care and cleanliness of articles supplied for use of prisoners.

17. Necessary refreshment for prisoners may be purchased out of money taken from them, providing the charge against them does not relate to the money. The amount expended for refreshments is to be entered in the Prisoner's Property Book.

18. When it is necessary for prisoners to have refreshments, either at their own expense or at the public expense, no beer or spirits whatever is to be given to them, or admitted into the cells, but only tea or coffee, with such eatables as are usually given in those cases.

19. When prisoners are detained pending inquiries before a charge is actually taken, the door of the room is to be kept closed, and a constable is to be posted specially to prevent their escape. When necessary for safe custody, a prisoner may be put in a cell pending any inquiry previous to the charge being entered; but the prisoner is to be present when statements are made against him on which the charge is founded.

20. A solicitor is to be allowed to communicate with a prisoner in custody of the police at a station. Facility, as far as practicable, is to be given that the communication may not be overheard by anyone; but care is to be taken that the prisoner shall not escape, and, if necessary for the purpose, one of the police may keep the prisoner in sight during the communication.

21. When a prisoner charged with any offence is taken to a hospital, and it is requisite that the prisoner should remain under medical treatment, a report of the circumstances of the case is to be made to the Inspector for directions as to whether a constable is to remain on duty at the hospital in charge of the prisoner.

22. Whenever a person is brought to a police station on a charge of felony, the sergeant on duty is not to suffer any statement in the nature of a confession to be extracted from the person charged, either by the police or by any other person. Should any private individuals attempt such a course, they are to be immediately prevented, and the circumstance is to be reported to the Inspector.

23. Prisoners are not to be cautioned by police that any statement they make will be given in evidence against them.

24. Any fact discovered in consequence of information obtained by a promise, threat, or inducement may not be given in evidence. (See "Evidence" and "Confessions.")

25. A statement made by a prisoner, when charged at a station, is to be accurately written down at the time by the sergeant on duty, and reported to the Magistrate who hears the case.

26. Prisoners are to be visited in the cells at least once every hour, and if drunk every half-hour; and in the latter case are to be spoken to and aroused on each visit.

27. If prisoners are insensible, or appear to be ill, or injured in any way, although they do not complain, the Police Surgeon is to be sent for immediately. This course relieves the police of responsibility, and is to be strictly observed. The Commissioner desires to impress most earnestly on the police the heavy responsibilities which they incur by deviating from this Regulation; and to warn them that in every instance of wilful disobedience and neglect, the officer will be visited with the severest punishment. (See also "Drunken Persons," and "Medical Aid.")

28. A sergeant, on commencing his tour of duty, in charge of a Police Station, is on each occasion to receive from the sergeant whom he relieves a statement of the number of persons then confined, and in company they are to visit the cells and make a personal inspection of each prisoner. The sergeant, for his own security, ought to see that the prisoners are in a proper state when he commences his tour of duty.

29. The property of prisoners convicted of felony, which has hitherto been delivered to the Sheriff, is to be retained by the police until further orders. An inventory is to be made in each case, and properly witnessed.

30. When prisoners are committed for trial, the Police are to make all necessary inquiries, at their late lodgings, and elsewhere, to ascertain their previous character.

31. Prisoners charged with indecent offences, or attempting to extort money by threats respecting unnatural offences, are to be confined in separate cells, and not placed with other prisoners.

32. In cases of prisoners committed by the Magistrates to prison, if the authorities of the prison refuse to receive the prisoner, he is to be taken back to the lockup. A report is to be made to the Commissioner of each case, and the Magistrate by whom the prisoner was committed is to be informed also.

33. Before a remanded prisoner is taken from the Gaol to the Police Court, in cases where the remand has not expired, an order from the Police Magistrate for the prisoner to be delivered up to the officer sent for him, is to be obtained.

34. When prisoners are identified, the police who can give evidence are to attend at the Police Court.

35. Whenever witnesses are brought to identify an accused person, that person is to be placed in the company of others of the same sex, preparatory to being seen by the witness expected to identify. The fact of a witness having a previous knowledge of the accused does not affect the rule. Police in uniform are not to be placed in company with accused persons for the purpose of identification.

36. The police are to be instructed to conform with this Regulation in all cases.

37. When prisoners are to be removed from Police Stations to the Police Courts, the officer on duty is to have a sufficient number of constables there, that all prisoners may be taken in a safe and orderly manner before the Magistrates.

38. In no case is one constable to be placed in charge of more than two prisoners. The constables on day duty are to be called in, if those going to the Police Court with charges are not sufficient.

39. Each constable must know, before he quits the Police Station, what prisoners are given in charge to him; and for them he is responsible until they are disposed of by the Magistrates. The officer on duty is likewise to attend to the prisoners at the Police Court, and see that they are securely and properly kept while waiting to be brought before the Magistrate.

40. For further particulars as to conveyance of prisoners, see "Vans."

41. Prisoners in custody of the police are not to be put into omnibuses, when there are other passengers. If it be necessary to provide a conveyance for a prisoner where the police vans are not available, a cab may be used, and if in a rural district where no cabs are to be had, a light cart is to be hired. The expenses in such cases may be charged to the Contingent Account.

42. Arrangements are to be made with the railway authorities for the safe custody of prisoners conveyed by railway.

43. Expenses incurred by the police in making inquiries and obtaining evidence against prisoners, prior to their committal, will be paid out of the Contingent Fund, and are to be submitted and approved, according to regulations.

PRISONERS' PROPERTY, DISPOSAL OF.

1. The police will make an inventory in triplicate of all property found in the possession of a prisoner at the time of his arrest, and which they are justified in seizing and retaining; the inventory to be signed by the constable who makes it, and countersigned by the Inspector or other officer in charge of police. The prisoner is also to be invited to sign the same. One copy will be forwarded to the Commissioner of Police, one to the officer in charge of the district, and one to the Gaol where the prisoner is confined.

2. Such property is to remain in the custody of the police until the prisoner shall have been either discharged or convicted, or found guilty.

3. The property itself is to be sent to the place of trial previous to the day appointed for trial, so that it may be accessible either (if necessary) for the purposes of identification, or to be returned to the prisoner, if discharged, or delivered to the Sheriff or Gaoler, if the prisoner be convicted, with a copy of the inventory.

4. Care is to be taken that property necessary for the purpose of identification remain, as much as possible, in the hands of the same constable or officer, so as to avoid rendering the evidence of identity complicated or embarrassing.

5. If the prisoner be discharged, the property is to be restored to him, with the exception of any portions necessary to be retained as proofs in any future proceedings, or any portions proved to belong to another person, and which may be delivered to such person on his indemnifying the police officer, Sheriff, or Gaoler, against any proceedings of the prisoner. It will be the duty of the Sheriff or Gaoler to inform the prisoner of the amount taken from him according to the duplicate inventory.

6. If the prisoner be convicted of a felony or a misdemeanor entailing forfeiture, all property found in his possession and all other property belonging to him are to be confiscated; and any such property identified as having been stolen may be restored to the owner. The remainder is to be delivered to the Sheriff, who will sell it, and pay the proceeds into the Treasury, unless His Excellency should consider it advisable to direct all or any to be given to the wife or children of the felon.

7. If the prisoner be convicted of a misdemeanor not punishable with forfeiture, the property found in his possession, and seized by the police, is to be delivered to the Sheriff or Gaoler, who will hold it at the disposal of the prisoner, subject to Gaol Regulations, either to be disposed of as he may wish (proper vouchers being taken) or retained by the Sheriff or Gaoler, and at the expiration of the sentence, returned to the prisoner.

8. In cases of summary conviction, a similar course is to be pursued before and after conviction, as before and after trial.

9. Members of the Force are strictly prohibited from having any dealings with prisoners in the way of buying, selling, or bartering any horse, saddle, or any other description of property whatever, and any member so offending will be dismissed the Service.

PRISONERS, REMOVAL OF, UNDER WRITS OF HABEAS CORPUS.

1. A prisoner who is in Gaol under committal for trial, or under sentence, cannot be temporarily handed over to the custody of the police for the purpose of giving evidence against some other offender, or of himself answering to another charge to be preferred against him, unless by writ of *habeas corpus*.

2. In order to obtain any such writ from a Judge of the Supreme Court, from whom alone it can be obtained, an affidavit must be prepared in accordance with one of the forms given in Appendix C; the first form being adopted for a writ *ad testificandum*, that is, where the prisoner is to be removed for the purpose of giving evidence; and the second, where for a writ *ad respondendum*, that is, to answer another charge.

3. If, when such a writ is required for the removal of a prisoner in any of the country districts, there be a Judge of the Supreme Court at hand, to whom the application can conveniently be made, the affidavit should be prepared in the district, and the application made to the Judge, through his Associate, without reference to this office; but if the application have to be made to a Judge in Brisbane, it is advisable that the full particulars should be sent to this office, when the necessary affidavit will be prepared, and the writ obtained, by the Detective Police. The police in the country districts, cannot always ascertain with certainty the particular Gaol in which the prisoner whose removal is required may be confined, and as the affidavit is useless unless it contain these particulars, it can be prepared with greater facility by the Detective Police, who, from the nature of their duties, are better acquainted with the various places of confinement, and their inmates, than the district police can be.

4. After obtaining any writ of the kind, the officer in charge of Detectives will at once forward it to the Commissioner's office for transmission to the district in which the prisoner may be confined, or to be otherwise dealt with as the circumstances of the case may require, unless it be for the removal of a prisoner in whose case

the Brisbane Detective Police are alone concerned, and no reference to the general police is necessary. In every such case the Officer in charge of Detectives may at once carry the writ into execution.

5. It must be carefully borne in mind that a prisoner who is removed from any Gaol by the police, under writ of *habeas*, has still to complete the period of punishment he was suffering at the time. Wherever the prisoner is taken, the writ should accompany him, as the warrant, by which the police retain him in their custody.

6. When the prisoner is removed to take his trial on another charge, and a conviction follow, he will be taken charge of by the gaol authorities present at the Court, and the writ should be at once handed by the police to those authorities, in order that they may be acquainted with the fact that the prisoner was under sentence at the time of his trial. In such a case, a report of the disposal of the prisoner, should be sent to the Commissioner's office, for the information of the Sheriff, or other authority from whose custody the police received the prisoner.

7. In all other cases, that is, where the prisoner has completed giving the evidence required of him, or has been acquitted of the charge preferred against him, he should be returned direct to the place whence he was taken, together with the writ for his removal.

PRIZE-FIGHTS.

1. The Law Officers of the Imperial Government having given their opinion that the police have legal authority to apprehend, detain, and charge before a Magistrate any person or persons against whom evidence can be produced to raise a presumption that the person who can be identified, intended to be concerned as a principal or accessory in a prize-fight in any part of the colony, the police are strictly to enforce the law.

2. Whenever it be known in sufficient time beforehand that parties are preparing for a prize-fight, the circumstances are to be reported to the Commissioner for directions as to the arrangements to be made, and numbers of police required to effect the apprehension; but if there

be not time for getting such directions, steps are to be taken at once to apprehend the parties, especially the principals, and the Inspector, sergeant, or constable, as the case may be, is responsible that the best measures practicable are adopted, and that a sufficient number of police be obtained.

3. Any of the police who hear that persons are in training, or preparing to fight, or accessory to an intended prize-fight, are immediately to report the circumstances to the Inspector or other superior officer.

4. Evidence to identify them and prove the intention, is to be obtained by all proper means.

PROMOTION.

1. All vacancies in the rank above that of constable, will, as far as may be practicable, be filled up by promotion from the next inferior rank; every inducement is thus held out for men of a good class to enter the Force, and to exert themselves while in it; for by zealously and efficiently performing their duties to the public they will be consulting their own interests.

2. At the same time, it must be understood that seniority, length of service, and good conduct, are not of themselves the main recommendation for promotion; for although they will always have their due weight, efficiency and adaptation for the particular vacancy will be the principal considerations. Hence those desirous of promotion must endeavor to merit it by a zealous attention to their duties, and the favorable report of their immediate superior officer will be an indispensable requisite for advancement to grades.

3. When vacancies in the higher ranks occur, and directions are given for men to be recommended to the Commissioner for promotion, those best qualified in all respects are to be selected, seniority of service being duly considered.

4. Police who are selected for promotion to higher ranks, prior to such promotion are to undergo an educational examination, to ascertain whether they are qualified

to discharge efficiently the duties which would devolve upon them. Each rank will be examined under the different heads, as hereafter stated.

5. Constables for sergeants :—
   (1.) Reading
   (2) Writing from dictation
   (3.) Writing a report of circumstances of supposed accident or occurrence
   (4.) Numeration and notation
   (5.) Compound addition.

6. Sergeants for Sub-inspectors :—
   (1.) Reading
   (2.) Writing from dictation
   (3.) Writing a report of case on which directions are given to a sergeant or constable, stating what the directions are
   (4.) Ordinary English composition, including punctuation
   (5.) Arithmetic; four first rules; reduction; proportion
   (6.) A supposed statement of facts will be made, on which a charge may be received or refused; the sergeant is to receive and enter same on a charge sheet, or refuse to receive the charge—according to his judgment—and enter the same on refused charge sheet.
   (7.) To make out a monthly report, the strength of district, and variations being supplied
   (8.) To make out an abstract for district pay from the numbers on the monthly report
   (9.) To abstract from a set of papers to be supplied, the leading points of a case necessary to be brought under the notice of the Commissioner, and embody the same in a special report.

7. Men selected for examination will be directed in police orders when and where to attend for such examination.

8. The names of those who have passed will subsequently appear in Police Orders, with further directions.

9. When police are being examined they are not to communicate in any way with each other, or copy any papers, or look over the papers of another man under examination.

10. When men are examined and are unable to pass, the paper in each case received from the Board of Education, is to be forwarded to the Inspector of the district (confidential), for a copy to be taken by the unsuccessful candidate, to enable him to perfect himself in those subjects in which he was deficient, so as to pass on a future examination. The paper is to be returned to the Commissioner.

11. They are also to be examined and reported on by the Police Surgeon as to their general sound state of health, and whether they have received any injuries or wounds likely to incapacitate them at any future time for the performance of police duty.

12. Sergeants recommended for promotion must be able to ride, and will be instructed during the time they are being taught foot drill.

13. All ranks prior to promotion must be able to drill, and will be certified by an Inspector who will see them at the Depôt.

14. When a constable is recommended for promotion to sergeant, the Inspector is to state whether the constable has been on the sick list during the last twelve months; and, if so, the date and for what number of days.

15. By the Regulations of the Service the police are to serve and reside wherever they may be appointed, and in all cases of anyone being recommended for promotion he is to be reminded that he may be required to serve in other districts.

16. Sergeants who are transferred to other districts on promotion are to remain in such districts, and the Inspectors are not to recommend their re-transfers to districts in which they served prior to promotion.

17. Some of the police having attempted to obtain promotion by means of applications made by private

friends, and such practices being injurious to the good order and discipline of the service, the police are to understand that their prospects of promotion must depend on the report which their superiors may make as to their qualifications and conduct in the performance of their duties.

18. Merit and not favor is the ground of advancement, and any of the police who attempt to bring interest to bear for the purpose of influencing the Commissioner, will be considered as disqualified for the promotion thus sought to be attained.

PROPERTY.

1. All articles of property found by the police, or given to them by the finder, are to be handed to the sergeant or other officer in charge of a Station, by whom full particulars are to be entered in the Occurrence Book, and the entry is to be signed by the officer as well as by the person who gives in the property.

2. The earliest opportunity is to be taken by this officer to make out a correct inventory of the property so found, which, after being signed by him he will forward, together with an explanatory report of the circumstances, to the officer in charge of the district, who will give directions as to its disposal.

3. Money or other property which may come into the possession of the police, and respecting the disposal of which there may be any doubt, is to be forwarded, together with a report of the circumstances, to head quarters, with a view to its being disposed of, as may be directed, by some competent authority.

4. The particulars of all property relating to charges, or found upon prisoners, or at their lodgings, or elsewhere, not disposed of by the Magistrates, but retained by the police, are to be entered in the Prisoners' Property Book under the several heads, and when subsequently disposed of or restored to the owner, the date and particulars are to be stated in the proper column.

5. A receipt is to be taken for each article given up.

6. A return, on the proper printed form, is to be made to the Commissioner each half-year, ending June and December, of all unclaimed property remaining in the hands of the police.

7. Skeleton keys, gambling instruments, and similar articles are to be deposited each half-year at the office of the Inspector, who will give directions as to their final disposal.

8. The Inspector may, if he consider it desirable, recommend that the description of property found be advertised in the newspapers.

9. The police are not to interfere in publishing any reward for the recovery of lost property, nor is a reference to be allowed for the payment of the reward in such cases to any of the Police Stations.

10. The police are not to interfere in any case of dispute as to ownership of property seized under legal process.

11. Any goods and chattels which have lawfully come into the possession of the police, and which are unclaimed, shall be sold and disposed of by the direction of the Commissioner of Police by public auction (a notice of such sale having been previously published thrice in the *Government Gazette*), and the clear produce of such sale shall, unless claimed within twelve months thereafter, be applied in aid of the Police Reward Fund; and every such sale shall be valid against all persons, and no persons selling any goods or chattels under this enactment shall be subject or liable to pay any auction or other duty in consequence of such sale. (See 27 Vic., No. 11, clause 31.)

PROSTITUTES.

1. Prostitutes cannot legally be taken into custody simply because they are prostitutes; to justify their apprehension they must commit some distinct act which is an offence against the law.

2. The police have no power to interfere with men and women talking together in the streets, so long as they behave themselves properly, and are not assembled toge-

ther in such numbers as actually to cause obstruction in the thoroughfares; but if it is absolutely necessary to interfere, then it is to be done civilly and firmly, without any offensive language or manners.

PUBLIC HOUSES.

1. It is the duty of the member of the Force in charge of a sub-district to minutely inspect any house for which an application for a publican's license is made, and make a full report to the Bench of Magistrates of its exact state.

2. The character of the applicant should be carefully ascertained before recommending him or her to the Bench as being a proper person to hold a publican's license.

3. The police are to enter licensed premises when required to do so by any licensed person, and are to act therein in the execution of their duty according to the following rules:—

4. The constable shall, on the demand of the licensed person, expel, or assist in expelling, from the licensed premises any person who is drunken, violent, quarrelsome, or disorderly, and any person whose presence on the premises would subject the licensed person to a penalty under "*The Licensing Act of* 1873," and may use such force as may be required for the purpose.

5. When the police shall take into custody any person charged as before-mentioned, the person making the charge is to be required to go to the Police Station and sign the Charge Sheet, and the police are not to take into custody any person upon the charge of another unless the person making the charge agree to do so.

6. Whenever a sergeant or constable enters any licensed premises, as directed by this Order, if no person be charged at the Police Station, a report of the cause of entering, and of the circumstances of the case, is to be made as soon as possible afterwards to a superior officer patrolling, or at the station, and a written report is to be made and kept for reference at the station.

7. Should such report not be made, or not be satisfactory, the sergeant or constable will be deemed to have

entered the house contrary to the Regulations of the Service, and be punished accordingly.

8. The constable is called on to see that there is no violation of the law by licensed persons.

9. In the sale of intoxicating liquors by any person at any place where he is not authorised by his license to sell the same, for example—in tents, at cricket matches, at races, and so forth.

10. In the permission of drunkenness, or any violent, quarrelsome, or riotous conduct on his premises, or the sale of any intoxicating liquor to any drunken person.

11. In the selling or exposing for sale, or opening or keeping open any premises for the sale of intoxicating liquors during the time that such premises are directed to be closed, or allowing during such time any intoxicating liquors to be consumed on such premises.

12. The above provision does not preclude a licensed person from selling intoxicating liquors to *bona fide* travellers, or to persons lodging in the house.

13. No holder of a license under this ("the Publicans") Act shall keep his house open for the sale of any liquor, or permit the same to be drunk or consumed in his house or premises, except between the hours of four in the morning and twelve at night on the six business days of the week, and except between the hours of six and nine in the morning and of one and three in the afternoon, and eight and ten at night, on Good Friday and Christmas Day, and except between the hours of one and three in the afternoon on Sundays, and on the three latter days only for the sale of liquors not to be drunk or consumed on the premises, and every such holder offending against any part of this enactment shall, for every such offence, be liable to a penalty not exceeding two pounds, and every separate sale shall be deemed a separate offence.

14 *Any person, whether licensed or unlicensed*, who shall sell or give to any aboriginal native any spirituous liquor, in any quantity whatever, or any fermented liquor in any quantity which shall produce intoxication is liable under the 51st clause " *Licensed Publicans Act*," to a penalty of five pounds.

15. And *any person* supplying Polynesian labourers with spirits is liable, under "*The Polynesian Labourers Act,*" clause 29, to a like penalty.

16. The permission knowingly of his premises to be the habitual resort of, or place of meeting, of reputed prostitutes, whether the object of their so resorting or meeting is or is not prostitution, and the allowing them to remain thereon longer than is necessary for the purpose of obtaining reasonable refreshment, is an offence.

17. Indecency in a public house is not necessary to be proved in order to convict for "knowingly suffering prostitutes to assemble and continue upon the premises." All that is necessary is, to prove facts fairly leading to the inference that women came to the house not merely to obtain refreshment, but for the purpose of meeting men, as prostitutes, and that the defendant knew it.

18. Justices may convict of this offence without proof of disorderly conduct, but they are not bound to convict on mere proof that prostitutes were allowed to remain in the house for a reasonable time.

19. Gambling is also prohibited, nor is any publican allowed to keep cards, dice, or other instruments of gaming, excepting billiard or bagatelle tables in his house.

20. The knowingly harbouring or suffering to remain on his premises any constable during any part of the time appointed for such constable being on duty, unless for the purpose of keeping or restoring order, or in the execution of the constable's duty; supplying any liquor or refreshments whether by way of gift or sale to any constable on duty, unless by authority of some superior officer of such constable.

21. A constable on beat duty or patrol will pay particular attention to all public houses within his walk or beat, reporting the hour which each is closed, and whether they appear to be conducted in an orderly manner.

22. On no pretence shall a constable in uniform enter any public house except in the immediate execution of his duty. Such a breach of positive order will not be excused, and he subjects the publican himself to a severe fine for allowing him to remain there while on duty.

23. The constable must report the name of any publican or keeper of any house, shop, room or place, of public resort, wherein provisions, liquors, or refreshments of any kind shall be sold or consumed (whether the same shall be kept or retailed therein or procured elsewhere), who shall wilfully or knowingly permit drunkenness or other disorderly conduct in such house, or knowingly suffer any gambling therein, or knowingly permit or suffer prostitutes or persons of notoriously bad character to meet together and remain therein.

24. In each case in which the right of entry into a public house is claimed or exercised, a report is to be made of the circumstances to the superior officer on the earliest occasion after.

25. Before an application to summon a person for refusing to admit the police, be laid before a Magistrate, the officer in charge of the station is to ascertain that the facts are strong enough to make it appear a proper exercise of this power on the part of the police.

26. When a sergeant or constable makes an application to summon a publican for any breach of the Publicans Act, he will make out a full report in writing of the circumstances of the case for the information of the officer in charge of the station.

27. It is strictly forbidden that the police, on any occasion, when visiting a public house in execution of duty, should ask for, buy, or take any drink.

28. It having been decided that playing skittles for money or beer is gambling, and consequently illegal, the holders of licenses for premises where gambling is so carried on are to be first cautioned by police, and, if the practice subsequently continues, they are to be summoned.

29. A register of all licenced premises, where thieves and suspected persons resort, is to be kept in each district.

30. Observation is to be kept on coffee stalls, to prevent and repress any assemblage of disorderly characters which causes obstruction to the thoroughfare, annoyance to passengers, or disturbance of the neighborhood.

31. Public houses in the neighborhood of the Police and Supreme Courts are to be visited by an Inspector or Sub-inspector.

32. In order to obtain a conviction against the holder of a license for offences specified, it is necessary that sufficient proof should be given before Magistrates that the landlord or person summoned was knowingly guilty of the offence.

PUNISHMENTS.

1. All constables have conferred on them by law powers superior to those of other members of the community, and as such powers are at all times liable to be abused, it has been rendered necessary to introduce certain penalties as punishments for such constables as shall offend against the Rules and Regulations that have been issued for the guidance of the Force.

2. In aggravated cases the officer in charge may take the offending party before a Bench of Magistrates to be dealt with in accordance with the 13th section 27 Victoria No. 11, and this course, from its being the more convenient, has been most frequently adopted, but as a general rule, it is necessary in those cases only in which the offences are of a serious nature, or have been committed against the public.

3. A return showing all fines and other punishments inflicted upon the members of the Force will be prepared by the Inspector in charge of each district, and submitted monthly for the information of the Commissioner.

4. The members of the Force in charge of stations will also return all defaulters in their sub-districts in the duty reports forwarded weekly to the Commissioner's office.

5. It is impossible to give any rule that would be of general application, as to the manner in which these punishments shall be awarded, as it must be left principally to the discretion of the parties inflicting them, who will see the necessity of in every case inquiring minutely into all the circumstances under which the offence was com-

mitted, so as to inflict a suitable punishment, taking into consideration the previous character of the individual, and the effect such punishment is likely to have on the Force at large.

QUARTERS OF MARRIED CONSTABLES.

1. The Sub-inspector, senior sergeant, or sergeant in charge of a station will visit the quarters of all married constables living out of barracks and ascertain that they are clean, that the locality in which they live is not disreputable, and that no calling or trade contrary to the Regulations is being carried on in such premises.

2. This inspection will take place once a-month, and an entry will be made in the Occurrence Book by the Inspecting Officer, who will concisely enter therein the state in which he found each man's quarters.

3. The address of each married constable will be entered in the Occurrence Book, after the date of inspection.

4. In case a married man removes from one street to another, he will at once report the fact to the officer in charge of the station, and the new address will be entered in the Occurrence Book.

RELIEFS.

1. The hours for duty are as follows :—
The day duty commences at 5 a.m. and continues till 9 p.m., for which purpose half the available duty men are told off, who are divided into two reliefs, with one sergeant or senior constable to each, and take street duty by four hours at a time.

2. The first relief goes on at 5 a.m., and remains on beat till 9 a.m.

The second goes on at 9 a.m. and remains till 1 p.m.

The first goes on at 1 p.m., and remains till 5 p.m.

The second goes on at 5 p.m., and remains till 9 p.m.

3. During the intervening four hours between their duties, the men so relieved are allowed to return to their barracks or homes, but must be ready at least a quarter of an hour before their tour of duty commences.

4. The night duty commences at 9 p.m., the men who go on at that hour remaining on beat until 5 c'clock the next morning, one sergeant or senior constable taking charge of each section.

5. In each relief, in addition to the number apportioned for beats, there is a reserve of one constable to remain at the station, ready to act, if required, in case of emergency. This duty will be taken in turn by the men.

6. The night and day duties change every fourteen days.

7. It is expected that all married constables will lodge as near as possible to the division to which they are attached, and that all members of the Force, (whether on duty or not) will be prepared to turn out in all such emergencies, as fires, accidents of any kind, disturbances, &c.

8. Officers in charge of divisions take their turn of day and night duty, but are not required to visit the barracks of any division except their own.

9. The duties of the police appointed to do duty in other large towns of the colony, with respect to hours, &c., will be carried out on the same system as at Brisbane.

10. Police attending Police Courts with prisoners, or in cases of summons, or at the higher courts, in their own time, are to be allowed reasonable "time off," according to the judgment of the officer on duty at the station.

11. Constables coming off duty are to be regularly assembled at the hours of relief, and marched to the places appointed by the Inspectors, there to be inspected by such Sub-Inspectors or sergeants as may be appointed for that purpose.

12. The police for duty in each relief are to assemble at the appointed station a quarter of an hour before the hour fixed for mounting duty.

13. The Sub-Inspector or sergeant on duty is to parade and inspect the men, to see that they are clean and properly dressed, and in all respects fit for duty.

14. The orders and informations are then to be read aloud, clearly and distinctly, so that each man may hear and understand them.

15. The section sergeants are then to march the constables to their respective sections and beats.

16. The reliefs are to march in single files, and are always to take the outer side of the footway. The police, when walking along the streets, are not to rudely shoulder past respectable people, but give way in a proper manner.

17. About one-half of the police being upon night duty, and one half on day duty. Constables are to be changed from night duty to day duty every fortnight.

18. The changes from night duty to day duty are to be made on the first Sunday in every fortnight. (See "Beats.")

REQUISITIONS.

1. All articles required will be supplied, and work to be done will be performed by means of the usual printed forms of requisition.

2. When work or repairs are urgent and require to be done immediately, a local tradesman may be employed. Requisitions are to be made out at once for such work, and forwarded to the Commissioner's office at the end of each month. The name and address of the tradesman who performed the work is to be entered in the proper place on the form of requisition.

3. Requisitions for all articles, including stationery, usually supplied from the Colonial Store, should be forwarded half-yearly through the officers in charge of districts, to the Commissioner of Police.

4. Such requisitions should be received at the Commissioner's office at least one month before the end of each half-year, in order that sufficient time may be allowed for making-up and forwarding the supplies to their destination.

5. The above Rules apply to requisitions for printed forms supplied by the Government Printer.

6. No requisition will be attended to unless it contains particulars of former supply, how disposed of, and the quantity and condition of stock on hand.

7. All members of the Force, below the rank of Sub-inspector, are strictly forbidden to sign these requisitions, as the Government do not hold themselves responsible for articles so supplied.

8. When a requisition is given for the conveyance of police, prisoners, &c., by coach, steamer, or otherwise, it is the duty of the member of the Force, proceeding in charge of such police, prisoners, &c., to have the exact amount charged duly entered on the back of the requisition before he certifies to its correctness.

9. Police or prisoners proceeding to different ports or destinations, although travelling by the same steamer or conveyance, on the same line of route, will not be put in one requisition. Each party will have a separate requisition.

10. The names of the police and prisoners will in every case be shown on the face of the requisition.

11. As it frequently happens that members of the Force receiving supplies neglect to certify on the back of the requisition that such supplies have been received, officers in charge of districts, and members of the Force in charge of stations, will carefully examine each requisition before forwarding the same to the Commissioner's office; and where any member of the Force has neglected to certify in the usual way, he will be reported for neglect of duty.

12. Members of the Force receiving supplies of any kind, will make sure, before signing the requisition on the back, that the amount charged is quite correct; for where an overcharge is made the person certifying to the accuracy of the amount will be held strictly responsible.

13. No member of the Force, excepting the officer in charge of a district, will (unless under exceptional circumstances) give a requisition for the purchase of any article or thing, or for the repair of anything, unless he is authorised to do so by the officer in charge of the district.

14. In case of an emergency, where it is impossible to obtain authority, the member of the Force giving the requisition will, when forwarding vouchers, attach a special report, giving full particulars of the circumstances which caused him to act without authority, and if the explanation is not considered satisfactory, he will be charged with the expenditure.

15. No officer in charge of a district will purchase any articles which can be obtained on requisition from the

Colonial Store, without the sanction of the Commissioner, unless in case of emergency, and then the price must not exceed current rates.

16. Requisitions to contractors for prisoners' rations will be made out daily, and be signed by the watchhouse-keeper, at the end of each month, and after the requisitions are compared with the Watchhouse Book, the officer in charge of the district will give one requisition, signed by himself, for the whole of the rations supplied, and attach it to the vouchers when forwarding them to the Commissioner's office.

17. Requisitions for shoeing troop horses will be signed at out-stations by the members of the Force in charge, but when sent with vouchers to the officer in charge of the district, it will be his duty to countersign all such requisitions, if correct, before he forwards them to the Commissioner's office.

18. When tradesmen call at Police Stations for information as to payment of any claim they may have on the department for work performed, the officer in charge is to inform them that they are to send their bills to the Inspector of the district, who will give due notice when they are to attend at his office to receive payment.

REWARDS.

1. In addition to special rewards which members of the Force may be entitled, under the authority of the Government, to receive from the Police Reward Fund for bravery or other meritorious conduct displayed in the performance of their duty, various sums are also from time to time offered, both by the Government and by private individuals, for the apprehension of notorious offenders, the recovery of lost property, &c., &c. Although these rewards are generally intended to act, not so much as a stimulant to the Police, as an inducement to the public to afford information or assistance; they are equally open to all the subordinate members of the Force, as well as to persons who have given information or assistance.

2. Any such rewards will be divided among the various claimants in proportion to the relative value of their

respective services; but it is to be understood that no officer is to participate in any reward, whatever part he may have taken, or however instrumental he may have been in effecting the object for which it was offered, unless under special authority.

3. At the same time, there should be no necessity for any reward to induce a member of the Force to exert himself to the utmost on all occasions for the public benefit, as it is for the purpose of preventing and detecting crime that the Police Force is maintained.

ROLL CALL.

(See "Barracks," par 17.)

SALUTING.

1. The police of all ranks are to salute His Excellency the Governor, the members of the Executive Council, Judges of the Supreme Court, President of the Legislative Council, Speaker of the Legislative Assembly, District Court Judges, within their districts, and the Commissioner of Police.

2. Inspectors, Sub-inspectors, sergeants, and constables, are to salute, when passing or addressing a superior officer, but if the nature of the duty, or other special circumstance make it undesirable to salute, it is not to be done.

3. Sergeants and constables are to salute, when passing or addressing a Police Magistrate, an Inspector, or Sub-Inspector.

4. Sergeants and constables in uniform are to salute Commissioned Officers of the Army or Navy in uniform.

5. The police are not to salute, but stand at attention only, when on parade, or posted in line on public occasions, such as the Opening of Parliament, &c.

6. When police, marching on duty, or assembled in a body, meet a superior officer, they are to be commanded, "Eyes right," or "Eyes left," as the case may be, but never salute except by word of command.

7. Police when mounted are not to salute in the same manner as when on foot, but in the following manner:—
On approaching a person entitled to a salute, the constable

will ride to attention. When within three horses leagths, he will bring the right hand quietly across the body, resting it lightly, with fingers extended on the top of the left hand, pause a moment, cut away the right hand smartly to the position of attention, and turn the head and eye at the same time in the direction of the person saluted.

8. The salute is to be acknowledged and returned by the superior officer.

9. Any of the police neglecting or disobeying these Orders are to be reported.

SEAMEN, ARREST OF, ETC.

1. It is the duty of a constable to apprehend any seaman given into his custody by the master of any British registered ship, for being drunk, riotous, or disorderly, on board his ship.

2. He may also arrest, without warrant, any seaman belonging to a British registered ship, given into his custody by the master, for desertion or absenting himself without leave.

3. The police have not the power to arrest a seaman belonging to a foreign ship, for any similar offence, without the written authority of the Consul of the nation to which such ship belongs, and even then a warrant is necessary, in each case, before the arrest can be lawfully effected.

4. No publican or lodging-house keeper, can detain the chest, tools, or other property of a seaman or an apprentice belonging to a Bristish registered ship.

5. Any person harbouring a seaman or an apprentice, is liable to a fine of £20 for each seaman or apprentice so harboured.

SEARCHING.

1. Prisoners charged with felony are to be searched, at the lock-up, with a view to discovering evidence bearing upon the charge.

2. Persons suspected of making, uttering, or having in their possession counterfeit coin, should be searched im-

mediately, at the place where taken into custody, when the circumstances admit of its being done. If the search cannot then be made, precautions are to be taken to prevent the prisoners from getting rid of base coin or other evidence of guilt before being brought to the Police Station, and when they are brought to the Police Station, they are to be immediately searched.

3. Persons reasonably suspected of having, or conveying in any manner, anything stolen or unlawfully obtained, may be searched.

4. Prisoners insensible from illness, drunkenness, or any other cause, are to be searched, solely for safe custody of their property, and its return to them.

5. Prisoners who are drunk and riotous, or known or suspected to be dangerous, are to be searched for the purpose of depriving them of arms or weapons by which they might make their escape, or inflict injury on themselves or those about them.

6. When prisoners are searched, it is to be done so effectually that all instruments or articles of property which they ought not to retain may be taken from them.

7. When prisoners are not searched, the officer taking the charge is to advise them to leave in his hands any article or property in their possession (for which a receipt enumerating each article is to be given to the prisoner) to whom it is to be returned when the charge is disposed of. In all such cases, an entry is to be made in the Occurrence Book, stating the names of prisoners, the particulars of each article handed to the police, and the number of the Charge Sheet on which the charge is entered.

8. When prisoners are searched, every article taken from them is to be distinctly called out by one of the police, and the particulars are to be entered on the Charge Sheet by the officer taking the charge. The amounts of notes, gold, silver, and copper monies are to be stated separately. The sergeant will be responsible for any loss that may happen through neglect or irregularity.

9. When prisoners are searched before arriving at a Police Station, every article taken from them is immedi-

N

ately handed, on arrival at the station, to the officer on duty, who is to enter the particulars on the Charge Sheet.

10. Female prisoners, charged with any offence for which they should be searched, are to be searched by a female appointed for the purpose.

11. The officer attending the Police Courts with charges, is to enter in the Prisoners' Property Book, when at the station and previous to going to the Court, the particulars of all articles described on the Charge Sheets; and after the cases are disposed of by the Magistrates, if the property is to be given up to the persons who were charged, every article is to be delivered to them, and a receipt taken, in the proper column.

12. If the property is to be detained by the police, by order of the Magistrate, an entry, stating particulars, is to be made in the proper column.

13. Property taken from prisoners is not to be returned to them until the decision of the Magistrates is known.

14. When property relating to a charge is given up to the owner, by order of the Magistrate or Commissioner, a receipt is to be taken in the proper column of the Prisoners' Property Book.

15. Property relating to a charge, which is found and brought to a Police Station subsequent to a charge being entered, is to be accurately described in the Prisoners' Property Book, with a reference to the Charge Sheet, and the former entry, if any, made in the book.

SERGEANTS.

1. To each district, and for the city or town police, one sergeant is selected to assist the officer in charge, by a personal supervision of the sergeants and constables; and he will be held responsible for the conduct and appearance of the constables, and for the state of the barracks and quarters, the arms, ammunition, appointments, &c., at the principal station in the district.

2. He is, to a great extent, responsible for the drill of the men of his station and is selected from the other sergeants expressly on account of superior knowledge of his duties.

3. He must keep a roster of duties performed by himself and the men under him, and will see that those constables who have to give evidence at the Police Court are in attendance, and properly dressed.

4. He will attend daily at the Inspector's office with reports of such constables under him as may have misconducted themselves, and will cause to be in attendance those parties who can give evidence.

5. He will inspect all carts or other conveyances belonging to the Force, which may arrive at and leave the station, and will see that the draught horses are properly groomed and attended to, and the carts and harness kept in proper order.

6. He will frequently, and at uncertain times, inspect the quarters of the sergeants and men, and will occasionally visit them during meals, for the purpose of seeing on such occasions that the men are properly and cleanly dressed, and conduct themselves with decency.

7. His position is looked upon, to a certain extent, as a confidential one; he will, therefore, do all in his power to preserve regularity and order, and to make himself acquainted with anything to the contrary which he thinks should be brought to the notice of the Inspector or other officer under whom he may be placed.

8. The remainder of his duties are similar to those of the other sergeants.

9. In the absence of the Inspector or Sub-Inspector, the sergeant is to represent that officer, and therefore what has been stated of the duties of those officers as to discipline applies equally to the sergeant when in the temporary charge of a sub-district or station.

10. It is his peculiar province to watch over the conduct of the constables, and to report every irregularity, neglect of duty, or breach of discipline, they commit, to the Inspector or Sub-Inspector, without delay.

11. His conduct towards the officers of the Force must be respectful and obedient.

12. He is held responsible for the general conduct and good order of the constables under his charge, and he is expected to know the character of each.

13. He is not to take any undue advantage of constables by hiding himself, or endeavoring to entrap them into the commission of an offence.

14. He is not to make himself too familiar with constables, but he is to instruct them in the duties they have to perform, and so conduct himself as to secure the respect of those over whom he is placed in command.

15. He is to parade at the station before the hour of the different reliefs, and form the constables of his section into rank for inspection by the Sub-Inspector.

16. He is to observe and report to the Inspector or Sub-Inspector whether each man is perfectly sober, neat, clean, and correct in his dress and appointments. Any absentees are to be reported, and the cause ascertained.

17. He is to "tell off" the constables to their several beats, and, unless the duty is performed by the Sub-Inspector, is to read the orders and informations aloud to the constables.

18. He is to march with the constables to his section, and see that each patrols his proper beat, and knows the ground.

19. He is constantly to patrol his section, and enforce the performance of duty by the constables. If at any time he finds a constable absent from his duty on the beat, he is to have him replaced if possible, and send for another from the reserve at the station, but this last only in case of necessity. He is immediately to ascertain the cause of the constable's absence, and report it to the Inspector or Sub-Inspector.

20. If any felony or disturbance occur, he is to send for such assistance as may be necessary to the station.

21. He is not to enter any public-house or beer-shop except in the immediate execution of his duty.

22. He is to notice hackney carriages and other vehicles at night which appear under any circumstances calculated to excite suspicion.

23. He is to pay particular attention to all public-houses, beer-shops, &c., on his section, and be prepared to state, when required, whether they are kept according to good order; he is to notice and report any which are

open during hours contrary to law, or in which any disorder is committed.

24. If he observe in the streets, &c., anything likely to produce danger or public inconvenience, or anything irregular or offensive, he is to report it to his Inspector or Sub-Inspector, taking such immediate steps at the time as may be necessary.

25. He is to notice and receive reports from the men as to the state of the gas lamps, whether any are broken or extinguished, and report the same to his Inspector.

26. In case a sergeant is absent from illness or other cause, his place is to be supplied by a constable or acting sergeant, who is to be named by the Inspector for that purpose.

27. He is to give all assistance in his power to persons applying to him, and he is expected to have a thorough general knowledge of the Police Regulations and Orders, and to aid in carrying them out effectively.

28. The sergeants are not to traffic, or have dealings or money transactions of any kind with constables.

29. The sergeant is never to absent himself from his station, except on duty, or by permission or direction of the officer of his station or division; and he must at all times be ready to meet any demand on his services.

30. He is to inspect minutely all parties or individuals going on duty, and if under arms is to count the ammunition in their pouches before they go out and when they return, noting in the Occurrence Book the hour of their despatch and return, the state in which they return, as well as the state of the horses if they or any of them be mounted, and all circumstances connected with the particular duty on which they had been employed, of which a record may appear in any degree necessary.

31. He must be perfectly impartial in the division of all the duties of his station, taking his own regular tour of them.

32. He will be held strictly responsible for the appearance of his men and barracks, the state of the arms, ammunition, appointments, and every article of Government property committed to his charge. He must show an example of neatness in his dress and appointments, and

of perfect cleanliness in his person and quarters; and if he suffers any disobedience of orders or neglect of duty, without immediately reporting it to his Inspector or Sub-Inspector, he shall be considered unfit for the position of sergeant, and be reduced accordingly.

33. He is occasionally to wait on the resident or local Magistrates to receive their instructions; and it is of the utmost importance that he should take every pains to inform himself of the several roads, passes, residences, and characters of his neighborhood.

34. He is to report to the local Bench, as well as to his officer, all outrages or other matters connected with the tranquillity of his sub-district, and shall visit all scenes of outrage as soon as possible after they have occurred, without reference to districts or stations, unless he shall have reason to know that the place had been visited by some other responsible party.

35. He will pay particular attention to the hotels and places of entertainment within the limits of his charge, and will report any irregularity he may observe, to the officer under whom he is placed.

36. When in charge of any station where there is no Inspector or Sub-Inspector, he will keep the same books, and make the same periodical returns, as are required to be kept and made by those officers.

37. When the number of sergeants in a district is insufficient to place one in charge of each station, the Inspector or officer in charge of the district, will select the best conducted and most efficient men as senior constables in charge; and on such senior constables will devolve all the duties of a sergeant, and they will receive a trifling addition to their pay, and as vacancies occur will be promoted to the rank of sergeant.

SERVANTS.

1. The police are to notice and report irregularities of servants in improperly admitting persons to, or letting them out of their masters' houses at unseasonable hours, especially when families are out of town, and the houses are left in charge of the servants.

2. If there are suspicious circumstances, and the police have good reason to suppose that persons are improperly in a house, they are to inquire at the house the name of the master or mistress; also state their suspicions (if there be any of the family or a trustworthy person in the house), and remain in the neighborhood in readiness to act if there be reason to suppose any crime is committed, or otherwise to ascertain the number and description of persons leaving the house, and the time they leave.

3. The greatest civility and caution is to be exercised in carrying out this order, so as not to give offence, or unnecessarily interfere with private domestic arrangements.

4. The police are not to gossip with servants, or loiter near houses with that object, or accept refreshment, or any other articles whatever, from servants as gifts.

SHERIFF.

Protection is to be afforded to the Sheriff and Deputy-Sheriffs in the execution of all writs from the Superior Courts, if in their written requisition they shall state that they have grounds to apprehend violence or opposition in the discharge of their duty.

SICK.

1. Any member of the Force consulting a medical man without having first reported himself to the officer of police in charge of the station and obtained an order for medical advice, must pay the fee himself.

2. Should any constable be suffering from the effects of his own misconduct, his whole pay will be stopped during the time he is unfit for duty—excepting the amount actually necessary for his support and medical treatment—and in such a case no order for medical attendance will be issued.

3. If the police are not capable of performing all their requisite duties, according to the rank they hold, they are to be returned as sick, and are to be seen by the surgeon.

4. All men incapacitated for duty by accident or illness are to be under the care of the police surgeon, and must be seen by him and reported as being really so incapacitated, within twenty-four hours of their declaring themselves sick. Without this report no man's name is to be entered on the sick list.

5. The sick men who are able to leave their homes are to be taken to the residence of the surgeon at 9 a.m. every morning, and each man being brought as often as the surgeon directs, provided that he is seen not less frequently than twice a week.

6. The sick who cannot leave home are there to be visited as often as the urgency of the case demands, but in no case less frequently than every other day.

7. If any man declares himself sick in the evening between 6 p.m. and 9 p.m., he is at once to be taken to the house of the surgeon, or the surgeon is to visit him as soon as practicable, if the sick man cannot go to the surgeon's house.

8. When the Surgeon is of opinion that hospital treatment is advisable, the sick man may be sent as in-door patient to the nearest public hospital, the charge of his maintenance in such establishment to be deducted from his pay.

9. In the case of any man wishing to be attended by a private practitioner at his own expense, this may be allowed, the Inspector's approval being first obtained.

10. Full pay may be granted to men on the sick list when seriously injured in the execution of their duty, and also in case of disease, when actually necessary in order to obtain requisite nourishment.

11. In cases of accident or sudden illness occurring to persons under the temporary charge of police, the nearest surgical aid is to be procured; but the police have orders, in all cases where it is possible, to send for the Police Surgeon; such visits are remunerated by a fee of 5s. for the first visit, and 2s. 6d. for every subsequent one in the same case. Only one visit is allowed under ordinary circumstances, the patient being transferred to the hospital

if further treatment is necessary. In all cases where the patient is able to pay, the medical attendant is to be paid by him.

12. If a man reports himself sick improperly, or if the Surgeon does not consider him sick, he is to be reported to the Commissioner for such misconduct.

13. In all cases of illness of any of the police from misconduct, a report is to be made for the decision of the Commissioner, whether any pay is to be allowed during such illness.

14. When any of the police have been on the sick list more than twenty-eight days, or have been more than four times sick during twelve months, or are in hospital, their names and other particulars required are to be sent to the Commissioner.

15. A case of sickness from fever or dysentery is not to be considered as one of four occasions occurring within twelve months, nor is inability to perform duty for a short time from injury received on duty to be considered as coming within the meaning of these orders, so far as to call for the opinion of the Surgeon.

16. Every case of severe injury occurring to any of the police on duty is to be reported to the Commissioner, with full particulars of the accident.

17. If any constable of short service be frequently sick, although not at any time for twenty-eight days together, the circumstances are to be reported.

18. The reports are to be made to the Commissioner, who will, if he thinks proper, refer them to the Surgeon.

19. A sick book is to be kept at each station, in which the name of every man who goes upon the sick list is to be entered.

20. The following particulars are to be entered by the Inspector or sergeant :—

21. The name, age, number, and rank; date of joining the force, previous sickness and sick leave, with dates, and date of going sick.

22. The other particulars stated in the book will be entered as often as he may judge necessary, by the Surgeon, to whom it is to be taken, along with the men on

the sick list. The Inspector, Sub-Inspector, or sergeant will call the attention of the surgeon to any omission in the entries.

23. The pages of sick books are to be numbered for ready reference.

24. When police, who are lame or suffering under any visible bodily disability are directed to be seen by the Surgeon, they are to attend in plain clothes, and not in uniform.

25. Sick or destitute persons are not to be removed from a dwelling by the police.

26. Police who are recovering from sickness or injuries, who have been directed to resume light or reserve duties, and are not sufficiently recovered to resume regular duty, are, at the end of every quarter to be seen by the Surgeon, who will report to the Commissioner on their condition.

27. When any of the police who become insane are admitted into a hospital or asylum, the usual rates of sick pay will be allowed during their illness until the period of sick leave granted for testing the probability of their recovery has expired.

28. If they are married, the pay is to be handed to their wives.

29. If they are widowers, with children depending on them for support, the pay is to be handed to some approved person for the benefit of the family of the insane man.

30. If they are single, sick pay will not be allowed while in the hospital or asylum, except for providing such necessaries as shall be satisfactorily shown to be required by them, in a report of the particulars and estimate of the amount made to the Commissioner, who will decide thereon in writing.

31. If the police, being married or single, are received by their wives or friends, the sick pay is to be handed to them, if the Commissioner is satisfied of their ability to provide the men with proper care and treatment during the term of sick leave; but the Commissioner's sanction must be obtained in writing.

32. If the police recover, or continue insane, and are obliged to quit the Service, their several claims for gratuity or pension will be considered, and it will be decided how such allowances are to be disposed of with reference to the men being placed under proper care.

33. When destitute persons in charge of the police are sick of an infectious disease a surgeon is to be called in, and an entry is to be made in the Occurrence Book.

34. If, however, such person has a home, and desires to be removed there, he or she may be taken there by the police, it being first ascertained that such person will be received at such home.

35. When police have been twenty-eight days on the sick list, the Surgeon may recommend them for sick leave for any period not exceeding twenty-eight days, with sick pay or full pay, according to his discretion, and the nature of each case. The Commissioner may grant sick leave when so recommended.

36. Any one of the police granted leave of absence for twelve months, on account of sickness or bodily injury, may employ himself in any trade or occupation which is not likely to prevent his restoration to health, or ability to resume his duty.

37. In ordinary cases of sickness, a constable will be considered as on leave of absence, and paid in accordance with clause 4 of "Leave of Absence."

38. Where there is a police hospital, half-pay only is allowed to constables while in it; but should they be suffering from the effects of their own misconduct, the whole of their pay is stopped. Where no hospital or medical accommodation is afforded, they will have to provide themselves with medical attendance and medicines.

SOLDIERING HORSES, &c.
(See "Cattle.")

STABLES.

1. The following stable regulations are printed and hung up for reference in each stable.

2. Directions to be observed at each station where horses are stabled. The stables will be frequently visited

by the Inspector, or Sub-Inspector, and daily by the station sergeant, to see :—

(1.) That the horses are well dressed, backs in sound state, in proper condition for work, and properly shod.
(2.) That the stable is thoroughly clean, and nothing out of repair.
(3.) That the stable utensils are complete, and in good condition.
(4.) That all the appointments are perfectly clean, in their proper places, and in good repair.
(5.) The qualities of forage contracted for are as follows :—

>Good sweet dry and clean maize, weighing 56½lb. to the bushel.
>Good sweet oaten hay, or lucerne hay.
>Good dry clean straw, or bush hay.
>Bran, of good quality.

3. When a horse is sick, green forage may be substituted for the hay, in quantity not exceeding the value of the hay, upon the authority of the Inspector.

4. Fitting of horse appointments.

The Bit.—The bit should be placed in the horses mouth so that the mouth piece may be one inch above the lower tusk ; in mares, two inches above the corner tooth (the head-stall parallel to the projecting cheek bone, and behind it).

The Bridoon.—To fit easy without gagging the throat-band, so as to admit three fingers between it and the jawbone.

The Curb.—Should be flat and smooth under the jaw; when properly fitted should admit of the play of one finger between it and the jawbone.

The Saddle.—To be placed in the middle of the horse's back, the front of it about the breadth of a hand between the play of the shoulder.

The Girth.—To admit of a finger between it and the horse's belly.

The Surcingle.—Placed neatly on the girth, and not tighter than it. In saddling, the surcingle *only* is to be put through the loop of the breast-plate, and the collar chains are to be worn through the centre cloak strap, and fastened round the neck of the horse.

The Crupper.—When properly fitted should admit the breadth of the hand between it and the croup of the horse.

The Breast-plate.—Upper edge of the rosette the breadth of three fingers above the sharp breast-bone, should admit the breadth of a hand on the flat of the shoulder.

The Stirrup.—The lower edge of the bar should reach two inches above the upper edge of the heel.

The Cloak.—The length of the cloak when rolled is to be thirty-six inches, or length of the sword from end of hilt to point of blade; the cloak is to be carried on the front of the saddle.

5. List of stable utensils:

  Corn bin
  Sieve
  Quartern measure
  Pail
  Lantern
  Fork
  Picker
  Sponge
  Horse cloth and roller
  Wheelbarrow
  Trimming comb
  Dandy brush
  Wash leather
  Oil tin and brush
  Steelyard or weighing machine
  Chain burnisher
  Mane Comb
  Scissors

Shovel
Horse brush
Curry comb
Water brush
Headstall and chain
Bass brooms
Horse scraper
Crest brush
Dung basket.

6. Stable utensils, when properly worn out, are to be condemned by the Inspector, and replaced.

7. The Inspectors are held responsible for the due observance of these regulations.

8. After returning from drill, or long tours of duty, or at any time when the horse is heated or wet with perspiration, it is to be placed in the stable, and its feet are to be washed out, and fore and hind quarters thoroughly dressed down. The girth is to be loosened, and the saddle allowed to remain on the horse's back, for at least one hour, until the horse has become cool, in order that its back may be kept sound.

9. On returning to stables the horses are always to be dressed down and their feet washed out. The proper care of the horses is the first consideration.

(See also " Forage," " Horses," &c.)

STREETS.

1. When constables are posted to a division, the sub-Inspector is to see that they are instructed, and ascertain that they make themselves perfectly acquainted with every street, &c., in the immediate neighborhood, and generally with all parts of the division.

2. The police when off duty are not to walk together in crowded thoroughfares, so as to cause an obstruction.

3. The attention of the sergeants and constables is to be specially directed to keeping the crossings of streets as clear as possible for foot passengers. No carriage is to be allowed to stop, or remain on any crossing. Drivers of omnibuses or cabs refusing to move are to be reported, that they may be summoned.

STRETCHERS.

1. A stretcher is supplied at every police station where required, and one is to be used in conveying persons who have been injured, or are incapable of walking to a police station. After being used, the stretcher is to be carefully cleaned.

2. Violent prisoners can be strapped down, and conveyed on the stretcher safely to the station.

3. A rug is supplied, to be used in covering persons conveyed by the police on stretchers, and when dead bodies are conveyed, the faces are to be covered.

4. When not in use, the rugs are to be neatly folded, and kept in the sergeant's room, to prevent their being improperly used, and when dirty they are to be washed, and the cost is to be charged in the contingent account.

SUB-INSPECTOR.

1. The Sub-Inspector is in his division what the Inspector is in his district, and should be governed by the spirit and principle of the foregoing instructions to that officer, and will be held equally responsible for the execution of his own duties, as well as for the general conduct, discipline, and appearance of his men, the state of his barracks, horses, arms, accoutrements, and ammunition; and also for the clothing and all other articles delivered to the Force of his division.

2. He will reside constantly within the boundaries of his division, and must not absent himself from it, except on duty, without permission from the Inspector.

3. He receives his orders and instructions from, and makes his report to, the Inspector, from whom he will obtain such information as may be required upon matters relative to the Police.

4. His position is looked upon, to a certain extent, as a confidential one; and he will therefore do all in his power to preserve regularity and order, and to make himself acquainted with anything to the contrary which he thinks should be brought to the notice of the Inspector, or other officer under whom he may be placed.

5. He will exact a ready obedience to his orders from the sergeants and constables placed under his command, and will best consult his own interests by a steady adherence to orders, and by following such a line of conduct as shall place him beyond the fear of censure or reflection in the event of being obliged to report any of his men for misconduct or breach of discipline.

6. He must respect and uphold the authority of his superiors, and must at all times observe a proper distance from his constables, so as not to forfeit their respect for his person or authority by undue familiarity.

7. As he is the channel of all communications to his constables, it is necessary that his orders to them be clear and explicit.

8. He is to make a true and precise entry in the weekly return of his division of all duties, by whom performed, and the hour of going on and returning from duty.

9. He is to pay strict and prompt obedience to all the lawful orders and directions of the Magistrates and superior officers of the Force, thereby showing those under him an example of respect for official rank which they must follow in their conduct towards others as well as himself.

10. He will pay particular attention to the manner in which cases are conducted by the police in the various Police Courts, and will personally attend, as often as possible, during the sitting of the Bench, for the purpose of assisting in carrying out the views of the Magistrates, as by them expressed; he will also report to the Magistrates, on their assembling, the results of all warrants and processes issued, and of the steps taken to give effect to their judicial proceedings.

11. If there are detached stations in his division he must frequently visit and inspect them, by night as well as by day, and is to note in the Station Occurrence Book the exact state in which he finds them.

12. In like manner, as the Inspector is expected to have a general knowledge of all matters connected with his district, the Sub-Inspector is expected to be particularly

acquainted with the pursuits, avocations, &c., of the inhabitants of the various localities within the limits of his charge.

13. He will inspect, as frequently as possible, never less than once per week, the arms, ammunition, accoutrements, &c., of the men under his charge, for the good order of which he will be held strictly responsible to his Inspector.

14. He will minutely inspect all men, horses, arms, saddlery, ammunition, and appointments, previous to their going out on any duty, to see that they are in all respects in a fit state, and in like manner on their return, and should any article be damaged, will immediately report the matter to the Inspector.

15. He will frequently, and at uncertain hours, inspect the quarters of the sergeants and constables, and will occasionally visit them during meals, for the purpose of seeing, on such occasions, that the men are properly and cleanly dressed, and conduct themselves in a proper manner.

16. He must take care that all orders are carefully read, and explained to his men, and that all rules and regulations are strictly adhered to, and he is immediately to report any infractions of them to the Inspector.

17. He will take occasional opportunities of drilling his sergeants and men, provided it does not interfere with their duties as police constables.

18. He will establish a well arranged system of patrols, in order that lines of communication and particular points in his division may be from time to time visited and guarded, and suspected places and persons watched; taking care, however, not to let this duty in any way needlessly harass the men or horses, or impair their efficiency for any sudden or urgent call.

19. He must cause particular attention to be paid to the saddles and to the horses' backs and feet, himself carefully and constantly inspecting them to satisfy himself that they are properly attended to, and always kept in a state fit for instant use.

o

20. Where there is a police paddock, he must take care that the fencing is kept in good order, making the constables execute any necessary repairs at times when not on duty.

21. A knowledge of individuals and characters is absolutely essential to the constitution of an efficient police in cities and towns, from the greater amount of vice that exists in them, from the greater adroitness of delinquents, and from the facilities presented for disposing of plunder and evading discovery; it therefore becomes a most important duty of the Sub-Inspectors in cities or towns to make themselves and their men well acquainted with the persons and haunts of all suspicious characters therein, in order to their being able to bring them forward without delay in the event of their being charged with the commission of any crime or misdemeanor, or by close observation of their movements deter them from committing depredations or other offences against persons or property.

22. They will also make themselves well acquainted with the several roads and passes, and with the bush generally in their respective neighborhoods.

23. The Sub-Inspector must be prepared to furnish the Inspector on all occasions with such information as may be required as to places, persons, and characters, and in short he should be in possession of such general intelligence respecting his Division as shall enable him to supply a report or a return on any point without waiting to collect materials for the purpose.

24. He should have a perfect knowledge of the characters, tempers, qualifications, and comparative merits of his constables, not permitting any private feeling to influence his opinion of them.

25. He is to keep a roster, and to see that there is an equitable division of duties throughout his division, and must never attempt to gratify any personal feeling towards his men or the public.

26. He must strictly avoid placing himself under pecuniary or personal obligations of any kind whatever to his subordinates, or to residents within the locality under

his charge, and must at all times, and in all ways, maintain a character for unimpeachable integrity.

27. Nothing will tend more to raise an officer in the estimation of his men than to prove that he is guided by a strict sense of duty and perfect impartiality, and that the slightest degree of favoritism cannot force itself into his official conduct. He will be firmly upheld in the correct discharge of his office, but will not be suffered to be overbearing and tyrannical, and it is expected that he will show to the men and to the public an example of general circumspection and propriety of demeanor.

28. It will be his duty to make himself acquainted with the characters of the several public-houses, or other licensed places of entertainment and amusement in his division, in order that he may be in a position to afford the necessary information to the Magistrates on the days appointed for granting or renewing licenses.

29. He will also direct the attention of the sergeants and constables to such establishments, and will question them from time to time as to the manner in which they are conducted.

30. When prisoners are remanded from one Bench of Magistrates to another, the Sub-Inspector will forward to the officer in charge of Police at the place to which the prisoner is remanded the full particulars of the case, stating why the prisoner has been remanded, with any other information he may be able to afford.

31. With regard to the disposal of property taken from prisoners on arrest, he will strictly adhere to the regulations.

32. Money or other property which may come into the possession of the police in any other way, and respecting the disposal of which there may be some doubt, he will forward, together with a report of the circumstances, to head quarters, with a view to its being disposed of as may be directed by some competent authority.

33. He is to report to the Inspector (and in cases of urgency also to the Commissioner) promptly and correctly all circumstances connected with or affecting in any way the peace of his locality.

34. He is to forward all notices of resignation, and all vouchers, accounts, correspondence, and returns intended for the Commissioner's office to the Inspector in proper form and at the regulated periods.

35. In case of criminal offences, however, a copy of the information to be communicated should be sent direct to the Commissioner's office, as the delay which would otherwise occur might be prejudicial to the public service.

36. Sub-Inspectors in charge of cities or towns are to be guided, as far as practicable, in the execution of their several duties therein by the instructions already given for the City Police.

37. They will make a proper division of such towns into walks or beats, according to the necessities, local circumstances, and strength of the Force; and will exercise a close, constant, and active supervision over the men in charge of the several beats, holding them strictly responsible for their state.

38. They must keep their men on the alert, both by day and night, for the prevention of crime and the detection of offenders; and must, by every means in their power, aid in the maintenance of peace and good order.

39. On any alarm of fire, they will cause the constabulary under their command (including those who are off duty) to turn out, and render every aid in their power which circumstances may demand.

40. Where there are fire brigades established, the duty of the constables will be simply to preserve order, protect property, and procure a free scope for the exertions of the firemen and the parties more immediately interested.

41. A more detailed account of the duties of police constables, and of the officer who directs their movements, at fires, will be found under that heading.

42. Each Sub-Inspector is to keep the following books:—

> General Order Book, to contain copies of all General Orders that may from time to time be received from the Commissioner's office.
>
> District Order Book, to contain copies of all other orders.

Letter and Minute Book.
Warrant Book.
Registry of Horses.
Miscellaneous Property Book.
Store Book.
Occurrence Book, to contain reports of duty performed, crimes committed, accidents, apprehensions, &c., and in which any officer senior to the one in charge will enter his name, with a remark as to the state in which he finds the station.

43. He will also make the following returns:—
Biennial property return.
Quarterly horse return.
Monthly cases of crime undetected.
Monthly warrant return.
Weekly duty return.
Weekly forage return.

44. He will keep a correct registry of all furniture and other Government property under his charge; and, in the event of his being transferred to another station, he will obtain a receipt for the same from the officer relieving him.

45. He will also forward, for the information of the Inspector of the district, a weekly journal of his own proceedings, stating—the particular duties he has performed; the state in which the men under his charge are; their general conduct, noting any complaints which have been brought against any of them, either by a member of the Force or by the public; the steps which have been taken to investigate such charges; any alteration which may have been made in the quarters or stables; any serious crimes which have been reported, and the steps taken; the general state of the locality under his charge, with regard to criminal and other offences; any drill or inspection which has taken place, and the state in which the men, horses, arms, accoutrements, &c., appeared at such inspection; and any other matter which he considers it necessary to notice—in fact, a comprehensive report of the general state of the division or station under his charge.

46. His conduct towards the Inspector must be respectful and obedient, whilst to the men he is to be civil and obliging, without compromising the respect due to his rank by improper familiarity.
(See "Inspector," par. 25, &c.)

SUICIDES—ATTEMPTED.

1. Persons who attempt to commit suicide are to be apprehended and charged with the offence.

2. If at the time of apprehension any injury has been inflicted, medical aid is to be obtained, or the person is to be conveyed to a hospital, according to the circumstances of the case.

3. If persons cannot be removed and charged, on medical grounds, they are to be kept under observation of police as may be necessary to prevent their escape, and they are to be charged when sufficiently recovered.

SUMMONSES.

1. In no case is application to be made to a Magistrate for a summons against a person without the approval of the Inspector or other sufficient officer having first been obtained on the proper printed form.

2. In all applications for the Inspector's authority to summon persons for offences against the law, the exact dates of offence and the statute under which proceedings are proposed to be taken, are to be fully and accurately stated.

3. All applications approved are to be entered in the Summons Register.

4. The results of summonses are to be entered on the proper printed form, and sent in on Monday in each week to be entered in the Register.

5. Summonses will be delivered to constables in duplicate, or with the original summons will be delivered a copy. The constable should, in the first instance, endeavor to serve the duplicate or copy, personally; that is, deliver it into the possession of the individual to whom it is addressed. Should it be a copy, he must produce the

original if required to do so by the party summoned. In case the constable is unable, from any cause, to serve the summons personally, it will be considered a legal and effective service if it be left at the then or last usual place of abode of the party named in the summons, or if it be affixed to one of the doors or some other conspicuous part of the outside of such abode; although a summons may be served either by day or night, constables will be careful to execute this duty between sunrise and sunset as much as possible, and in serving on the premises, they are not to require admittance into the dwelling-house. After service of a summons, the constable will make before a Magistrate an affidavit of the service (which must be indorsed in the back of the original smmons), as follows:—

6. " Colony of Queensland }
   to wit.   }
    of   police constable, maketh oath and said that on the day of   instant, he this deponent did (personally) serve the within named with a true copy or this summons, by leaving the same (with) at his usual place of abode.
    Sworn before me at   this day of   1876."

7. And will then return the original, without delay, to the party from whom he originally received it.

TEMPER, COMMAND OF.

1. A perfect command of temper is absolutely indispensable to the proper discharge of police duty.

2. A constable must not allow himself to be moved or excited by any language or threats, however insolent; the cooler he keeps himself the more power he will have over his assailant.

3. Idle or silly remarks are unworthy of notice, and if the persons making them see that they have no effect upon the constable, they will soon leave off.

4. Forbearance and moderation will always be understood and appreciated by the public, the Magistrates, and the Commissioner.

(See "Civility.")

THEATRES.

1. A careful watch is to be kept on all saloons and theatres, and a report is to be made of any irregularities or immoral conduct.

2. The police on duty at theatres are, if required, to assist the manager and his servants in removing any person from a seat or box which has been regularly let to another.

3. Great forbearance is to be shown in not using more force than is necessary, and that no offensive language be used.

4. The person is only to be removed from the seat or box which he wrongfully persists in occupying; he may, however, be removed out of the house at the desire of the manager if he makes a disturbance, and continues to do so; but he is not to be taken to the Police Station or detained in custody, unless charged with some offence for which he may legally be apprehended.

THIEVES.

1. A Register Book of thieves and suspected persons known to the police is to be kept at stations in each district. It is to be open to inspection, in order that the information it contains may be as widely known as possible to police.

2. The Register kept at the head-quarters of each district is to contain the names, &c., of all thieves and suspected persons known throughout the district.

3. The Register at each station is to contain only the names, &c., of those known on the station.

4. All the columns of the Registers are to be properly and carefully filled in, and the names indexed. Under the head of "Apprehensions and previous Convictions," the offence, date of each conviction, and the Courts where the prisoner was convicted, are to be shown.

5. Any subsequent convictions or particulars are to be carefully entered as they occur or are ascertained. One name only is to be entered under each register number.

6. The Inspectors are to examine these Registers, and enter their initials, and date of having done so.

7. When any of the police observes a person known to him as a convicted thief, or the associate of such, or a suspected character, to be in the service of or employed by any one, a report of the facts is to be made to the Inspector; no communication is to be made to the employer or master concerning the character of the person, unless by directions of the Inspector.

8. The Inspector will judge whether the case calls for such a communication to the employer; and if, from the length of time since the conviction or periods of suspicion, there may be reason to suppose the individual is a reformed character, and of honest habits, the case is to be brought before the Commissioner for his decision as to any communication being made to the master.

TRANSFERS.

1. Transfers from one district to another are permitted, if satisfactory reasons are assigned, and the Inspectors concerned have no objection.

2. When application for a transfer is received by an Inspector, he is to attach the man's defaulter's sheet, and forward it, with any remark or objection of his own, to the Inspector of the district to which the man wishes to be transferred, who will make such remarks as he considers necessary, and forward the whole to the Commissioner.

3. If the transfer is approved, it will appear in police orders.

4. A form is issued from the Commissioner's office with every newly-appointed constable, containing the particulars for entry in the District Register, and is kept in the Inspector's office, and sent with the men, in case of transfer.

5. The defaulter's sheet of a man is always to be sent with the form of particulars, to the district to which the man is transferred; also, the particulars of entries in Sick Book, and certain articles of clothing.

6. Inspectors and sergeants who are transferred to other districts on promotion are to remain in such districts, and the Inspectors are not to recommend their re-transfers to districts in which they served prior to promotion.

7. A man who is reported for misconduct, and then applies for transfer will not be considered deserving the indulgence.

8. When any of the police, for misconduct, are transferred by the Commissioner from one district to another, they must bear the expenses incurred on account of their removal.

UNIFORM.

1. Patterns of the uniform and appointments to be worn both by the officers and the men of the Force are kept at the Depôt, Brisbane, where they can be seen at any time.

2. Members of the Force will be held strictly responsible that only uniform and appointments of the regulation pattern are worn by them.

UNINHABITED HOUSES.

1. Particular attention is to be paid to uninhabited houses, which thieves may enter, and passing along the parapet of other houses enter an open window, commit an attic larceny, and escape.

2. The constables on beats should carefully mark all empty or uninhabited houses.

3. The sergeants will instruct constables how to mark the houses.

VAN.

1. There is one van attached to the Brisbane Police, for the purpose of conveying prisoners from Police Stations to the Courts and gaols.

2. The van is to be carefully driven through the streets, at the rate of not more than six miles per hour.

3. The constable who acts as driver is responsible for the safety of the horses, but not for the safe custody of the prisoners. He is not to leave the box while the horses are attached.

4. The escorting sergeant or constable is held responsible for the safe custody of the prisoners. He is to take a receipt for the prisoners delivered by him.

5. The receipts are to be filed in the Inspector's office.

6. The van is to be completely washed inside and outside every night, and cleaned in the morning before being taken out; if the streets are very dirty, the van is to be partly cleaned between the journeys. The harness is also to be properly cleaned and attended to.

7. The police are always to be properly dressed in uniform when out with the van.

8. No communication is to be permitted between the prisoners conveyed, or by any of them with any other persons.

9. No delay on the journeys, or impropriety, is to be permitted with the van.

10. The journeys are so arranged that the prisoners arrive at and leave the Police Court in proper time, to meet the arrangements of the Police Magistrate.

11. On no pretence whatever is any person (except prisoners) not in the police to ride in or upon the van.

12. Prisoners are not to be taken out of the van at the Police Court until the gaoler or some of the police are ready to receive them and take the responsibility of their safe custody.

13. The escorting sergeant or constable in charge of a van is to carefully notice the condition of prisoners when handed over to him for conveyance, and if in an instance it appears to him that a prisoner is under the influence of drink, a report is to be made to the Inspector.

WARRANTS.

1. The constable is bound to follow the directions contained in a warrant, and to execute it with secrecy and despatch. The power given to him for the purpose of arresting has been already shown. If the warrant cannot

be executed immediately, it should be executed as soon as possible afterwards.

2. The constable must execute the warrant himself, or, when he calls in assistance, must be actually present. Upon all occasions he ought to state his authority, if it be not generally known, and should show his warrant when required to do so, but he should not part with the possession of the warrant, as it may be wanted afterwards for his own justification.

3. As it frequently happens that the warrant is in the hands of one constable, whilst another constable having undoubted information of such warrant may find the accused person (or a person whom he has good ground to suppose to be such person), the latter ought in such cases to make the arrest, and if it be provable that a warrant has been issued, although it was not in his hands, he will be justified in his act, and will be entitled to the protection of the law. In such case he should communicate to the prisoner his information respecting the warrant.

4. The constable may enter a house to search for stolen goods, having received a search warrant from a Magistrate for that purpose. He should, when it is possible to do so, execute it in the daytime. If he finds the goods mentioned he is to take them to a magistrate, and when the warrant so directs, he must take the person also in whose possession they are found. To avoid mistakes, the owner ought to attend at the search, to identify the goods, but this is not indispensably necessary in all cases.

5. When a constable executes a distress warrant he should be careful to seize a sufficient quantity of goods, for he is responsible for the full amount marked on the warrant once he makes distraint. If he cannot find sufficient goods whereupon to levy, the warrant will be endorsed " *Nulla bona*," giving the date search was made, and signed by the constable to whom it was given to be executed.

6. On the other hand, care must be taken by the constable that he does not make an excessive distraint.

7. The goods of a husband are not distrainable for the penalty imposed upon the wife.

8. If the defendant pay or tender the sum mentioned in the warrant, together with the legal expenses of distress, the constable should cease to execute the warrant, and the defendant, if in custody, should be forthwith discharged.

9. The constable who sells under authority of a distress warrant should sell for ready money, or he becomes responsible for the same, and certify a return of the warrant within a reasonable time.

10. The defendant should be served with the copy of Minute of Order before a warrant of commitment, or warrant of distress issues in all cases whereby statute authority is given to commit or to levy by distress any sum for not obeying the order of the Justices. But if the defendant has a certain time given him to pay, *a demand for payment must be made* after the time has expired before the warrant can issue. If by not paying forthwith defendant is liable to a distraint, then no demand is necessary.

11. A constable may arrest under warrant on a Sunday in cases of felony, treason, or breach of the peace; but there is a breach of the peace on all indictable offences, and on all misdemeanors; of course a warrant of arrest may be executed in the night.

12. He cannot break open doors to execute it. Before he commences to search he might ask "whether he has any property there not his own?" and he should take the occupant with him as he searches. Should he find any stolen property, his duty is *not to question* the party, *unless simply to exhort him to tell the truth*, but to listen and note what the party wishes to say about it.

WARRANT OF COMMITMENT.

In cases where a constable executes a warrant of commitment for want of distress, it often happens that the defendant is arrested subsequent to the date of the warrant; it is therefore always necessary to endorse on the back of the warrant the date of arrest, after which the constable will sign the endorsement.

WARRANTS, CUSTODY OF.

1. In arresting offenders without warrant, a constable is frequently exposed to the risk of being made a defendant in an action for false imprisonment. This applies more particularly to the arrest of offenders who are attempting to escape from the colony, and to this risk is sometimes added the difficulty that the constable does not know at what Police Station a warrant may be lying, and is at a loss to know where to send for it.

2. Moreover, uncertainty and delay have often arisen where warrants have been issued at places where there is no Police Station, or at a place that has a name common to several other parts of the colony, without it being stated which place is intended to be understood.

3. The latter difficulty will be removed if attention be paid to these instructions, viz. :—That the Bench by which each warrant is issued, and the name of the nearest Police Station shall be inserted in the report of the offence, and there will seldom be any difficulty in tracing how a warrant has been disposed of, or where it is to be found, if the following instructions be observed,

4. The Warant Book at each station should contain an entry of the full particulars of every warrant that passes through the hands of the police at that station, and if a warrant, after having been forwarded elsewhere, be returned to them again, a further entry of it should be made. If the warrant has been received from any other station or place, the entry should also state (in the column for remarks if necessary) whence, and from whom it has been received.

5. Every warrant issued for any person who is suspected of being about to leave the colony, and which the police of the station at which it has been issued have failed to execute, should be forwarded to the officer in charge of Detectives, at Brisbane, to be filed in his office, from which it can easily be obtained whenever required.

6. Every other warrant should as a rule be filed in the office of the Inspector, or other officer in charge of the district in which it has been issued, and should never be allowed to remain in any other district, or at any other

station in the same district, unless with the prospect of its early execution, or some other special reason.

7. But all warrants issued in the Brisbane Police District should, failing early execution, be deposited and filed in the office of the officer in charge of Detectives, whence they can be obtained at any time, whether by day or by night.

8. In criminal cases, whether in themselves of an important character or not, so much may depend upon the production or non-production of a warrant, that the greatest care must be shown by the police in the transmission, registration, and filing of all warrants that come into their hands.

WARRANT, REMAND.

1. On a remand warrant being received by a watchhouse, keeper, or other member of the Force having charge of a prisoner, it will be his duty to read over the warrant and ascertain that the dates are correct and that the warrant has been signed by the Magistrate who granted the remand.

2. When any member of the Force is instructed to escort a prisoner under a remand warrant to any Gaol or place of detention it will be the duty of such member of the Force to carefully examine the warrant, whether of remand or commitment, and see that it is in proper order, and duly signed by a Magistrate before taking over the prisoner from any watchhouse-keeper or other member of the Force having prior custody of the prisoner.

3. A constable escorting a prisoner under warrant of remand or commitment long distances through the bush or on board steamers should be very careful that no opportunity is given the prisoner to steal or do away with the warrant.

4. When travelling by steamer it is generally safest to ask the captain of the vessel to lock up in his cabin all such documents until the prisoners arrive at the port of destination. (See "Escorts," and "Property forms.")

WATCHHOUSES.

1. There will always be a sergeant or constable on duty at the watchhouse, who will on no account quit it during his time of duty.

2. Strict order, discipline, and cleanliness are to be observed at watchhouses.

3. Irregularities, noises, or disturbances by prisoners or others within the watchhouse are to be avoided as much as possible, so as to prevent annoyance to the neighborhood.

4. Persons coming in a proper manner to the door of a watchhouse are to be admitted by the constable without enquiry as to the nature of their business, if they state they wish to see the sergeant or constable on duty.

5. Persons not connected with the Police Service are not to be permitted to remain at a watchhouse longer than is absolutely necessary for the completion of the business they come upon.

6. The wife of a sergeant is not to be employed in cleaning, or working in any other manner, for payment, at a watchhouse; the wife of a constable may be so employed, on the approval of the Inspector.

7. The sergeant or constable on duty at the watchhouse will receive all charges against prisoners brought in by the different constables or other individuals, ascertain their nature, and when he is satisfied that it is a proper charge, cause the name of each prisoner to be entered in the Charge Book, with the particulars of his offence.

8. He will admit to bail, with the consent of the officer on duty, persons charged during the night-time with any petty misdemeanor, such as trifling assaults, committing trifling wilful mischief, and others of a similar description; also persons charged with drunkenness may, when they become sober, be admitted to bail, as in other cases of petty misdemeanor.

9. Persons against whom charges of assault, attended by cutting and wounding, have been received, or for felonies, or aggravated misdemeanors, when the charge has been received and entered in the Charge Book, are to be detained in custody at the watchhouse until they can be taken before a Magistrate for examination; and no

prisoner can be detained in the custody of the Police after he has been once brought before a Magistrate to answer the charge preferred against him, without a warrant for his detention.

10. Persons apprehended on warrant should only be admitted to bail with the sanction of the Magistrate by whom the warrant was signed, or by an order from the Inspector or officer in charge of the district.

11. If any property be brought to the sergeant or constable on duty at the watchhouse, either taken from persons apprehended, or otherwise, he will immediately make an entry of the same in the Watchhouse Book; the several articles of property should be marked at the time they are received, so that they may be afterwards certainly known to be the same; they should be taken by the watchhouse-keeper himself from the party bringing them, and not allowed to be out of his sight until marked in the manner directed; they should then be locked up in the place for the purpose, or in certain cases, when required as evidence, given back to the charge of the constable who took possession of them.

12. When any person brought to the watchhouse in a state of intoxication is searched, which should be at the watchhouse (except in particular cases, when immediate search becomes necessary), the articles should always be taken by one person, and called out distinctly, and entered in the book by another, and when the person from whom they are taken is discharged he should sign a book or receipt for the whole. No part of such property is to be returned to the prisoner until the decision of the Magistrate on the case is known.

13. In the case of persons of known respectability being arrested for some trifling misdemeanor, they need not be searched, but should be requested to produce such property as they may have on their persons, and should, if possible, be placed in a cell by themselves.

14. The only provisions allowed by Government to prisoners in watchhouses are twenty-four ounces of bread, sixteen ounces of meat, and one quarter of an ounce of salt, and two ounces of soup per day for each

P

prisoner under sentence of confinement with hard labor, and twenty-four ounces of bread each for all other prisoners. The officers in charge of police at the stations where there are lockups will call for tenders for these supplies, according to the above scale, and will transmit such tenders as they may receive to the Commissioner's office in the usual manner. As soon as the acceptance of any tender has been notified, the rations may be ordered by the officer in charge of the station, and the account should be rendered to the Inspector of the district.

15. No person in the employment of Government shall have any interest in such contracts.

16. When it is necessary for prisoners in confinement to have other refreshment than what is provided by Government, no beer or spirits can be admitted into the cells, but only tea or coffee, with such eatables as are usually given in those cases, but this cannot be permitted without the sanction of an officer of police.

17. Prisoners in the watchhouse must be frequently visited, and immediate attention is to be given to any case requiring assistance or medical aid. (See "Cells" and "Charges.")

WATER POLICE.

1. The Water Police consists of an Officer, sergeants, and constables.

2. The members of the Force are stationed at Moreton Bay on board a Hulk, of which they have charge, and are responsible that the vessel is at all times kept clean and in good order.

3. They are amenable to the same rules for the maintenance of discipline, and have by the law the same powers as other constables.

4. The duties particularly devolving upon them are, to afford police protection and maintain order among the shipping in Moreton Bay; to enforce the Port Regulations; to supervise the transhipment of powder; to board immigrant and other vessels on their arrival at the anchorage; to serve summonses; excute warrants, and other legal

processes on parties in the Bay and on the neighboring coast; to convey prisoners to and from vessels in the Bay; to attend the Police Court when required, &c., &c.

5. They are supplied with the same arms as the foot police.

6. All signals from vessels in the Bay for police protection, &c., will be registered in the Occurrence Book, stating the vessel's name, night or daytime when made, and when signal is hauled down answered.

7. The same record will be made of all signals from the Gaol at St. Helena.

8. When it is signalled from St. Helena that a prisoner has escaped, the fact should be at once telegraphed to the Brisbane Police.

9. When exact information has been received from the island, the circumstances should be fully detailed, *i.e.*, if the escaped prisoner is supposed to be making for the mainland. In all cases, the fullest description of the prisoner should be forwarded by wire to Brisbane, Cleveland, and Sandgate.

10. In the event of a fire occurring in the harbor, all the available Force will proceed immediately to the spot, in readiness to render such assistance as may be necessary, either in extinguishing the fire or saving and protecting property.

WEIGHTS AND MEASURES, ILLEGAL.

The summonses of Magistrates, in cases of persons charged with using illegal weights or measures, may be served by the police.

APPENDIX A.

INDICTABLE OFFENCES—A TABLE OF.

Offence.	Felony or Misdemeanor.	Statute.
ABDUCTION—		
1. Forcible abduction from motives of lucre	Felony	29 Vic., No. 11, s. 54.
2. Abduction of a girl under 16 years of age	Misdemeanor	*Ibid.*, s. 56.
ABORTION—		
1. By administering drugs	Felony	29 Vic., No. 11, s. 59.
2. By using instruments	ditto	*Ibid.*, same s.
ACCESSORY AND PRINCIPAL—		
Principal in second degree	Same as principal in first degree.	
ACCESSORY BEFORE THE FACT IN FELONY—		
In treason and misdemeanors all are principals	Same as principal.	
ACCESSORY AFTER THE FACT IN FELONY—		
In treason all are principals; in misdemeanors accessory after the fact not punishable	Felony.	

ACCUSING OF CRIME—		
1. Letter threatening to accuse, or accusing with intent to extort	Felony	10 and 11 Vic., No. 66, s. 1.
2. Accusing, or threatening to accuse, with intent to extort	ditto	29 Vic., No. 6, s. 52.
3. Inducing a person to alter or destroy any document by threatening to accuse of crime	ditto	*Ibid.*, s. 53.
AFFRAY	Misdemeanor	C. L., 2 Ed. III., c. 3.
AGENTS, BANKERS, ETC.—		
1. Embezzlement of money by	Misdemeanor	29 Vic., No. 6, s. 80.
2. Selling, &c., chattels or securities entrusted to him	ditto	*Ibid.*, same s.
3. Factor pledging, &c., property of his principal	ditto	*Ibid.*, ss. 81, 83
4. Frauds by trustees	ditto	20 and 21 Vic., No. 54, s. 1.
5. Frauds by bankers, brokers, &c. ...	ditto	*Ibid.*, s. 2.
6. Frauds under powers-of-attorney...	ditto	*Ibid.*, s. 3.
7. Frauds by bailees	Felony	30 Vic., No. 22, s. 2.
8. Frauds by director, &c., of public company...	Misdemeanor	20 and 21 Vic., No. 54, s. 5.
9. Frauds in keeping fraudulent accounts	ditto	*Ibid.*, s. 6.
10. Frauds in wilfully destroying books, &c. ...	ditto	*Ibid.*, s. 7.
11. Frauds in publishing fraudulent statements	ditto	*Ibid.*, s. 8.
12. Receivers of property fraudulently disposed of	ditto	*Ibid.*, s. 9.

INDICTABLE OFFENCES—A TABLE OF—*continued.*

Offence.	Felony or Misdemeanor.	Statute.
ASSAULT—		
1. Common assault and battery	Misdemeanor	C. L, 29 Vic., No. 11, s. 40.
2. Upon justices, &c., in case of wreck	ditto	29 Vic., No. 11, s. 35.
3. Upon peace or revenue officers	ditto	*Ibid.*, s. 36.
4. To prevent apprehension	ditto	*Ibid.*, s. 36.
5. In pursuance of conspiracy to raise wages	ditto	*Ibid.*, s. 39.
6. With intent to commit felony	ditto	*Ibid.*, s. 36.
7. Indecent assaults	ditto	*Ibid.*, ss. 52, 53, 63.
8. Assaulting police in execution of their duty	ditto	2 Vic., No. 2., s. 8.
ATTEMPT TO MURDER—		
1. By poison	Felony	29 Vic., No. 11, s. 8.
2. By stabbing, cutting, or wounding, shooting, drowning, suffocating, &c.	ditto	*Ibid.*, s. 11.
ATTEMPT TO DO BODILY INJURY—		
1. By shooting, attempting to shoot, cutting, or wounding	Felony	*Ibid.*, s. 15.
2. Doing bodily injury with or without weapon, or cutting or wounding	Misdemeanor	*Ibid.*, s. 17.
3. By explosive substances, or corrosive fluids	Felony	*Ibid.*, s. 25.

ATTEMPTS TO COMMIT OTHER OFFENCES—

1. Attempt to commit rape	...	Misdemeanor	*Ibid.*, s. 51.
2. Attempt to carnally know a girl under 10 years		ditto	*Ibid.*, s. 50.
3. The same, between 10 and 12 years	...	ditto	*Ibid.*, s. 52.
4. Attempt to commit sodomy	...	ditto	*Ibid.*, s. 63.
5. Throwing wood, &c. on a railway, or meddling with same with intent to endanger the safety of any person		Felony	*Ibid.*, s. 29.
BARRATRY ...	...	Misdemeanor	C. L.
BIGAMY ...	...	Felony	29 Vic., No. 11, s. 58.

BLASPHEMY OR PROFANENESS—

1. Blasphemy	...	Misdemeanor	C. L.
2. Scoffing at Scripture	...	ditto	C. L.
3. Blasphemous libel	...	ditto	C. L.

BRIBERY—

1. At common law	...	Misdemeanor	C. L.
2. At elections	...	ditto	31 Vic., No. 37, s. 54.
3. Being bribed	...	ditto	*Ibid.*, s. 53.

BRIDGES—
1. Destroying or damaging them by fire.
2. The same by any other means.

Indictable Offences—A Table of—continued.

Offence.	Felony or Misdemeanor.	Statute.
Burglary and Housebreaking—		
1. Burglary	Felony	C. L.
2. Burglary and attempt to murder ...	ditto	29 Vic., No. 13, s. 47.
3. Burglary by breaking out of a house	ditto	29 Vic., No. 6, s. 65.
4. Breaking and entering a church or chapel ...	ditto	*Ibid.*, s. 55.
5. House-breaking and stealing ...	ditto	C. L.
6. Breaking and entering a building within the curtilage	ditto	29 Vic., No. 6, s. 58.
7. Being armed with intent to break and enter	Misdemeanor	*Ibid.*, s. 63.
Burning—		
1. Church or chapel	Felony	29 Vic., No. 5, s. 1.
2. Dwelling-house, any person being therein ...	ditto	*Ibid.*, s. 2.
3. House, outhouse, farm buildings, manufactories, &c.	ditto	*Ibid.*, s. 3.
4. Hay, straw, implements, &c., in farm buildings	ditto	*Ibid.*, s. 7.
5. Stack of corn, hay, wood, and crops of corn, trees, &c.	ditto	*Ibid.*, ss. 17, 18, 19.
6. Coal mines	ditto	*Ibid.*, s. 27.
7. Ships, whereby life endangered ...	ditto	*Ibid.*, s. 44.
8. Ships, to prejudice owner or underwriter ...	ditto	*Ibid.*, s. 45.

BUTCHER—		
1. Slaughtering, &c., any animal unfit for human food	Misdemeanor	15 Vic, No. 13, s. 5.
2. Selling, or exposing for sale, the same	ditto	*Ibid*, s. 7.
BUYING OF TITLES	Misdemeanor	C. L.
CARNALLY KNOWING FEMALE CHILDREN—		
1. Under 10	Felony	29 Vic, No. 11, s. 48.
2. Above 10, and under 12	Misdemeanor	*Ibid*, s. 49.
CARRIAGE—		
1. Person in charge causing bodily harm by furious or wanton driving	Misdemeanor	*Ibid*, s. 33.
CARRIERS—		
1. Fraudulently taking, &c., property entrusted to him	Felony	29 Vic., No. 6, s. 3.
CATTLE—		
1. Stealing, or killing with intent to steal	Felony	*Ibid*, ss. 10, 11.
2. Maliciously killing or wounding	ditto	29 Vic, No. 5, s. 42.
CHALLENGE TO FIGHT—		
1. Sending or giving	Misdemeanor	C. L.
2. Provoking a person to send or give	ditto	C. L.

Indictable Offences—A Table of—continued.

Offence.	Felony or Misdemeanor.	Statute.
CHEATING—		
Selling, unwholesome provisions, using false weights, passing spurious for genuine articles, cheating at cards, dice, &c.	Misdemeanor	C. L.
CHILD STEALING	Felony	29 Vic., No. 11, s. 57.
CLERGYMEN ARRESTING	Misdemeanor	*Ibid.*, s. 34.
COIN—		
1. Counterfeiting gold or silver coin	Felony	29 Vic., No. 4, s. 2.
2. Gilding or silvering coin	ditto	*Ibid.*, s. 3.
3. Impairing the coin	ditto	*Ibid.*, s. 4.
4. Buying, selling, or importing counterfeit coin	ditto	*Ibid.*, ss. 6, 7.
5. Uttering counterfeit coin	Misdemeanor	*Ibid.*, s. 9.
6. Uttering, and having other base coin in possession	ditto	*Ibid.*, s. 10.
7. Uttering twice in 10 days	ditto	*Ibid.*, s. 10.
8. Uttering after a former conviction	Felony	*Ibid.*, ss. 2, 12.
9. Having base coin with intent to utter it	Misdemeanor	*Ibid.*, s. 11.
10. Same, second offence	Felony	*Ibid.*, ss. 2, 12.

235

11. Counterfeiting copper coin ...	ditto ...	*Ibid.*, s. 14.
12. Uttering base copper coin ...	Misdemeanor ...	*Ibid.*, s. 15.
13. Making or having, &c., coining tools, &c.	Felony ...	*Ibid.*, s. 24.
14. Conveying tools, &c., out of the mint	ditto ...	*Ibid.*, s. 25.
15. Accessories ...	...	*Ibid.*, s. 34.
COMPOUNDING FELONY ...	Misdemeanor ...	C. L.
COMPOUNDING PENAL ACTIONS ...	Misdemeanor ...	31 Vic., No. 20, ss. 21, 35.
1. Taking reward for helping to stolen goods ...	Felony ...	29 Vic., No. 6, s. 106.
CONCEALING BIRTH ...	Misdemeanor ...	29 Vic., No. 11, s. 61.
CONSPIRACY ...	Misdemeanor ...	C. L.
1. Conspiring to cheat, defraud, falsely to accuse of crime, to obstruct, &c., course of public justice	ditto	29 Vic., No. 13, s. 38.
CRUELTY TO CHILDREN, APPRENTICES, ETC.—		
1. Children of tender years under one's control	Misdemeanor ...	C. L.
2. Apprentices ...	ditto ...	29 Vic., No. 11, s. 23.
3. Animals ...	ditto ...	14 Vic., No. 40, s. 1.
DEAD BODY—		
Disinterring or selling ...	Misdemeanor ...	C. L.

INDICTABLE OFFENCES—A TABLE OF—*continued.*

Offence.	Felony or Misdemeanor.	Statute.
DESERTING CHILDREN— 1. Deserting child under 16 years old	Misdemeanor	22 Vic., No. 6, s. 9.
DISORDERLY HOUSE— Keeping such	Misdemeanor	C. L.
DISSENTERS— 1. Disturbing their congregation	Misdemeanor	52 Geo. III., No. 155, s. 12.
DOGS— 1. Stealing 2. Receiving money to restore stolen dogs	Misdemeanor ditto	29 Vic., No. 6, s. 18. *Ibid.*, s. 20.
EMBEZZLEMENT— 1. By clerks and servants	Felony	*Ibid.*, ss. 72 to 78.
EMBRACERY	Misdemeanor	C. L., and Jury Act, ss. 40 to 44.

ESCAPE—		
1. Party escaping...	Misdemeanor	C. L.
2. Aiding prisoners to escape	ditto, (or felony if party in custody for treason or felony)	C. L., and 16 Geo. II., c. 31, ss. 1, 2, 3.
3. Officers allowing escape—negligent	Misdemeanor	C. L.
voluntary	ditto	C. L.
4. Aiding the escape of prisoners of war	Felony	52 Geo. III., c. 156, s. 1.
EXTORTION	Misdemeanor	C. L.
FALSE IMPRISONMENT	Misdemeanor	C. L.
FALSE PRETENCES	Misdemeanor	C. L., and 29 Vic., No. 6, ss. 93 to 95.
FORCIBLE ENTRY AND DETAINER	Misdemeanor	5 Richd. II., c. 7; 21 Jas. I., c. 15.
FORGERY—		
1. Of seals or sign manual...	Treason	29 Vic., No. 3, s. 1.
2. Of signature of Governor, Colonial Secretary, &c.	Felony	*Ibid.*, s. 2.
3. Of transfer of stock, power-of-attorney, &c.	ditto	*Ibid.*, ss. 3 to 7.
4. Of East India bonds, &c.	ditto	*Ibid.*, s. 8.
5. Of exchequer bills, bonds, &c.	ditto	*Ibid.*, ss. 9 to 12.
6. Of stamps, false dies, &c.	ditto	*Ibid.*, ss. 13, 14.
7. Of bank notes, bank bills, &c.	ditto	*Ibid.*, ss. 15, 16.

Indictable Offences—A Table of—continued.

Offence.	Felony or Misdemeanor.	Statute.
Forgery—continued.		
8. Of plates, &c., for bank notes, &c.	Felony	29 Vic., No. 3, ss. 17 to 22.
9. Of deeds, wills, bills of exchange, money orders, &c.	ditto	Ibid., ss. 22 to 29.
10. Of records, process, instruments of evidence, &c.	ditto	Ibid., ss. 30 to 32.
11. Of court rolls, or copy thereof, relating to copy-hold	ditto	Ibid., s. 33.
12. Of registers of deeds	ditto	Ibid., s. 34.
13. Of orders, &c., of justice, recognizances, &c.	ditto	Ibid., s. 35.
14. Of marriage licenses	ditto	Ibid., s. 38.
15. Of registers of births, marriages, and deaths	ditto	Ibid., ss. 39, 40.
16. Demanding property on forged instruments	ditto	Ibid., s. 41.
17. Forging any instrument which in law is a will	ditto	Ibid., s. 42.
18. Forging, in Queensland, documents purporting to be made out of, or payable out of England	ditto	Ibid., s. 43.
Gaming—		
1. Cheating at cards, dice, &c.	Misdemeanor	14 Vic., No. 9, s. 7.
2. Gaming house keeping	ditto	Ibid., s. 1.

GOLDFIELDS			20 Vic., No. 29.
HOMICIDE—			
1. Murder	...	Felony	C. L.
2. Manslaughter	...	ditto	C. L.
HORSE-SLAUGHTERING—			
1. Putting hide into lime	...	Misdemeanor	26 Geo. III, c. 71, s. 9.
INDECENCY—			
1. Public indecency	...	ditto	C. L.
2. Printing or publishing indecent books, prints, &c.	...	ditto	C. L.
JUSTICES' ORDER, DISOBEYING	...	ditto	C. L.
LARCENY—			
A. Of Goods and chattels	...	Felony	29 Vic., No. 6.
B. Of valuable securities	...	ditto	*Ibid.*
1. Deeds relating to real property, wills, records, &c.	...	ditto	*Ibid.*, ss. 27 to 30.
C. Of animals—			
1. Horses, cows, sheep, &c.	...	ditto	*Ibid.*, s. 10.
2. Killing cattle with intent to steal them	...	ditto	*Ibid.*, s. 11.
3. Dogs	...	Misdemeanor	*Ibid.*, s. 18.
4. Killing pigeons	...	Felony	C. L.
5. Fish	...	Misdemeanor	29 Vic., No. 6, ss. 24, 25.
6. Oysters, or dredging for	...	ditto	*Ibid.*, s. 26.

Indictable Offences—A Table of—continued.

Offence.	Felony or Misdemeanor.	Statute.
Larceny—continued.		
D. Things growing on or attached to land	Felony	29 Vic., No. 6, ss. 31 to 38.
E. From mines	ditto	*Ibid.*, ss. 39, 40.
F. From the person	ditto	*Ibid.*, s. 41 to 54.
1. Assault with intent to rob	ditto	*Ibid.*, s. 43.
2. The same by persons armed	ditto	*Ibid.*, s. 44.
3. Using chloroform for the purpose of robbing	ditto	29 Vic., No. 11, s. 19.
G. In a dwelling-house	ditto	29 Vic., No. 6, ss. 65, 66.
H. In manufactories	ditto	*Ibid.*, s. 67.
I. From ships, boats, docks, &c.	ditto	*Ibid.*, s. 68 to 71.
K. By clerks, servants, &c.	ditto	*Ibid.*, s. 72 to 78.
L. By tenants, lodgers, &c.,	ditto	*Ibid.*, s. 79.
Letter Threatening—		
1. To murder, or to burn or destroy property	Felony	29 Vic., No. 5, s. 52.
2. To accuse of crime		10 and 11 Vic., No. 66, s. 1.
Libel—		
1. Seditious or blasphemous	Misdemeanor	11 Vic., No. 13, s. 5.
2. Defamatory	ditto	*Ibid.*, ss. 8, 9.

241

LIENS ON CROPS, WOOL, ETC.—		
1. Lienor defrauding by sale	Misdemeanor	31 Vic., No. 36, s. 42.
2. The same by any other means	ditto	*Ibid.*, s. 35.
LUNATICS—		
1. Illtreatment, &c., of	Misdemeanor	33 Vic., No. 12.
MAINTENANCE—		
1. Deserting child under 16 years old, &c.	Misdemeanor	22 Vic., No. 6, s. 9.
2. Abandoning child under 2 years	ditto	29 Vic., No. 11, s. 24.
MALICIOUS INJURIES—		
A. To houses—		
1. Setting fire to church, &c.	Felony	29 Vic., No. 5, s. 1.
2. Setting fire to a dwelling-house, any person therein	ditto	*Ibid.*, s. 2.
3. Setting fire to a house, outhouse, manufactory, &c., hovel, shed, fold, &c.	ditto	*Ibid.*, s. 3.
4. Attempting to set fire to buildings	ditto	*Ibid.*, s. 8.
5. Riotously demolishing church, house, &c.	ditto	*Ibid.*, ss. 11, 12.
6. Destroying or damaging house with gunpowder, &c., any person therein	ditto	*Ibid.*, ss. 9, 10.
7. The same, with intent to murder	ditto	29 Vic., No. 11, s. 9.
8. Attempting to destroy buildings, &c., with gunpowder	ditto	*Ibid.*, s. 27.
9. Making or having gunpowder, &c., with intent to commit said offences	Misdemeanor	*Ibid.*, ss. 65, 66.

Indictable Offences—A Table of—continued.

Offence.	Felony or Misdemeanor.	Statute.
MALICIOUS INJURIES—continued.		
B. Manufactures, machinery, &c.—		
1. Destroying goods in process of manufacture, machinery, &c.	Felony	29 Vic., No. 5, ss. 14, 15, 16.
c. To individuals—		
1. Burning, disfiguring, or disabling a person with gunpowder, &c.	ditto	29 Vic., No. 11, s. 25.
2. Exploding, or sending explosive substances, or throwing corrosive fluids with intent, &c.	ditto	Ibid., s. 26.
D. To corn, trees, fences, &c.—		
1. Setting fire to crops of corn, stacks, &c.	ditto	29 Vic., No. 5, ss. 17, 18, 19.
2. Destroying hopbinds	ditto	Ibid., s. 20.
3. Destroying or damaging trees, &c., in pleasure ground to the value of £5	ditto	Ibid., s. 21.
E. To mines—		
1. Setting fire to a coal mine	ditto	Ibid., s. 27.
2. Attempting the like	ditto	Ibid., s. 28.
3. Conveying water into a mine, &c.; obstructing a shaft, &c.	ditto	Ibid., s. 29.

4. Damaging steam-engines, staithes, wagon-ways, &c.	ditto	*Ibid.*, s. 30.
F. To rivers, canals, ponds, bridges, toll-gates, &c.:—		
1. Injuries to sea-banks, river-banks, and works on rivers, canals, &c.	ditto	*Ibid.*, ss. 31, 32.
2. Injuries to ponds, reservoirs, &c.	Misdemeanor	*Ibid.*, s. 33.
3. Destroying or damaging bridges	Felony	*Ibid.*, s. 34.
4. Toll-gates, weighing machines, &c.	Misdemeanor	*Ibid.*, s. 35.
G. To railways, telegraphs, &c.:—		
1. Placing wood, &c., on rails with intent, &c.	Felony	29 Vic., No. 11, s. 29.
2. Throwing stone, &c., upon an engine, &c., with intent, &c.	ditto	*Ibid.*, s. 30.
H. To works of art	Misdemeanor	29 Vic., No. 5, s. 41.
I. To animals:—		
1. Killing or wounding horses, cattle, sheep, &c.	Felony	*Ibid.*, ss. 42, 43.
K. To ships:—		
1. Setting fire to ships whereby life is endangered, or casting away, or anywise destroying	ditto	*Ibid.*, s. 44.
2. The like, with intent to prejudice owner, &c.	ditto	*Ibid.*, s. 45.
3. Attempting either of the two last-named offences	ditto	*Ibid.*, s. 47.
4. Damaging buoys, signals, &c.	ditto	*Ibid.*, ss. 48 to 51.

INDICTABLE OFFENCES—A TABLE OF—*continued.*

Offence.	Felony or Misdemeanor.	Statute.
MARRIAGE—		
1. Minister celebrating without being registered	Misdemeanor	28 Vic., No. 15, s. 29.
2. Marrying a minor without consent of parent or guardian	ditto	*Ibid.*, ss. 25, 27.
3. Forging such consent	Felony	*Ibid.*, s. 28.
MAYHEM	Misdemeanor	C. L.
MISPRISION OF TREASON, ETC.—		
1. Of treason	Misdemeanor	C. L.
2. Of felony	ditto	C. L.
3. Helping to stolen property without trial of offender	Felony	29 Vic., No. 6, s. 106.
MUTINY, INCITING TO	Felony	1 Vic., c. 91, ss. 1, 2.
MURDER. (See "HOMICIDE")	Felony	C. L.
NUISANCE	Misdemeanor	C. L.

OATHS, UNLAWFUL—		
1. Administering or taking oath to commit treason, &c.	Felony	52 Geo. III., c. 104, s. 1.
2. Oath to engage in any mutinous or seditious purpose	ditto	37 Geo. III., c. 123, s. 1.
OBSCENITY—		
1. Printing or publishing obscene writings or prints	Misdemeanor	C. L.
2. Publicly selling, or exposing for sale, or to public view, any obscene book, print, picture, &c.	ditto	C. L.
OFFICE, REFUSING TO EXECUTE ...	Misdemeanor	C. L.
ORDER OF JUSTICE, DISOBEYING ...	Misdemeanor	C. L.
PARLIAMENT—		
Offences at elections ...	...	See 31 Vic., Nos. 21 and 37.
PERJURY AND SUBORNATION—		
1. Perjury or subornation of perjury	Misdemeanor	29 Vic., No. 13, s. 27.
2. Perjury by statute law ...	ditto	*Ibid.*, s. 23; 5 Eliz., c. 9, s. 3.
PERSONATING—		
1. Soldiers or seamen ...	Felony	5 Geo. IV., c. 107, s. 5.
2. Officers in army or navy ...	ditto	7 Geo. IV., c. 16, s. 38.
3. Constables	ditto	27 Vic., No. 11, s. 18.

Indictable Offences—A Table of—continued.

Offence.	Felony or Misdemeanor.	Statute.
Piracy—		
1. At common law	Felony	7 and 8 Geo. IV., c. 28.
2. And cutting and wounding	ditto	1 Vic., c. 88, s. 2.
3. By statute	ditto	*Ibid.*, s. 5 ; 11 and 12 Wm. III. c. 7, ss. 7, 8, 9 ; 8 Geo. I., c. 24, s. 1 ; 18 Geo. II., c. 30.
Post Office—		
1. Stealing or embezzling letters	Felony	1 Vic., c. 36, s. 26.
2. Stealing a letter-bag or a letter from it, or stopping a mail	ditto	*Ibid.*, s. 28.
3. Stealing from a letter-bag in a post office packet	ditto	*Ibid.*, s. 29.
4. Stealing from a letter	ditto	*Ibid.*, s. 27.
5. Receiving letter so stolen	ditto	*Ibid.*, s. 30.
6. Opening or delaying letter	Misdemeanor	*Ibid.*, s. 25.
7. Retaining letters lost or mis-delivered	ditto	*Ibid.*, s. 31.
8. Stealing or detaining newspapers	ditto	*Ibid.*, s. 32.
9. Forging the hand of the Receiver-General	Felony	*Ibid.*, s. 33.

PRISON-BREAKING—		
1. Breach of prison	Felony, if party in custody for felony; misdemeanor, if party in custody for misdemeanor	C. L, and 1 Ed. II., c. 2, s. 1.
2. By convicts in penitentiary	Felony	1 Vic., c. 91, s. 1.
3. Assisting prisoners to escape	ditto	2 and 3 Vic., No. 56, s. 8.
QUEEN'S STORES—		
1. Unlawfully having them	Misdemeanor	9 and 10 Wm. III., c. 41, s. 2; 9 Geo. I., c. 8, s. 4; 17 Geo. II., c. 40, s. 10.
2. Same, second offence	ditto	39 and 40 Geo. III., c. 89, s. 7.
3. Selling or concealing	Felony	55 Geo. III., c. 127, s. 39; 40 Geo. III., c. 89, s. 1.
4. Defacing the marks	ditto	*Ibid.*, s. 7.
5. Stealing or embezzling them	ditto	22 C. II., c. 5; 4 Geo. IV., c. 54.
RAILWAY—		
Offences under Railway Act	...	See 27 Vic., No. 8.
RAPE—		
1. Rape	Felony	29 Vic., No. 11, s. 46.
2. Procuring defilement of girls under 21	Misdemeanor	*Ibid.*, s. 47.
3. Attempt to commit rape	ditto	*Ibid.*, s. 51.

Indictable Offences—A Table of—continued.

Offence.	Felony or Misdemeanor.	Statute.
Receiving Stolen Goods—		
1. Where principal is guilty of Felony	Felony	29 Vic., No. 6, s. 96.
2. The same, guilty misdemeanor	Misdemeanor	*Ibid.*, s. 100.
Registration—		
1. Wilfully making any false statement	ditto	19 Vic., No. 34, s. 34.
2. Destroying books, counterfeiting copies, giving false certificates, forging seal, &c., of Registrar-General, &c.	Felony	*Ibid.*, s. 35.
Rescue—		
1. Party rescued convicted of felony	Felony	C. L.
2. Party rescued convicted of misdemeanor	Misdemeanor	C. L.
3. If not convicted and afterwards acquitted	ditto	C. L.
4. Rescue of murderer or his body after execution	Felony	25 Geo. II., c. 37, s. 9.
Rescue of a Distress—		
Breaking the pound to rescue a distress for rent impounded	Misdemeanor	C. L.

Riot—		
1. Riot	Felony	C. L.
2. Opposing proclamation under Riot Act, or 12 or more persons remaining one hour after proclamation	ditto	1 Geo. I., c. 2, s. 5.
Robbery. (See "Larceny")	Felony	C. L.
Seamen—		
Forcing a seaman on shore, or leaving him abroad	Misdemeanor	7 and 8 Vic., No. 112, s. 47.
Sedition—		
1. Seditious words	Misdemeanor	C. L.
2. Seditious meetings	ditto	C. L.
Ship—		
1. Purchasing anchors, boats, goods, &c., found at sea, &c.	Felony	9 and 10 Vic., c. 99, s. 29.
2. Taking to a foreign port and there selling	ditto	*Ibid.*, s. 31.
3. Cutting away or defacing buoys, &c.	ditto	*Ibid.*, s. 38.
Smuggling—		
1. Making signals	Misdemeanor	16 and 17 Vic., c. 107, s. 244.
2. Armed assemblies for	Felony	*Ibid.*, s. 248.
3. Shooting at boats, &c., or wounding officers	ditto	*Ibid.*, s. 249.
4. One of several smugglers being armed or disguised	ditto	*Ibid.*, s. 250.
5. Assaulting or resisting officers with violence	Misdemeanor	*Ibid.*, s. 251.

Indictable Offences—A Table of—continued.

Offence.	Felony or Misdemeanor.	Statute.
Sodomy	Felony	39 Vic., No. 11, s. 62.
Soliciting to the Commission of an Offence	Misdemeanor	C. L.
Stage Coaches— 1. Injury by furious driving	Misdemeanor	29 Vic., No. 11, s. 83.
Stamps— 1. Having forged dies, &c., stamps, &c.	Felony	29 Vic., No. 3, ss. 13, 14.
Subsequent Felony	Felony	29 Vic., No. 14.
Suicide— Attempt at	Misdemeanor	C. L.
Transportation— 1. Aiding convicts to escape 2. Rescuing them 3. Being at large before the expiration of sentence	Felony ditto ditto	16 Geo. II., c. 31, ss. 1, 2, 3. 4 Vic., No. 29, s. 14. 4 and 5 Wm. IV., c. 67.

TREASON—		
1. Compassing death of king	Treason	25 Ed. III., c. 2, s. 5.
2. Violating king's wife	ditto	*Ibid.*
3. Levying war, &c.	ditto	*Ibid.*
4. Felony in compassing the death, &c., of the Queen	Felony	11 Vic., No. 12. s. 3.
5. Attempting to fire at, or do injury to the Queen	High misdemeanor	5 and 6 Vic. c. 51, s. 2.
UNNATURAL OFFENCES—		
Sodomy or bestiality	Felony	29 Vic., No. 11, s. 62.
WITNESS—		
Tampering with	Misdemeanor	C. L.

APPENDIX B.

Depot Stud Book.

Registered No.	Name.	Color.	Sex.	Age.	HEIGHT.		BRANDS.		Particular Description, Marks, &c.	Where Bred or Purchased	TRANSFERS.		DISPOSAL OF.		Remarks.
					Hands.	Inches.	Police.	Other.			Date.	District	Date.	Cause.	

APPENDIX C.

QUEENSLAND POLICE.
Brisbane Station, Moreton District.

REPORT of HORSES under VETERINARY TREATMENT at the POLICE DEPOT   day of   187 .

Register No.	Name.	Color.	Sex.	Date admitted.	Nature of Disease.	Remarks.

I hereby certify the above to be a correct return.

Brisbane Police Depôt,   day of   187 .

_____ Farrier.

APPENDIX D.

FORMS OF AFFIDAVITS NECESSARY IN OBTAINING WRITS OF HABEAS.

No. 1.

In the Supreme Court of the Colony of Queensland.

I, (*name*), (*rank*) of Police, in the Colony of Queensland, make oath and say,—

First: That (*name*), now a prisoner confined in (*gaol or penal establishment*), at (*place of confinement*), in the said colony, is and will be, as this deponent is advised and verily believes, a material and necessary witness on behalf of the prosecution in an inquiry into a charge against one (*name*), for (*offence*), which said charge stands for inquiry on the (*date*) day of (*month*), A.D. 187 , at (*place*), in the said colony.

Second: That the Crown cannot safely proceed with such inquiry without the testimony of the said prisoner (*name of witness*).

(*Signature of party making affidavit.*)

Sworn before me, at (*place*), in the Colony of Queensland, this (*date*) day of (*month*), Anno Domini 187 .

A Commissioner of the Supreme Court of the Colony of Queensland for taking Affidavits.

NOTE.—All erasures to be initialled by the Commissioner.

APPENDIX D.

FORMS OF AFFIDAVITS NECESSARY IN OBTAINING WRITS OF HABEAS.

No. 2.

In the Supreme Court of the Colony of Queensland.

I, (*name*) (*rank*) of Police in the said Colony of Queensland, make oath and say,—

First: That (*name*), now a prisoner confined in (*gaol or penal establishment*) at (*place*) in the said colony, is charged with (*offence*).

Second: That from information received, the said (*name of party making affidavit*) hath reason to believe, and doth believe, that the said (*name of prisoner*) committed the offence in question.

Third: That the said offence was committed in the Police District of (*name*), in the said colony, and it is requisite for the purpose of enquiry into the said charge that the said (*name of prisoner*) should be brought before the Bench of Magistrates at (*place*), in the said colony, on the (*date*) day of (*month*), A.D. 187 .

(*Signature of party making affidavit.*)

Sworn before me, at (*place*), in the Colony of Queensland, this (*date*) day of (*month*), Anno Domini 187 .

A Commissioner of the Supreme Court of the Colony of Queensland for taking Affidavits.

NOTE.—All erasures to be initialled by Commissioner.

APPENDIX E.

QUEENSLAND POLICE.

STATEMENT of all FORAGE issued in the _____ District during the month ending _____ 187 , to Horses, Cattle, &c., not belonging to the Department of Police, or if belonging to the Department, not used in Police service.

Station.	Particulars of Animal			Date of coming into Possession of Police.	Under what circumstances.	Date of Disposal.	How disposed of.	No of Rations issued.	Dates of Issue.	Amount received.	Remarks.
	Color.	Sex.	Brands.								

I certify the above to be a correct return.

Police Department, Inspector's Office, _____ 187 .

_____
Officer in Charge.

APPENDIX F.
QUEENSLAND POLICE.

MORETON DISTRICT.—Forage issued at Goodna Station, week ending 11th March, 1876.

Days of the Week.	Issues of Forage in Thirds.			Total Rations Issued to Horses.		Rider or Driver.	On what Duty.	From what Station.	Hours of		Quantity.				TOTALS.				Remarks.
	Morning.	Noon.	Evening.	Belonging to the Station.	Belonging to other Stations.				Arrival.	Departure.	Corn.	Bran.	Hay.	Straw.	Corn.	Bran.	Hay.	Straw.	
Sunday				1											8	1	14	4	
Monday				1	¼	Con. White, 62	Court duty Retd. to Station	Gatton	4 p.m.						10½	1⅓	21	8	
Tuesday				1	⅔					3 p.m.					13½	1⅓	21	4	
Wednesday				1	1½	S. con. Saudes, 72, and Con. Judge, 409	In search of an offender Retd. to Station	Harrisville	11 a.m.	11 a.m.					18½	2⅓	28	12	
Thursday				1	⅓										13½	1⅓	28	4	
Friday				1											8	1	14	4	
Saturday				1											8	1	14	4	
TOTALS	3½	3½	3½	7	3										80	10	140	40	

FOR POLICE SERVICE.   FOR OTHER THAN POLICE SERVICES.*

* Requisitions must be attached for any forage issued under this head, signed by the party drawing it, or a note made of the sum reimbursed for the supply.

B

APPENDIX G.

CLASSIFICATION OF OFFENCES.
Offences against the Person.

High treason
Murder
Murder, attempt to
Shooting at, stabbing, wounding, &c., with intent to maim
Manslaughter
Feloniously attempting to procure abortion
Concealing birth of their infants
Sodomy
Assaults with intent to commit sodomy
Extorting money under threats, &c.
Rape
Assault with intent to commit rape
Indecent assault
Abduction
Bestiality
Bigamy
Child dropping
Child stealing
Feloniously demanding money with menaces
Threatening a witness
Assaults and inflicting bodily harm
Assaults, common
Assaults on police
Rescue from custody, and attempt to
Obstructing police constables on duty
Attempt to commit suicide
Feloniously throwing over a person a corrosive fluid.

Offences against property committed with violence.

Burglary
Burglary, attended with violence to persons
Breaking into a dwelling-house, and stealing
Breaking into a dwelling-house, with intent to steal
Breaking within the curtilage of a dwelling-house, and stealing
Breaking into shops, warehouses, counting-houses, &c.
Conspiracy to break into a dwelling-house, with intent to steal
Robbery
Robbery, accessory before the fact

CLASSIFICATION of OFFENCES—*continued.*

Robbery, accessory after the fact
Assault with intent to rob
Sacrilege
Feloniously breaking into a church, and stealing
Feloniously breaking into a church, with intent to steal.

Offences against Property committed without violence.

Cattle stealing
Horse stealing
Sheep stealing
Illegally using horses and cattle
Larceny in a dwelling to the value of £5
Larceny in a dwelling
Larceny from the person
Larceny by servants
Larceny from letters containing bank notes, &c.
Larceny, simple
Misdemeanor with intent to steal
Embezzlement
Receiving stolen property
Frauds
Conspiring with intent to defraud
Unlawful possession of goods
Dog stealing.

Malicious Offences against Property.

Arson
Feloniously wounding cattle
Wilful damage.

Forgery and Offences against the Currency.

Forgery, and uttering forged instrument
Feloniously selling and having in possession forged stamps
Coining
Coin (counterfeit), putting off, uttering, having, &c.

Other Offences, not included in the above Clauses.

Accessory to felony before the fact
Accessory to felony after the fact
Advertising for recovery of stolen property with promise that no questions shall be asked
Apprentice runaway

CLASSIFICATION OF OFFENCES—*continued.*

Being unlawfully on the premises
Breach of corporate and municipal bye-laws
Breach of mining regulations
Breach of ticket-of-leave regulations
Bribery
Compounding a felony
Contempt of court
Crown lands—illegal occupation of, removing sand, loam, &c., from, cutting timber on, &c.
Cruelty to animals
Deserters, military and naval
Deserters from merchant service
Deserting their families
Disorderly characters
Disorderly prostitutes
Drunk and disorderly characters
Drunkenness
Endeavoring to obtain a situation by false characters
Furious driving
Gambling, and found in gambling houses
Indecently exposing the person
Keeping a common brothel
Libel
Lunacy.

Miscellaneous Offences under—

Fire (prevention careless use of) Act
Fisheries Act
Game (protection of imported) Act
Health Act
Insolvent Act
Licensed Butchers Act
Licensed Carriages Act
Licensed Distilleries Act
Licensed Hawkers Act
Licensed Pawnbrokers Act
Licensed Publicans Act
Masters and Servants Act
Merchant Seamen Act
Police Regulation Acts
Railway Acts
Registration of Births, Deaths, &c., Acts

CLASSIFICATION OF OFFENCES—*continued*.

Roads and Streets Act
Town and Country Police Act
Scab Act
Small Debts Act
Vagrant Act.

Mutiny
Nuisances
Obscene language
Perjury, and subornation of perjury
Personation at elections
Personating a police constable
Prison breaking and escape from custody, and harboring or aiding escaped felons
Riot, breach of the peace, pound breach
Sedition
Selling and exposing obscene prints for sale
Sending a threatening letter
Smuggling
Threatening language
Unlawfully opening graves
Unlawfully removing a dead body for anatomical examination, without the authority required by law
Unlawfully solemnising a marriage
Unlawfully soliciting and inciting a person to commit a felony
Unlicensed theatres, found in.

APPENDIX H.
QUEENSLAND POLICE.

RETURN of Cases Committed for Trial to the _____ Court, held at _____ on the _____ day of _____ 187 . _____ District.

PRISONER.						CONSTABLE.		
Name.	Committed for Trial		Offence.	Sentence.		Name.	Register No.	Remarks.
	Place.	Date.						

Forwarded for the information of the Commissioner of Police.

Police Department, _____ Office, _____ 187 .

_____ Officer in charge.

APPENDIX I.

QUEENSLAND POLICE.

REPORT of HORSES considered unfit for Service. _____ District.

Register No.	Name.	Color.	Sex.	Age.	HEIGHT.		Police Brands.	Other Brands.	Particular Description, Marks.
					Hands.	Inches.			

Special Report.

We hereby certify that we are of opinion that the horse above described is, for the causes assigned, unfit for further police service.

Dated this   day of   187 .

DECISION.

} Members of the Board.

APPENDIX K.

QUEENSLAND POLICE.

RETURN of FINES and other PUNISHMENTS inflicted upon MEMBERS of the FORCE stationed in the   District, during the month of   187   .

District Letter and No.	Names of Defaulters.	Rank.	Where stationed.	Date of Offence.	Particulars of Offence. (To be recorded as fully as practicable.)	Plea.	Names of Witnesses; that of reporting witness being given first.	Decision.	By Whom.	Remarks.

I certify the above to be a correct return.

_____
Inspector in charge of District.

To the Commissioner of Police

APPENDIX L.

QUEENSLAND POLICE.
Sick Register.

_____ Station, _____ District.

Name.	Age.	District Letter and No.	Rank.	Date of Joining Service.	Previous Sickness.	Date of Previous Sickness.	Length of Sick Leave.	By whom recommended.	Name of Police or other Surgeon in attendance upon sick man.	REMARKS. The Police, or other Surgeon will enter here shortly the treatment necessary in each case, with any other remarks he may think proper to make.

APPENDIX M.

QUEENSLAND POLICE.
Transfer Statement.

THE Constable undermentioned is, by order of the Commissioner of Police, herewith forwarded to _____ Station, to fill vacancy caused by _____

The statement of his account is as under.

Date when paid, to inclusive.	Signature.

Name:
Register No.:
Age:
Height:
Eyes:
Hair:
Complexion:
Country:
Calling:
Religion:
Date of Appointment:

To the Officer in Charge of Police.

By Authority: JAMES C. BEAL, Government Printer, William street, Brisbane.

www.ingramcontent.com/pod-product-compliance
Lightning Source LLC
Chambersburg PA
CBHW032008230426
43672CB00010B/2288